YOUTH BLOOM IN GCC

MEI-KW Middle East Series 02

YOUTH BLOOM IN GCC

Edited by
SAMEENA HAMEED

KNOWLEDGE WORLD

KW Publishers Pvt Ltd
New Delhi

MEI@ND

Series: MEI-KW Middle East Series 02

ISBN 978-93-91490-80-5 Hardback
ISBN 978-93-91490-88-1 ebook

Published in India by Kalpana Shukla

KNOWLEDGE WORLD
KW Publishers Pvt Ltd
4676/21, First Floor, Ansari Road
Daryaganj, New Delhi 110002
Phone: +91 11 43528107
Marketing: kw@kwpub.in
Editorial: production@kwpub.in
Website: www.kwpub.in

Printed and Bound in India

Dedicated to

My Mother, Abeda Paiker
With Love and Affection

Contents

About MEI@ND

Formally launched in February 2010, the Middle East Institute, New Delhi seeks to promote the understanding of contemporary Middle East. It is India-based but not India-centric. Its main research focus is geopolitical dynamics of the Middle East including, but not limited to, military matters, economy, energy security, political system and institutions, society, culture and religion, and conflicts in the region. The institute also encourages research on bourgeoning Asian interest in and engagements with the Middle East. MEI@ND documents bilateral relations amongst the Middle Eastern states and strives to produce an updated analysis of the region's changing strategic landscape. Besides a host of web-based activities, the premier publications of MEI include, *Contemporary Review of the Middle East* (a quarterly by Sage) and *Persian Gulf: India's Relations with the Region* (an annual by Palgrave). Professor P R Kumaraswamy is the Honorary Director of MEI@ND.

MEI Middle East Series is the latest step in promoting Middle Eastern studies in India and seeks to be a platform for younger scholars to develop and showcase their academic pursuits. Books both edited and authored of about 75,000 words on contemporary Middle Eastern developments will be published under the series. Fresh Ph.D. holders are especially encouraged to convert their doctoral theses into books as part of the series. The MEI@ND has partnered with KW Publishers, New Delhi to publish books under this series, and strives to publish 2-4 books annually. Honorary Director of MEI is the editor of the Series. Queries and proposals should be addressed to mei.newdelhi@gmail.com.

The edited volume ***Youth Bloom in GCC*** is the second in the series and presents a constellation of essays on political, economic and social developments in MENA since Arab Spring.

Acknowledgements

This volume on the youth in the GCC, is written mostly by young scholars, who could understand the possibilities and problems of their generation. The book borrows its life from the exposure of the young scholars to niche areas under discussion. It was indeed challenging to combine their knowledge with scientific analysis and academic rigours. When I reflect upon its journey, the book is about youth both in letter and spirit. With initial shaky start, and concern even about its viability, it gained momentum with the smooth exchange of ideas, arguments and chapters, also facilitated by the promptness and commitments of the contributors. I express my deep gratitude to all the contributors, for their valuable contribution and timely cooperation for the project to come to its fruition.

I would like to sincerely thank MEI@ND and KW Publishers for agreeing to publish the book as the second in their series. Special thanks to Kalpana Shukla and the KW team for facilitating the publication. My deepest appreciation to MEI@ND for creating an ecosystem that breeds scholarship and my association with its team had been extremely enriching and engaging.

I have been fortunate to have teachers and mentors Prof Gulshan Dietl, Prof Girijesh Pant, Prof Zikrur Rahman and Ambassador Talmiz Ahmad who have not only shaped and sharpened my abilities to understand the subject but have provided gainful opportunities. I extend my deepest gratitude for their constant blessings for my academic pursuits. I am deeply grateful to my colleagues, seniors and contemporaries at the Centre for West Asian Studies, JNU for giving me comfort, confidence and intellectual stimulus to pursue my academic work. Prof A K Ramakrishnan, Dr Mahendra Pratap Rana and

Dr Vrushal Ghoble have always been supportive and available and my special thanks to them.

I extend my appreciation to my students, especially Rohit Sharma and Shadia Khan for their association with the book and their commitment to its successful completion. I am equally grateful to my friends and well-wishers, for the goodwill and best wishes that have generated positive vibes and good omen. Special mention must be made for my friends Ayem, Ritu Sain, Azra Khanam, Bushra Sabri, and Tarrunum

I thank with appreciation and gratitude to work-family Prof P R Kumaraswamy and Dr Md. Muddassir Quamar for their rigorous reviews, critical discussions and meticulous organisation of the manuscript. Our academic trio has yielded immense work synergy and timely deliverables.

My academic journey had been eventful, and each milestone bears several names of friends, well-wishers and supporters, which is impossible to list at any amount of available space, but I should express my gratitude to Ambassador Sanjay Singh, Ambassador Swashpawan Singh, Ambassador R. Rajagopalan, Prof Azhar Mohammad, Prof Javed Iqbal, Prof Javed Ahmed Khan, Prof Nazim Ali, Prof Shamir Hasan, Dr Sreeradha Datta, Dr Rafiullah Azmi, Dr Nazmi, Qamar Aga Sir and Aftab Alam.

My parents and my brothers and sisters have been a constant source of support, on whom I often have relied upon to take care of my family responsibility, while I spent days in finishing my academic commitments. Without their backstage role, this book would not have seen the light of the day. I am equally thankful to my little daughter Sidra for patiently enduring my absence, sacrificing her rights over my time, attention and care. My elder daughter, Heba deserves a special appreciation and pride for designing the book cover.

All the above persons that could be mentioned and all those whom I could only remember have facilitated the fruition of this book project. My heartiest gratitude is to my beloved mother, whose courage, relentless drive and unwavering support have been the engine of my academic journey and to her, with deep love and affection, I am dedicating this book to her. The errors and omissions are totally mine.

Sameena Hameed

List of Tables and Figures

Contributors

Sameena Hameed is Assistant Professor in Middle Eastern Studies in Jawaharlal Nehru University, New Delhi. Her areas of specialisation include the Middle Eastern economy, India's economic relations with the Middle East and energy security issues and has contributed monographs, journal articles and chapters to edited volumes. She has prepared research papers and study reports for the Ministry of External Affairs and other trade and commerce organisations like ASSOCHAM. She has been a member of the MEA-constituted Select Group on Gulf and West Asia. She was also a member of the Indian team for 'India-GCC Strategic Partnership' project and the Indo-Saudi Dialogue. She is the co-author of *Persian Gulf 2020: India's Relations with the Region* (Palgrave Macmillan).

Lakshmi Priya is Research Analyst at Manohar Parrikar Institute for Defence Studies and Analyses, New Delhi. She has a Ph.D. in West Asian studies from Jawaharlal Nehru University. Prior to this, she was associated with the Indian Social Institute and Office of the Cultural Attaché, Embassy of the Kingdom of Saudi Arabia, as a researcher. She completed her masters in Arabic language from the School of Languages, Jawaharlal Nehru University. In addition to area studies, she also has an interest in international relations and political theory. She has published a research article on the legitimacy of the Baath in Syria and the Gramscian idea of Cultural Hegemony.

M.H. Ilias is Professor and Dean, Faculty of Social Sciences, Mahatma Gandhi University, Kottayam. His areas of research interest include South Asian Migration to the Gulf Region, Islamic Movements in South Asia, Religion and State in the Gulf States, Hadrami migration on the

Malabar Coast, Religion and Visual Culture in West Asia, Sociology of Conflict, and Muslims and New Media. His recent publications include, *Society and Change in the Contemporary Gulf* (co-edited) and *Off-Campus Orientalism: Western University Branch Campuses in the Gulf, India-West Asia Relations: Understanding Cultural Interplays* (co-edited), *Arabi-Malayalam: Linguistic-Cultural Traditions of Mappila Muslims of Kerala* (co-authored) and *Space Memory and Jewish National Identity*. He was a recipient of Ford Foundation Fellowship for Postdoctoral Research (2007) at Oxford University; Postdoctoral Visiting Research Fellowship (2008) at the Centre for Modern Orient, Berlin; and SUSI Fellow (2019) at Temple University, Philadelphia.

Md. Muddassir Quamar is Associate Fellow at Manohar Parrikar Institute for Defence Studies and Analyses, New Delhi and holds a Ph.D. in Middle East studies from Jawaharlal Nehru University. He has a wider interest in politics and societies in the Arabian Gulf, political Islam, Middle East strategic affairs and India's relations with the Middle East. Dr Quamar is the author of *Education System in Saudi Arabia: Of Change and Reforms* (2021) and co-author *India's Saudi Policy: Bridge to the Future* (2019). He has published several research papers in reputed international journals and contributed chapters for edited volumes. In 2014-15, he was Visiting Fellow at the King Faisal Center for Research and Islamic Studies, Riyadh. Dr Quamar has been associated with the MEI@ND in various capacities since its inception in 2010.

Melissa Cyrill is Deputy Managing Editor at a Hong Kong-based FDI consultancy. She has previously worked at Manohar Parrikar Institute of Defence Studies and Analyses, New Delhi. She obtained Doctorate from JNU for her thesis *New Media and State-Society Relations in Bahrain and the United Arab Emirates, 2011-2016*. Her areas of research interest include labour migration and political economy of the GCC, role of social media after the Arab uprisings, Gulf digital diplomacy narratives, and changes in the socioeconomic status of women and youth in the UAE. Her publications include "Examining the Interventionist Logic in the Arab Uprisings" (*Strategic Analysis*), and "Diplomacy in the Internet Age—Challenges and Opportunities for the UAE" (co-authored chapter).

N Janardhan is Senior Research Fellow, Gulf-Asia Programme, in Anwar Gargash Diplomatic Academy, Abu Dhabi, that offers PGD and MA courses on foreign policies of the Gulf and Asia. His academic publications include, *The Arab Gulf's Pivot to Asia: From Transactional to Strategic Partnerships* (Ed, Gerlach, 2020); *A New Gulf Security Architecture: Prospects and Challenges for an Asian Role* (Eds, Gerlach, 2014); *India and the Gulf: What Next* (Eds, GRC Cambridge 2013); and *Boom amid Gloom: Spirit of Possibility in 21st Century Gulf* (Ithaca, 2011). With a Ph.D., from Jawaharlal Nehru University, New Delhi, he is Assistant Managing Editor of *Journal of Arabian Studies* (Routledge).

Nawar Kassomeh is a doctoral candidate in Politics and International Relations at Lancaster University, UK. He is working on his thesis *Shia Minority between Inclusion, Exclusion and the Geopolitical Tensions in the Pakistani Elitist Islamic State*. His research interests include the Middle East, GCC states, political Islam, identity, nationalism, and geopolitics. His recent publication includes co-authored journal article "Wealth and the Persistence of Authoritarianism in Singapore and Gulf States."

P R Kumaraswamy is teaching contemporary Middle East at Jawaharlal Nehru University (JNU), New Delhi. From 1992-1999 he was a research fellow at the Harry S., Truman Research Institute for the Advancement of Peace, Jerusalem. Since joining JNU in September 1999, he has been researching, teaching, and writing on various aspects of the contemporary Middle East. His works include *Squaring the Circle: Mahatma Gandhi and the Jewish National Home* (2018), *India's Israel Policy* (2010), and *Historical Dictionary of the Arab Israeli Conflict* (2015, second edition). In February 2010, he set up the virtual Middle East Institute, New Delhi and serves as its honorary director. He is the editor of *Contemporary Review of the Middle East* (Sage India) and the series editor of *Persian Gulf: India's Relations with the Region* (Palgrave Macmillan).

Prabhat Jawla is a doctoral candidate at the Centre for West Asian Studies, Jawaharlal Nehru University. He obtained his Master's in International Relations from the South Asian University, New Delhi. He also holds a Post-Graduate Diploma in International Environmental Law. His principal research interests include security issues in the Persian Gulf and the activities of Iran's Islamic Revolutionary Guard Corps (IRGC). He has written various commentaries and published book reviews on these themes in academic journals including *Strategic Analysis*, *South Asia Research* and *Contemporary Review of Middle East*. His issue-brief titled, *Iraq Under Mustafa Al-Kadhimi: Turning Over a New Leaf* was published by Manohar Parrikar Institute for Defence Studies and Analyses (MP-IDSA).

Priyanka Chandra is a political theorist and Assistant Professor of Political Science and International Relations at the Jindal School of International Affairs, O.P. Jindal Global University. She holds Ph.D., M.Phil and MA degrees from Jawaharlal Nehru University and BA from University of Delhi. Her specialisation is on the state, democratisation and political Islam. Her research interests include nationalism, public sphere, civil society, women movements, with a focus on West Asia, North Africa and more recently, South Asia. Her works have been published as chapters in edited books as well as journals and online platforms.

Priyanka Mittal is teaching at Delhi University. She has completed her Ph.D. from Centre for West Asian Studies, School of International Studies, Jawaharlal Nehru University, New Delhi, India for her thesis on "Saudi Media after September 11 Attacks". Her research area includes Saudi domestic and transnational media, women, religion, public broadcasting services in authoritarian states and digital media. She has presented papers at various national and international seminars and conferences.

Raahat Verma is an independent research consultant with expertise in Open Source Analytics (OSINT) and Social Media Intelligence. Her research interests include Grey Zone exploring technological advancements and their real-time effect on statecraft. She has provided consultancy to several firms in the preparation of related documentaries, development modules, learning software and strategic communication projects. She has a Master's degree in International Relations and Area Studies from Jawaharlal Nehru University, New Delhi.

Rhea Abraham is a MENA analyst for a private risk consulting firm in India. She previously worked as Associate Fellow at the Centre for Air Power Studies, New Delhi. Her research interests include the Middle East, India-Gulf relations and migration. She has a doctorate in Gulf Studies from India-Arab Cultural Centre, Jamia Millia Islamia, New Delhi and has completed a course on International Migration from Oxford University. She has several publications to her credit including a chapter on "Indian Diaspora in the Gulf".

Rohit Kumar Sharma is a doctoral candidate at the Centre for West-Asian Studies, JNU. He is a law graduate and holds a master's in international relations from South Asian University. He also holds a Postgraduate Diploma in Human Rights, International Humanitarian and Refugee Laws. Currently, he is working on the Cyber Security policies in Israel for his Ph.D. He has contributed chapters to various edited volumes.

1. Introduction

Sameena Hameed

Youth has no age.

—Pablo Picasso

The Arab streets since the last decade have been reverberating with swelling masses, mostly youth and have refused to be quietened by the resurrecting authoritarian regimes. Many countries in Middle East North Africa (MENA) region inhabited predominantly by young population have descended into chaos, disorder, civil wars and internal strife, while some others are crippled by corruption and incomplete and ineffective transition in the aftermath of the Arab uprising in 2011. However, the GCC countries, comprising Bahrain, Kuwait, Oman, Qatar, Saudi Arabia, and the United Arab Emirates (UAE), have been grabbing global attention for their rapid transformation and burst of entrepreneurial energy. The salience of this transformation in the GCC is its young population.

Youth as an analytical category has been difficult and problematic and is intertwined with various issues. This can be gauged with the lack of uniformity in defining what constitutes the youth population and the linkages drawn to various social, cultural and economic aspects. However, youth is a biological category and a social one characterised by common values, goals, and distinct behavioural responses (Buchmann, 2001) to opportunities and deprivation, to changes and challenges. It is the spirit of adventure, enterprise, non-conformity, creation and going in the wilderness, can be as destructive as wildfire.

In less than a year, after the world celebrated the first International Youth Day on 12 August 2000, it was stunned by the gruesome 11 September 2001 terrorist attacks, in which all 19 perpetrators except four were Saudi youths. This catapulted the global discourse on Arab youths being attracted towards terrorist organisations (National Commission on Terrorist Attacks upon the United States, 2004). Links were being made to the problems of youth about lack of freedom and productive opportunities leading to radicalisation (Diwan, 2014). However, at the regional level, since the escalation of youth-led opposition during the 2011 Arab uprising (Boghardt, 2013), the GCC regimes began to cultivate them as an important constituency. The GCC governments have been projecting their pro-youth strategies and policies. At present, despite several challenges, GCC youth operate from the vantage point of relative stability, wealth, global connectivity and encounters with diversely skilled, multi-national workforce. This book is an attempt to look at the contours of potentials and possibilities for the GCC youths from this vantage point, their adaptations and the challenges posed to their development. The GCC region has been transformed twice in recent history; although some constants are enduring, changes have been phenomenal.

As of 2018, the GCC countries were endowed with about 30 per cent of the proven global oil reserves and 20 per cent of the global gas reserves (British Petroleum, 2019). The boom in oil revenues had previously transformed their urban landscapes. In a few decades, the skylines of the small pearling towns are dotted with skyscrapers. Oil wealth and globalisation brought in the most modern and cosmopolitan consumption patterns. However, the societal relations were fossilised in the increasing Islamisation of the region after the Islamic revolution in Iran in 1979. The windfall gains from successive oil booms gave the relatively small population of the region one of the highest per capita incomes in the world. Yet, most of it accrued as distributed rent rather than productive income. The successive generation of the 'versatile tribesmen' (Fattah, 2016), who toiled in the desert and the distant sea to make a tenuous living, eventually were sustained and supported by their states' oil rent distribution. After the first oil crisis in 1973, the boom in oil revenues concurred with the formation of modern GCC states after their (except Kuwait in 1961) independence in 1971. As the oil wealth flowed, the regimes could provide their populace, without levying taxes on them, extensive social services, subsidised commodities, credits, and high-paying jobs in the public sector. In exchange, the people accorded legitimacy to the rulers without any rights of representation or participation in matters of state governance. However, the demand for these rights was never completely surrendered or silenced.

The transformation that is currently underway is the engagement of its young population with what is commonly called the fourth industrial revolution. The fourth industrial revolution amalgamates the physical and digital world and has amplified the scale, scope and speed of production, distribution and consumption of a whole range of activities, information, ideas and innovation. It rides on the energy and enterprise of the younger population and would not have been possible without their catalytic engagement with the frontier technology. As a result, young men and women are now known to make business propositions of diverse needs and consumptions, including art and culture, and have developed several start-ups in niche areas.

The social ecosystem that the second transformation calls for has aggravated the push and pull forces over the region's traditional social structures and unrepresentative political institutions. The pressures for substantive reforms have been sustained by youth activism. Much of this was already underway since the early 21st century. The most widespread call for political restructuring has come from the youth in the small states of Kuwait and Bahrain (Boghardt, 2013). In Kuwait, their activism led to the electoral reforms in 2005 and the prime minister's resignation in 2011. In Bahrain, the 14 February coalition was a loosely organised confederation of youth networks, predominantly Shia, that sprang up during the 2011 Arab uprisings. Oman also witnessed substantial unrest during and in the aftermath of the Arab uprisings as local youths in Sohar clashed with the police during 2012 and 2013 (Valeri, 2015).

The GCC youths continue to face common challenges like their regional peers but are advantaged over them thanks to the relative political stability, larger wealth, better infrastructural development and global connectivity. The regimes have made bolder commitments for technological and infrastructural development. The GCC youths are equally innovative in continuing their activism despite massive state surveillance through innovative use of traditional spaces, digital forums, cultural spaces and volunteering. In many ways, they complement and supplement the states' efforts towards growth and development. At the same time, the GCC states have been struggling to maintain their social contracts with the population due to the fluctuating oil revenues. There are increasingly looking towards the potential of the young population to engage with the frontier technology and create new business opportunities. The encounters between the regimes and the young people in the region are both interesting and perplexing.

Youth and Unemployment

The Arabs were famous as maritime traders and started early on. While the region did not have much production except for dates and pearls, it leveraged its geographic location at the crossroads of Asia, Africa and Europe and en route to the long-distance trade in the Indian Ocean. It prospered through the entrepot trade before oil. The predominance of the oil industry eventually stymied other economic activities and created an oil-based economy. The vibrant merchant class that existed before the dawn of the oil era was eventually co-opted by the regimes through privileges, positions in bureaucracy, government contracts, land purchases and marriages into the ruling class families. There was not much to trade besides oil, which was under the state's ownership.

At the same time, the massive inflow of oil revenues has pushed rapid industrialisation and urbanisation that attracted a large expatriate workforce to the region. The GCC nationals preferred high-paying jobs in the public sector provided by the states. However, it became increasingly difficult for the regimes to maintain the commitment of providing the population with jobs and other social services due to fluctuating oil revenues and high population growth rates.

The GCC population had higher fertility rates than the global average until the dawn of the 21st century. However, since then, the fertility rates in many GCC countries (Qatar, UAE, Kuwait and Bahrain) have fallen steeply and have been lower than the global average (World Bank, n.d.). Oman had a high fertility rate of about 2.8 in 2019 against the global average of 2.4 (World Bank, n.d.). The high fertility rates in the earlier decades have led to the predominance of adolescents and youth in the population pyramid of these countries. This also confers a demographic opportunity to the region, but adequate capacity building and productive deployments are prerequisites to reap its dividend. For want of gainful opportunities, the youth potential often goes unharnessed even diverted towards undesirable or destructive channels.

Providing gainful employment has been a major challenge for the oil-based GCC economies, which had conventionally relied on expatriate workers. The expatriate workers are the majority resident populations in most GCC countries ranging from 88 per cent in UAE to 45 per cent in Oman. They constitute an even larger percentage of the workforce. Fewer jobs existed for the GCC nationals in their undiversified economies. More skilled and low-cost expatriate workers mostly took up those in the private sector with a consequential rise in nationals' unemployment. The GCC countries have been trying to diversify their economies and develop new industries and sectors with varying degrees of success.

Policies to increase the employment of the nationals by increasing their job quotas have seen limited success (Gulf Labour Market and Migration, 2014). Youth unemployment in Bahrain has been consistently rising since the turn of the present century to reach 7.3 in 2019 (Table 1.1). In Qatar, it has generally been low and declining to reach 0.5 in 2019. In more populous Saudi Arabia, the problem of youth unemployment is more acute and has been at a higher level of about 25 per cent or above in the past two decades. According to the International Labour Organisation (ILO), youth unemployment in Saudi Arabia has increased since 2016 to 29.6 per cent in 2019. The situation in Kuwait is equally troubling, with a continuous increase in youth unemployment to reach 15.7 per cent in 2019.

Table 1.1: Socio-Economic Indicators: GCC States

Country	National population* (in a million) (2020)	Average median age (in years) (2021)	GDP (at current prices, in US$ billion) (2019)	Unemployed youth as % of total labour force aged 15-24 years)** (2019)
Bahrain	0.8 (46)	32.3	37.5	7.3 (15.7)
Kuwait	1.3 (31)	29.3	128.3	15.7 (29.4)
Oman	2.7 (55)	25.6	79.3	8.4 (36.3)

Qatar	0.32 (11.6)	33.2	188.1	0.5 (2.1)
Saudi Arabia	20.7 (2018) (48.8)	27	802.9	29.6 (64.4)
UAE	1.2 (12)	32.5	414.2	7.0 (13.4)

Sources: Kingdom of Saudi Arabia, General Authority for Statistics; UAE Federal Competitiveness and Statistics Centre, www.fcsc.gov.ae; World Bank database; World Population Review; Kumaraswamy, Quamar and Hameed (2020)

Notes: *Figures in bracket are per cent of the total population.
** Figures in bracket are that of female unemployment.

Women and their Visibility

In the GCC region, the female population is equally educated as their male counterparts but is not visible in the labour force. As a result, female youth unemployment is generally two to three times more than males. For example, in Saudi Arabia, more than two-thirds of the female labour force of the age group 15 to 24 years were unemployed in 2019 (Table 1.1). *Saudi Vision 2030*, architected by Crown Prince Mohammad bin Salman (popularly called MbS), has focused on boosting employment opportunities for women. As a result, the national estimates on female employment have increased in the last few years. However, the ILO estimates (World Bank database) do not corroborate the same and shows an increase in female unemployment since 2016.

Besides not getting enough job opportunities, their labour force participation rates (which means the per cent of women in the working-age 15-65 years employed or actively looking for work) have been low by global standards. This reflects the cultural baggage where women's primary role is viewed as homemakers and caregivers. The women labour force participation rates have ranged between 19-36 per cent. Bahrain, Kuwait and Qatar have higher female labour force participation rates (above 30 per cent) than the others. In recent years, consequent to the state policy of increasing employment among females, female labour force participation rates have generally increased in all the countries except Kuwait. On the contrary, in Kuwait, it has been broadly declining between 2011-16 (Figure 1.1). The case of Kuwait clearly illustrates the pessimism among females that sets in with the general decline in employment opportunities and manifests itself in their withdrawal from the labour force.

Figure 1.1: Female Nationals Labour Participation Rate in the GCC countries (in per cent)

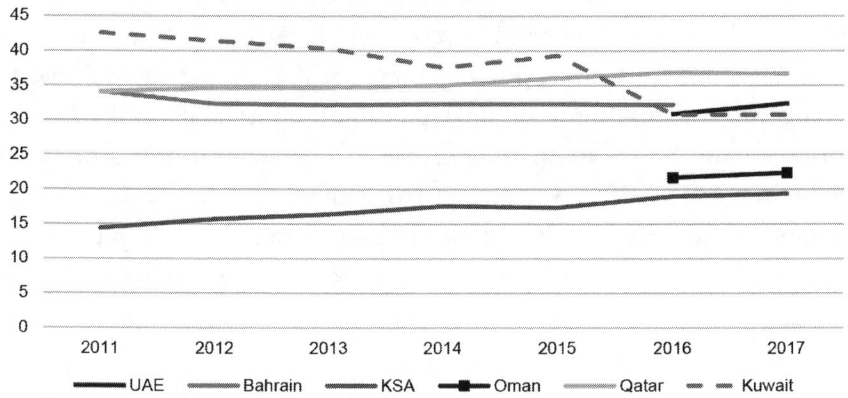

Source: GCC-Stat, https://dp.gccstat.org/en/DataSearch

Youth and Skill Development

The education system in the GCC region is lagging in generating required skills that could enhance the nationals' employability. Even though there is near total literacy in the region, the Gulf youth lack professional skills required in the job market. The educational reforms that produce marketable skills are a vital concern in all the GCC states. The governments aimed to build a knowledge economy and recognised the importance of improving the quality and curriculum of their education systems. Private schools offering international curricula are emerging as the preferred choice over public schools. The enrolment ratios in primary and secondary education have been about 90 per cent. They are free and compulsory, but tertiary education was about 57.6 per cent in 2019; they range from 70.9 per cent in Saudi Arabia to 18.9 per cent in Qatar (Statista, 2021). The ranking of the GCC states in the Programme for International Student Assessment (PISA) scales in Reading, Mathematics and Science has been low in the Global Innovative Index (Commonwealth, 2020).

However, the relatively affluent population has widespread ownership of computers and access to the internet and mobile-enabled technology, and therefore the digital connectivity is fast transforming the scope and output of education and the learning experience in the region. The academics and others are exploring innovative pedagogy through ICT-mediated technology. As a result, there is a burst of interest, activity and experimentation with diverse teaching content and interactive modules. For example, in the American University of Sharjah, courses are designed on problem-based learning and encourage critical and creative thinking among the students, promoting deployable market skills (Al Musawi, 2016). There is also an increasing use of mobile learning and social media in education (Al Musawi, 2016). However, even the adoption of technology in education is not culturally neutral. For example, female students find it culturally uncomfortable to show face online (Hurley, 2020) and difficult to post their audio or video recordings for their educational assignments.

Youth and Discursive Politics

Youth in the region have been politically charged and have actively mobilised around issues of social concern. For example, several youth groups in Kuwait merged to form the Democratic Civil Movement to press for a full parliamentary system. In recent years, several youth groups have promoted discussion over issues that concern their future, like unemployment, corruption, political and judicial reforms. In addition, they transformed traditional spaces of *Diwaniya*—social gatherings restricted to Kuwaiti men—into venues of open dialogue with members of other communities like the expatriates (Abraham, 2020). In Bahrain, youth engagement with politics has been deeply rooted since the civil unrest in the 1990s. Despite state repression after the youth activism during the Arab uprisings, new youth societies emerged, and some participated in the two rounds of the national dialogue for reconciliation. However, youth societies have to choose between lack of resources or lack of freedom due to state support (Watanabe, 2019).

While substantial political reforms remained unachieved, political engagements have shifted to informal, digital and cultural spaces. The Bahrainonline.org, launched in 1998, was visited by 100,000 times and had long been the source of political activism (Jones and Sehabi, n.d.). At the same time, popular culture and art have become the vehicles to communicate politically sensitive issue to the audience. They are becoming new sites of sensitive discussions, voicing dissent, discontent or support to various causes among the Gulf nationals and expatriates in the region.

Youth as Social Capital

Volunteerism is a multi-faceted sector and offers many activities that play an essential role in the community development process. The pandemic of COVID-19 has highlighted the importance of volunteerism in meeting social needs. It provides a fertile ground for people to participate in their progress and plays an active role in societal regeneration. Besides, volunteerism inculcates diverse skills, ultimately benefiting the individual and the country. Volunteerism is the social capital that the GCC governments have increasingly looked upon to enlist youth support in meeting the national vision targets and sustainable development goals (SDGs).

One of the goals of Saudi *Vision 2030* aims to enlist one million male and female volunteers by 2030. The number of volunteers in Saudi Arabia has increased from 23,000 in 2015 to more than 409,000 in 2020, exceeding the target for the year (Al Fouti, 2021). Bahrain and Saudi Arabia have national policies that mention volunteerism's importance in youth development and employability. The UAE and Saudi Arabia have national volunteering portals to promote awareness and list volunteers for various social projects. National centres for volunteerism have also been set up in Kuwait and Qatar. In addition, there is interest in the region to develop statistical tools to measure volunteer work.

Civil society organisations or non-government organisations (NGOs) also provide the platform for youth volunteerism to participate in social life. They have significant engagement with the youths in Kuwait. In January 2015, the Ministry of Public Affairs in Kuwait allowed the formation and registration of volunteer groups with at least five Kuwaiti members. However, young members have less power and influence than the elders due to their relatively weaker positions and lesser access to resources and influential networks. The young voices have generally been absent from the official discourse, but they have created their own spaces and means of participation. There had been tensions between the youth perspectives and the official discourses about rights and participation.

Youth and women showed a higher tendency to respond to social needs. Women accounted for about 57 per cent of the total volunteering in the MENA region, even though their participation in the workforce is significantly low (UN Volunteer Programme for Arab Regional Office, n.d.). Besides, the youth in the region are increasingly attracted to be social entrepreneurs (Osman, 2016) who seek to address the social and economic problems of the society through a business approach. They show their eagerness to pursue ways that yield greater meaning in work rather than personal profit. Moreover, people's religious/cultural orientations have traditionally envisioned their participation in public life to accumulate spiritual capital for worldly life and beyond. In their efforts, they are also facilitated and funded by private companies like Venture 7 and Dow Chemicals, who have supported local organisations and academic institutions engaged in incubating social entrepreneurs.

The Arab youth have been actively pressing for climate change-related actions. For example, Nashier Shafi of the Arab Youth Climate Change Qatar was listed in the 100 most influential people in climate change policy by *Apolitical* 2019. In addition, there is a push for green entrepreneurship that encourages youth to co-create environmental solutions. However, youth NGOs face significant challenges of credibility and a lack of appreciation for their community role because of public perception that the government alone was responsible for the well-being of the society.

The global forces have reshaped cultural experience in the GCC societies. UAE is already on its way to reaping the dividend of embracing global values and cosmopolitan culture. Its openness and tolerant policies have significantly enhanced the comfort of doing business, and the Emiratis are making business opportunities out of cultural events. UAE and Saudi Arabia are now espousing their cosmopolitan cultural hue rather than an Arab one. They project themselves as a cultural bridge located at the crossroads of multiple cultures. Interfaith dialogues were held in Saudi Arabia and Qatar. Pope Francis arrived in the UAE in 2019 and became the first Pope to visit the Arabian Peninsula. Digital connectivity has fostered cross-cultural communications and acculturation, and youths are the torch bearers of this change.

Social Settings

The Arab societies have been based on lineage identities and group associations. The struggle of youth to create their identities navigating traditions and modernity has been daunting. This is more prohibitive for the women, who have traditionally been identified in familial relations as someone's mother, wife or daughter. Art, culture and social media have provided women with non-conformist space to increase their visibility and change their performative roles. Creative industries are exalting talents and merit in a society infested with patronage.

An overriding concern among the people is that the access to jobs and other opportunities, and resources have been based on patronage and not merit. The GCC states had been seeking legitimacy through their allocative or distributive roles. Thus, the access to vital resources and economic opportunities had been mediated by the state and had been driven by the patron-client relationship. The prevalence of '*wasta*' (mediation) based on tribal and family associations has been pervasive in the GCC region (Ramady, 2016) even though these countries ranked among the less corrupt in the CPI Transparency Index (Transparency International, 2018).

The negative effect of *wasta* had been the placement or promotion of individuals with the 'right connection' to positions independent of their education, merits, or capabilities. Even the nationalisation of the job market generally operated on *wasta*, and the citizens with the strongest *wasta* connections rather than the one with the best profile were often selected (Budhwar and Mehllahi, 2016, p. 151). The corrosive effect of *wasta* in Arab societies comes from its acceptance as the normal and often the only way of doing things. The Saudi King made strong statements to tackle corruption and nepotism, emphasizing that no one was above the law, including the king, the crown prince and the royal family members, and that anyone can file a lawsuit against them (Al Arabiya, 2015). However, much of the anti-corruption drive against members of the royal family was seen as an attempt to facilitate the rise of MbS to power and control.

The GCC region, until recently, had maintained a dichotomous structure, where a traditional social structure continued to rest on most modern consumption patterns. The social contract has been mediated through Islam, tribal affiliations and distribution of oil rents. In the past, successive attempts towards economic diversification have been limited due to their dependence on the investments funded from oil revenues. Therefore, a paradigm shift was required to create an ecosystem where the creative potential of the young population, especially women, could be harnessed. For a country like Saudi Arabia that heralds itself as the leader of the Muslim world, this would not be possible without redefining Islam in the Saudi context, and MbS's 'moderate Islam' dismantles some of the most restrictive aspects of its Wahabi version. Various Arab youth surveys converge on the declining share of youth, who consider religion important for their identity, and overwhelming proportions in Oman and Saudi Arabia want religious institutions to reform (Arab Youth Survey, 2021). From economic liberalisation, the GCC states are now toying with social and religious liberalisation, but would this lead to political liberalisation, still eludes an easy answer.

Youth Development Index

The Youth Development Index (YDI) ranks the countries according to their development in six indicators: education, employment and opportunity, health and well-being, equality and inclusion, peace and security, and political and civic participation. Table 1.2 gives the score of the GCC countries in the YDI 2020. The relative performance of the GCC countries shows that most of the GCC countries rank higher in YDI, education, health and well-being, equality and inclusion, and political and civic participation.

Table 1.2: GCC Score in Youth Development Index 2020

	Edu-cation	Employ-ment & Opportunity	Health & Well being	Equality & Inclusion	Peace & Security	Political & Civic Parti-cipation	Overall YDI*
Bahrain	0.840	0.848	0.903	0.877	0.594	0.265	0.779 (47)
Kuwait	0.847	0.855	0.870	0.941	0.882	0.279	0.814 (27)
Oman	0.823	0.817	0.843	0.898	0.861	0.108	0.769 (52)

Qatar	0.775	0.914	0.866	0.952	0.906	0.161	0. 802 (32)
Saudi Arabia	0.896	0.836	0.815	0.836	0.575	0.250	0.760 (57)
UAE	0.785	0.870	0.756	0.885	0.891	0.198	0.763 (56)

Source: The Commonwealth (2020).
Note: * figures in the bracket are global ranks among 181 countries.

UAE has had a marginal improvement in its YDI score since 2014 (The Commonwealth, 2020). Oman has consistently improved its YDI score since 2012, while Qatar's had inconsistent performance and had three years of declining scores between 2012-14 (The Commonwealth, 2020). Saudi Arabia's score improved significantly between 2012-15 and then broadly declined until 2017 while significantly improving in the next two years. Some of the thrust given to the youth in the *Vision 2030* document were bearing fruits, especially regarding the young women in the Kingdom. On the other hand, almost all GCC countries have a low political and civic participation score.

Productivity of the young population is also linked to their health. Studies suggest increasing the use of tobacco among the youth. The adolescent population in the region is about 25 per cent. The causes of their mortality rates have shifted from non-communicable diseases to road injuries, mental health issues, and other attitudes that compromise their health and well-being (Al Makadma, 2017). There is also a concern about the increasing use of synthetic hallucinogens in the UAE. Exposure to diverse cultures in the region has also led to the increasing incidence of phyco-social stress. The consumption of drugs and naturally occurring mood-alternating substances has been an increasing concern (Al-Harthi and Al-Adawi, 2002).

State Policies

UAE has made the most institutional efforts to harness the potential of its youth population. It has a Federal Youth Authority and laws for the inclusion of youth in the decision-making of the federal government entities. The UAE's Minister of State for Youth Affairs, Shamma bint Suhaïl bin Faris Al Mazr, became the youngest government minister globally at the age of 22 years in 2016. She has established 'youth councils' to allow young people to register in consultative council meetings. Among initiatives to engage the young population are Emirati Youth Opportunities, Youth Hub, Interactive Youth Lab and Arab Youth Centre, which serves as a regional centre for larger connectivity and collaboration. These initiatives and institutions provide a two-way flow to listen to the youth's aspirations, needs, and challenges and engage them to generate ideas and practical solutions in the decision-making.

Vision 2030 of MbS is pivoted on youth energy. It recognises that the nation's real wealth is its young people. While a host of programmes have been launched to provide opportunities and enhance the capabilities of young men and women, engaging them in the decision-making process is the major reform to watch out for. Like the UAE, Kuwait also has the official website for the youth and a Youth General Authority regulating its affairs. The National Youth Project, established in 2012, was a consultative project in which the Kuwaiti youth were asked to submit policy recommendations on issues such as health, education, economic development, health and housing, among others. The outcome of this initiative was the establishment of the Ministry of Youth Affairs. The recommendations submitted by the Kuwaiti youth under the project were considered in the special meeting of a Council of Ministers presided by the Emir (*Kuwait News Agency*, 2013). The Kuwaiti Youth Council was created in 2012 to help implement the National Youth Project, but the council's first meeting took place only in 2019 (Roy, 2019). Despite this, youth issues like the housing crisis and jobs did not figure in the 2020 election campaign (Al Mullah, 2020).

In Oman, youth affairs are covered under the Ministry of Culture, Sports and Youth. In 2013, the National Youth Commission carried out nationwide consultations with people aged 15 to 39 years over a wide range of issues. Only in 2018, it developed a National Youth Policy and 26th October is annually celebrated as Omani Youth Day. However, the issue of jobs had remained the most prominent cause of youth unrest in the Sultanate in the last few years. The country has faced economic downturns due to low oil prices since 2014 and, unlike its peers, does not have substantial financial reserves to fall back upon. In addition, the high cost of employing the Omanis under Omanisation policy put additional strain on the profitability of the private sector.

There is no clear definition of the youth in Bahrain's legislation or policies. In 2011, the *National Strategy for Youth 2011-15* was launched with much fun fare. The Supreme Council for Youth and Sports under the Ministry of Youth and Sports is one of the important institutions mandated with the development, implementation, monitoring and evaluation of the programs concerning the youth. Other programmes to support the Bahraini youth include the Hope fund, King Hamad Award for Youth Empowerment and a multi-skill development initiative called e-Shabab. However, it is unclear whether Bahrain has an active National Youth policy or strategy. The Supreme Council for Youth and Sports website only mentions different goals and objectives, and that too, in the framework of sport, missing out on other pressing issues concerning the youth.

Digital infrastructure and E-governance have created venues for an interactive governance process. The 'digital natives' of the region have also pushed their states to reorient their foreign relations toward techno-strategic partnerships. UAE and Bahrain signing the Abraham Accord with Israel could be an inflexion point in their countries' attempts to harness youthful energy. However, it also brings in the concerns of increased states' surveillance over their population. The youth themselves are the fountainhead of the transformation currently underway in the region by pressing for reforms, engagement with frontier technology, creative commerce with culture and the upsurge of entrepreneurial energy.

In the middle of all these changes, challenges and complexities, the GCC youth continue to be concerned about getting a suitable job, starting a family, and leading a decent life or worried about the rising cost of living. The following chapters provide glimpses of how the GCC youth interact with the powerful agents of globalisation, technology and cross-cultural encounters and in negotiating their immense possibilities and participation with the state. The young digital generation in the region is prompting the states to respond in unconventional ways. The different chapters bring for the readers the breeze of change that came with youth bloom in the region.

Structure of the Book

Professor P R Kumaraswamy, in Chapter 2, looks at the analytical category of who constitutes an Arab youth. Dr Md. Muddassir Quamar, in Chapter 3, examines the demographic and governance aspect of the Saudi *Vision 2030*. Dr Rhea Abraham, in Chapter 4, looks at the digital transformation and governance in Bahrain. Nawar Kassomeh, in Chapter 5, looks at the limitation of political participation of GCC youth with consequent adaptations. Professor M H Ilias, in Chapter 6, examines the contour of popular politics in the GCC and ways of dressing, becoming the political statement of the Gulf youth.

Rohit Sharma, in Chapter 7, illustrates how the fintech environment is empowering the youth and is driven by the GCC Millennials, including women. In Chapter 8, Raahat Verma, looks at the uniqueness of the GCC states' engagement with the crypto-currency as the younger age groups are enthusiastically looking at its investment potential. Dr Mellissa Cryill, in Chapter 9, gives social and cultural aspects of the digital communities in the UAE and their encounters in the virtual world.

Dr Priyanka Chandra, in Chapter 10, dwells on the social and cultural narratives emanating from lived experiences of women and transgender and questions the state-sponsored narrative of gender reforms. In the next chapter, Dr Lakshmi Priya throws light on women becoming visible and vocal through art. Dr Priyanka Mittal, in Chapter 12, examines the role of Saudi women as cultural intermediaries, who, through a variety of production of marketable goods and services, are subtly acting as creative managers or tastemakers in society. Prabhat Chawla, in Chapter 13, throws light on the role of youth activism in the field of climate change and how it complements and supplements government initiatives. Finally, Dr N Janardhan, in Chapter 14, throws light on 'data as new oil' and the GCC countries striving to be AI hubs, prompting the governments to seek relations with new foreign partners.

References

Abraham, Jethu (2020), "Kuwaiti Youth Shake Up Traditional Diwaniya Concept," *Arab News*, October 16, https://www.arabnews.com/node/1749976/middle-east, accessed on December 28, 2021.

Al Arabiya (2015), "King Salman: Even Saudi King is Not Above Law," June 4, https://english.alarabiya.net/News/middle-east/2015/06/04/King-Salman-Even-the-King-not-above-law, accessed on December 29, 2021.

Arab Youth Survey.com (2021), "Arab Youth Survey 2020," http://arabyouthsurvey.com/en/findings/

Al Fouti, Abeer (2021), "The Role of Volunteerism in Meeting National Government Agendas," *Gulf Business,* December 7, https://gulfbusiness.com/the-role-of-volunteerism-in-meeting-national-government-agendas/ accessed on December 29, 2021.

Al-Harthi, Abdullah and Al-Adawi, Samir (2002), "Enemy Within?: The Silent Epidemic of Substance Dependency in GCC Countries," *SQU Journal of Scientific Research: Medical Science,* vol. 4, no. 1 and 2, pp. 1-7.

Al Makadma, Abdulkarim S. (2017), "Adolescent Health and Adolescent Healthcare in the Arab Gulf Countries: Today's Needs and Tomorrow's Challenges," *International Journal of Pediatrics and Adolescent Medicine,* March, vol. 4, no. 1, pp. 1-8, https://doi.org/10.1016/j.ijpam.2016.12.006, accessed on December 30, 2021.

Al Mullah, Yasmina (2020), "Kuwait Elections: Youth Issues Absent From Political Discourse," *Gulf News,* November 18, https://gulfnews.com/world/gulf/kuwait/kuwait-election-youth-issues-absent-from-political-discourse-1.75355684, accessed on December 27, 2021.

Al Musawi, Ali S. (2016), "Use of Social Media in Technology Enhanced Learning," *Transforming Education in the Gulf Region,* Routledge.

British Petroleum (2019), *BP Statistical Review of the World Energy 2019,* https://www.bp.com/content/dam/bp/business-sites/en/global/corporate/pdfs/energy-economics/statistical-review/bp-stats-review-2019-full-report.pdf, accessed on December 22, 2021.

Boghardt, Lori Plotkin (2013), "Breaking Taboos: Youth Activism in Small Gulf States," The Washington Institute for Near East Policy, https://www.washingtoninstitute.org/policy-analysis/youth-activism-small-gulf-states accessed 27 December 2021, accessed 28 December 2021.

Buchmann, M. (2001), "Sociology of Youth Culture," in N. J. Smelser, P. B. Baltes (eds.), *International Encyclopaedia of Social and Behavioural Sciences*, pp. 16660-16664, Elsevier.

Budhwar, Pawan S. and Mahllahi, Kamel (2016), *Handbook of Human Resource Measurement in the Middle East,* Cheltenham and UK: Elgar Publishing.

Diwan, Kristin S. (2014), "The Contest for 'Youth' in the GCC," The Project for Middle East Political Science, https://pomeps.org/, accessed on December 28, 2021.

Fattah, Hala (2016), "Social Structures and Transformation in the Gulf and Saudi Arabia Until 1971," in J. E. Peterson (ed.), *The Emergence of the Gulf States Studies in Modern History,* pp. 241-262, London: Bloomsbury, http://dx.doi.org/10.5040/9781474295741.ch-008, accessed on December 30, 2021.

Foster, James E. and Handy, Christopher (2008), "External Capabilities," Oxford UK: Oxford Poverty and Human Development Initiative.

Gulf Labour Market and Migration (2014), "Arab Gulf States: An Assessment of Nationalisation Policies," Research Paper no. 1/2014.

Hurley, Zoe (2020), "Showing their Faces Online is Difficult for Some Arab Students Educators Must Respond," Al Fanar Media, https://www.al-fanarmedia.org/2020/06/showing-their-faces-online-is-difficult-for-some-arab-women-educators-must-respond/, accessed on December 29, 2021.

Jones, Toby C. and Shehabi (n.d.), "Bahrain's Revolutionary," Foreign Policy, https://foreignpolicy.com/2012/01/02/bahrains-revolutionaries/, accessed on December 27, 2021.

Kumaraswamy P. R., Md. Muddassir Quamar and Sameena Hameed (2020), *Persian Gulf 2020: India's Relation with the Region*, Singapore: Palgrave Macmillan.

Kuwait News Agency (2013), "The National Youth Project Concluded Honouring Ceremony," June 4, https://www.kuna.net.kw/ArticleDetails.aspx?id=2314911&language=en, accessed on December 27, 2021.

National Commission on Terrorist Attack Upon the United States, USA (2004) *9/11 Commission Report*, Washington DC.

Osman, Aziza (2016), "Arab World's Pioneer of Social Entrepreneurship," *Arabian Business*, March 16, https://www.arabianbusiness.com/startup/arab-world-s-pioneers-of-social-entrepreneurship-625018, accessed on December 29, 2021.

Ramady, Mohamed A. (2016), *The Political Economy of Wasta: Use and Abuse of Social Capital Networking*, Springer.

Roy, Chetali (2019), "National Youth Council Panel Holds Meet to Choose Youth Counsellors," *Arab Times*, December 4, https://www.pressreader.com/kuwait/arab-times/20191204/281530817889339, accessed on December 27, 2021.

Shires, James (n.d.), "The Implementation of the Digital Surveillance Infrastructures in the Gulf," The Project on Middle East Political Science, https://pomeps.org/the-implementation-of-digital-surveillance-infrastructures-in-the-gulf, accessed on December 28, 2021.

Statista (2021), *Tertiary Student Gross Enrolment Ratio in the Gulf Cooperation Council Countries in 2019 by Segment*, https://www.statista.com/statistics/1227269/gcc-tertiary-student-ger-enrolment-by-country/access 29 December 2021, accessed on December 28, 2021.

The Commonwealth (2020), *Youth Development Index 2020*, https://thecommonwealth.org/media/news/new-global-youth-development-index-shows-improvement-state-young-people, accessed 27 December 2021, accessed on December 28, 2021.

Transparency International (2018), *Corruption Perception Index 2018*, https://www.transparency.org/en/cpi/2018/index/dnk, accessed December 30, 2021.

UN Volunteer Programme for Arab Regional Office (n.d.), "Plan of Action to Integrate Volunteering into the 2030 Agenda: Re-imagining Volunteering in the Arab States," https://www.unv.org/sites/default/files/Rimagining%20Volunteering%20in%20the%20AS-web.pdf, accessed on December 29, 2021.

Valeri, Marc (2015), "Simmering Unrest and Succession Challenge in Oman," Carnegie Endowment for International Peace, https://www.jstor.org/stable/pdf/resrep13074.pdf?ab_segments=0%252FSYC-6168%252Fcontrol&refreqid=excelsior%3Adff92065db8cc8972ee5820fe0c1e96, accessed on December 27, 2021.

Watanabe, Shun (2019), "Challenges for National Dialogue in Post Arab Spring Era: The Case of Bahrain," *Journal for Asia Japan Research Institute of Ritsumeikan University*, vol 1, pp. 56-72, https://www.jstage.jst.go.jp/article/asiajapan/1/0/1_56/_pdf, accessed on December 2, 2021.

World Bank (n.d.), *Fertility Rates Total (Birth Per Women)*, https://data.worldbank.org/indicator/SP.DYN.TFRT.IN, accessed on December 29, 2021.

2. Who is an Arab Youth?

P R Kumaraswamy

When he set himself alight and became the unintended catalyst for popular protests in Tunisia and beyond, Mohamed Bouazizi was 26 years old. The protests he began in Sidi Bouzid in the centre of the country sparked off the Jasmine Revolution and soon spread to different parts of the Arab world. Over time, the phenomenon is known by different names, including Arab uprising (Abusharif, 2014), Arab awakening (Pollack & Byman 2011), Arab Revolution (Prashad, 2016; Bayat, 2017), dignity revolution (Cohen, 2011), Twitter revolution (Kassim, 2012), Facebook Revolution (Cohen, 2011), Arab Spring (Lynch, 2011), a revolt of the educated unemployed (International Labour Organisation (ILO), 2011), Islamic awakening (Lutz, 2011), youth revolution (Al-Sakkaf, 2011) and above all youth-led uprising (UNDP, 2016, p. 21).

While these nomenclatures have a strong rationale, it is essential to recognise that youth made up a large portion of the protesting population, and this raises an interesting query: who's an Arab youth? Can Bouazizi, a 26-year-old vegetable vendor by vocation, be classified as an Arab youth? Interestingly, there is no universal definition for Arab youth; the United Nations (UN) agencies and individual Arab states adopt a stretchable age yardstick to define the Arab youth. The age limit ranging from 15 to 35 makes most countries 'young' and comes with higher rates of youth unemployment. How do different countries and UN agencies define the Arab youth?

Defining Criterion

One could use several variables to identify and define the youth, such as age, education, employment, marriage, etc., Unlike age, the rest are subjective and elastic. If one uses compulsory education—a defining feature of the youth—as the criteria, it covers primary and secondary education. However, due to popular demand and yearning, a vast majority do not content with graduating from schools but pursue higher education in universities, colleges and other technical institutions. This means that youth definition would include pupils beyond the age of 18. As part of their reform drives, several Arab countries have established scores of higher education institutions and off-campuses of premier western universities. Hence, the upper age of an Arab youth could no longer be 18 but goes up to mid/late 20s. Bouazizi, the catalyst for the Arab Spring, for example, left high schooling without graduating. According to his mother, "He had that dream himself when he was younger, but he had a brother and sisters to support, so he quit school at 18 to work" (Beaumont, 2011).

Defining youth as the period when a person finds his/her first job is equally problematic. Family conditions and poverty contribute to children being unable to complete schooling and start earning their livelihood even before completing schooling. The first jobs of the school dropouts would be menial and subsistence; Bouazizi, for example, dropped out of school to support his large family after the death of his father. The Arab Spring highlighted the larger problem: educated unemployed. The expansion of higher education in the Arab world was not commensurate to employment opportunities. The spate of measures taken by rich Gulf-Arab countries such as Arabisation of the labour force, expanding the scope for female employment, expatriate taxes, limits of social service benefits to overseas employees, etc., are partly a response to youth unemployment which triggered Arab Spring protests.

As highlighted by several Arab countries, youth unemployment is often higher than the national average and is seen as a major social challenge facing Arab societies. According to a Brookings study, youth unemployment in MENA countries "have been highest in the world for over 25 years, reaching 30 per cent in 2017" (Kabbani, 2019, p. 1). It is as high as 42 per cent among Saudi nationals and 36 per cent in Jordan and Tunisia. The Arab Spring exposed the problem of educated unemployed youth. This partly explains and justifies the age-definition of youth going up in some countries. Even the UN, which had earlier set 24 as the upper age of the youth, had to move it to 29, in its AHDR report published in 2016, a few years after popular unrest.

Marriage could be another variable to define the Arab youth. Can a married person—male or female—with children be considered a youth, even for statistical purposes? Parenthood and childcare responsibilities significantly cloud the status of being a youth. Child marriages, teenage pregnancies, and challenges of raising children add severe social, emotional, and financial burdens for the younger population. Child marriage robs young girls of their adolescence and suddenly thrusts parenthood upon them. Thus, their transition from childhood to parenthood happens without the adolescence stage. The UN Convention on the Right of the Child of 1989—which all Arab countries have signed up and ratified—defines anyone under the age of 18 as a child (Office of the High Commissioner, United Nations [OHCHR, UN], 1990); yet several countries consider those within the age of 15-18 as youth; in the Jordanian case, it is 12 years. Moreover, in several countries, females were married before they reach 18 or even while they were just children. Though education and financial hardship have increased the marriage age of men and women in several Arab countries, considering young mothers and fathers as 'youth' looks odd.

Discussing the prevalence of child marriage in MENA countries, a UNICEF report concluded that the region "is home to nearly 40 million child brides, including currently married girls and women who were first married in childhood" (United Nations Children's Fund [UNICEF], 2019, p. 2). It also observes that around "one in five young women in the Middle East and North Africa were married before their 18th birthday" (UNICEF, 2019, p. 2). Indeed, 32 per cent of the women in Yemen between the age of 20 and 24 were first married or were in union before they turned 18, including 9 per cent who married or were in union before they turned 15. The number for Iraq stands at 24 and 5 per cent, respectively (UNICEF, 2019, p. 4).

Thus, age appears to be the least contentious variable to identify the Arab youth. As would be discussed, even this is not without its share of confusion and conflicts. However, what is the age-based definition of the Arab youth?

Age of an Arab Youth

There is no universal definition for the Arab youth. Even the UN has changed the yardstick over time, and so did several Arab countries. The inaugural issue of the Arab Human Development Report (AHDR) on the *Arab Youth* published in 2002 conducted a survey among Arab youths of "15-20 years of age" (United Nation Development Program [UNDP], 2002, p. 29), but its statistics on employment and productivity covered people in the 15-24 age group (UNDP, 2002, p. 159). The second report on *Knowledge Economy* referred to the youth constituting "two-thirds of the Arab world's population" but did not offer any age definition (UNDP, 2003, p. 164). The 2004 AHDR on *Freedom* used the 15-24 age framework to assess literacy and school enrolment (UNDP, 2004, p. 239). The fourth report on the *Arab Women* talked of female youth but did not offer any specific definition but once again offered literacy and enrolment data for the female population within the age of 15-24 (UNDP, 2005, p. 296).

The fifth report on *Human Security* published in 2009 offered a tentative definition and included those under the age of 25 and concluded: "Some 60 per cent of (Arab) population is under 25 years old, making this one of the most youthful regions in the world, with a median age of 22 years compared to a global average of 28" (UNDP, 2009, p. 3). Highlighting the growing unemployment among this segment of the population, it warned of 'youth bulge', which became a catchphrase after the outbreak of the Arab Spring. Citing Arab Labour Organisation (ALO) figures for 2005-06, AHDR placed youth unemployment ranging from a low of 6.3 per cent in UAE to a high of 46 per cent in Algeria (UNDP, 2009, p. 109). However, its literacy and enrolment figures were for the 15-24 age group (UNDP, 2009, p. 239).

A more detailed discussion of the scope of Arab youth had to wait until after the Arab Spring. The 2016 AHDR on *Youth and Prospects for Human Development in A Changing Reality* significantly expanded the scope of the Arab youth and flagged the 15-29 age bracket. Using this definition, the report estimated "the number of young people in the region at over one hundred million" (UNDP, 2016, p. 7). The first report since the Arab Spring also observed that "two-thirds of the Arab region's population is below thirty years of age, half of which falling within the 15-29 age bracket" (UNDP, 2016, p. 7). Unlike earlier reports, its assessment of the youth covered the 15-29 age group. Responding to the youth-led Arab uprising, AHDR defined youth as "the stage during which a person moves out of dependence (childhood) and into independence (adulthood)." For the purposes of statistics, the UN "defines youth as individuals of ages 15-24 years. This range encompasses people who are officially recognised as a youth in the UN Millennium Development Goals and people whom many would classify as adolescents."

However, the Middle East Youth Initiative[1] "defines youth as people of ages 15-29 years," and the AHDR 2016 uses this range to "reflect the prolonged transitions to adulthood faced by many in the region" (UNDP, 2016, p. 22). Furthermore, the AHDR admitted that the Arab youth is not 'a homogeneous group' and even though their "socioeconomic, demographic and geographical situations vary widely within and across countries," a "regional analysis can provide a broad understanding of the development profile of youth" (UNDP, 2016, p. 22).

Furthermore, AHDR 2016 admitted that the popular protests in the Arab world "underline the significance of the Arab region's youthful demographic profile. Never has the region had such a large share of youth; youth of age 15-29 make up around 30 per cent of the population, or some 105 million people" (UNDP, 2016, p. 22) or 60 per cent of the Arab population "have not reached the age of 30" (UNDP, 2016, p. 22). However, even while focusing on the youth, the AHDR was realistic and observed:

> Social change is not engineered by youth, but it is most manifest among youth, who must be at the centre of any movement forward in the Arab countries. The future not only belongs to them, but will be shaped by them. It is therefore urgent to focus on youth as subjects and agents of human development in the region because no account can be complete without considering how those who mediate such tensions in their daily lives perceive and respond to their situations. (UNDP, 2016, p. 22)

Reiterating one of the causes for the Arab Spring protests, the AHDR of 2016 observed that the youth unemployment in the Arab countries was the highest in the world in 2013 with 29 per cent as against the global average of 13 per cent (UNDP, 2016, p. 31) and the need to create "more than 60 million" jobs in the next decade to stabilise the situation (UNDP, 2016, p. 32).

Unlike the earlier version AHDR 2016 provides greater details concerning the age group of the Arab youth in its statistics; its details concerning unemployment cover 15-24 age group; maternal mortality for 15-19 and 20-24 age group; health issues 18/19 to 24; use of drugs and alcohol 13-15 (UNDP, 2016, p. 226). Thus, while discussing health habits and their fallouts, the AHDR offers three subgroups of the youth; 15-19, 20-24 and 25-29 (UNDP, 2016, p. 116).

While discussing early marriages among females, the age bracket goes down even further as the AHRD notes "some (Arab) countries still have significant proportions of 15-19-year-olds marrying" (UNDP, 2016, p. 111). In its assessment, 15 per cent of the Arab women "in the 20-24 age-group had married prior to the age of 18 ... (and) 0-14 per cent of the girls in the Arab countries marry by the age of 15, and from 2-34 per cent marry by the age of 18" (UNDP, 2016, p. 111). A disturbing observation of the AHDR concerns the "minimum age of marriage"; in Saudi Arabia, Sudan and Yemen, it is 'below 15' for both the genders; is between 15-17 for both the genders in Kuwait and Palestine; is 15-17 for females in Bahrain, Lebanon, Qatar and Syria; and is 18 and above for females only in Algeria, Egypt, Iraq, Jordan, Morocco, Oman, Tunisia and UAE and for men in other countries (UNDP, 2016, p. 265). Thus, despite their acceptance of 18 as the lower age of the youth, several countries have legalised marriage before their population enters the youth.

The voting age in most Arab countries is 18 (UNDP, 2016, p. 188) but is 20 in Bahrain; 21 in Kuwait and Oman; 25 in UAE; but is 17 in Sudan.[2] Only Morocco has an age-based reservation in parliament; out of the 395 members of the lower house, 30 seats are reserved for "candidates under the age of 40" (UNDP, 2016, p. 188).

Other UN Agencies: One of the earliest attempts to define the youth was made in 1985, which the UN declared as Year of the Youth. It defined them "as those persons between 15 and 24 years of age, without prejudice to other definitions of Member States" (United Nations General Assembly [UNGA], 2001, p. 2). As admitted by the Secretary-General Report of 2001, since 1985, all the statistics put out by the UN used this classification, and this framing was reiterated by subsequent UN resolutions and steps (UN, n.d.). At the same time, the UN recognised that beyond the statistical definition, "the meaning of the term 'youth' varied in different societies around the world and that definitions of youth had changed continuously in response to fluctuating political, economic and socio-cultural circumstances" (UN, n.d.).

In 2001, the UN warned that as "the world's populations are ageing, the medium variant projection for the share of youth in the global total is expected to decrease further." From 18.1 per cent in 1995, it would be 13.2 per cent in 2050 (UNGA, 2001, p. 2). In 2000 nearly 85 per cent of youth were living in the developing parts of the world while more developed countries would witness a larger share of the ageing population. Justifying the age criteria, a UN factsheet observed that "age is the easiest way to define this group, particularly in relations to education and employment, because 'youth' is often referred to a person between the age of leaving compulsory education and finding their first jobs" (UN, n.d.).

The UN uses youth and young people as 'interchangeable' to mean the 15-24 age group (UN, n.d.). It also highlights the other age-based definitions for youth:

• UN Habitat (Youth Fund)	15-32 years
• UNICEF/WHO/UNFPA	Adolescent 10-19; Young People 10-24; Youth 15-24
• UNICEF/ Convention on Rights of the Child	Child until 18
• The African Youth Charter	15-35

Article one of the Convention of Rights of the Child of 1989 (came into force September 1990) reads as follows: "For the purposes of the present Convention, a child means every human being below the age of eighteen years unless, under the law applicable to the child, majority is attained earlier" (OHCHR, 1990). Some definitions include even those below 18 as youth (UNGA, 2001), though 'child' would be the most appropriate expression. Discussing the rights of the refugees, UNHCR considers a minor to be under 16 as "a person of 16 or over may be regarded as sufficiently mature to have a well-founded fear of persecution" (UNHCR, 1992, p. 35). Other definitions, however, state the adolescent to be a person of 18 or above. The ILO defines anyone within the 15-24 age group as 'young workers' and those above 25 as 'adult workers' (ILO, 2021, p. 24).

Individual countries add further confusion to defining the Arab youth. In 1978 Jordan became the first country in the Middle Eastern region to establish a Ministry of Youth and Culture (UNGA, 2001, p. 8). In UAE, the Supreme Council of Youth and Sports created in 1971 became a ministry a decade later (UNGA, 2001, p. 9). As part of its efforts for sustainable development, in December 2004, Jordan came out with National Youth Strategy and this defined youth as those "young Jordanian males and females who are aged 12 and 30 years old." Within this, it offered four distinct age brackets "to differentiate actions, namely 12-15, 16-18, 19-22 and 23-30" (Higher Council for Youth and UNDP, 2004, p. 4). Interestingly, Jordan included 12-15 age groups, normally considered children within its youth definition. This broader, both minimum and maximum age, enabled Jordan to claim that it is 'very youthful' and those below 30 "represent 74 per cent of the entire population. Young people (12-30) represent 40 per cent of Jordan, approximately 2.2 million in numbers. They are the single largest population group in the country" (Higher Council for Youth and UNDP, 2004, p. 4).

The vision documents outlined by some of the Arab countries offer varying definitions of youth. Egypt, which witnessed the galvanisation of youth leading to the overthrowing of the Mubarak regime, did not go beyond a passing reference to sustainable development teams including representatives "from all groups including youth, women and disabled" (Government of Egypt, 2016, p. 4). Setting out its desire for a world-class 'education system' and knowledge economy, Qatar merely spoke of "A national network of formal and informal educational programs that equips Qatari children and youth with the skills and motivation to contribute to society, fostering" through a series of social goals and agenda but does not define the Qatari youth (State of Qatar, 2008, p. 20).

Oman Vision 2040, launched in December 2020, was a 'repacking' of the earlier *Vision 2020* launched by Sultan Qaboos in 1995 (Diwakar, 2019) and frequently refers to Omani youth but without defining them (Sultanate of Oman, 2020). *New Kuwait 2035*, unveiled in March 2018, does not even make a passing reference to the youth (Mahdi, 2018). Bahrain has been witnessing unrest since March 2011, but its *Economic Vision 2030* makes one innocuous reference to "supporting and developing talented youths throughout the course of their education" (Kingdom of Bahrain, 2008, p. 22).

The *Economic Vision 2030* unveiled by Abu Dhabi in November 2008 is primarily focused on preparing the Emirati youth for the new demands of the labour market and the need to make them technically skilled. Part of this goal is also aimed at reducing the Emirati dependence upon the expatriates, who make up more than 90 per cent of the workforce. Accepting the general UN benchmark, it observes that nearly "two-thirds of the (Emirati) Nationals are aged 24 and younger, while two-fifths are beneath the age of 15." Flagging its younger population, it observes that Abu Dhabi has a "significantly higher proportion of youth than that seen in other transformation economies" (Government of Abu Dhabi, 2008, p. 36).

Since King Salman took over the reins of power in January 2015, his son Mohammed bin-Salman—more commonly known as MbS—has emerged as the key figure in the modernising efforts. Several of the measures—women's right to drive, return of movies, music and other forms of entertainment, relaxed implementation of dress code, clipping the powers of the religious police (mutawa)—are aimed at securing the support of the youth for his political and social agenda. Hence, youth figures prominently in the *Vision 2030* unveiled in April 2016. "While many other countries are concerned with aging populations," it proudly claims, "more than half of the Saudi population is below the age of 25 years." The Kingdom will leverage "this demographic dividend by harnessing our youth's energy and by expanding entrepreneurship and enterprise opportunities." Moreover, conscious of its historic treatment and widespread criticisms, it claims "Saudi women are yet another great asset" (Kingdom of Saudi Arabia, 2016, p. 37).

The *African Youth Charter* of 2006 says, "youth and young people shall refer to every person between the ages of 15 and 35 years" and with a caveat: "young people aged 15 to 17 years subject to each country's laws" (African Union, 2006). Out of 22 states of the Arab League, as many as ten countries, namely, Algeria, Comoros, Djibouti, Egypt, Libya, Mauritania, Morocco, Somalia, Sudan and Tunisia, are also members of the African Union. Thus, youth being people up to the age of 35 also binds them.

If one compares the later benchmark of 29 or 35 years, the picture is rather gloomy. Under the *African Youth Charter*, Arab youth includes those up to the age of 35; the life expectancy in Arab-African Comoros (2019), Mauritania (2019) and Sudan (2019) are 63 (2019); Yemen (2019) is 64; Djibouti (2019) is 65; Syria (2019) and India (2019) is 68; Iraq (2019) is 69.[3] Thus, if one accepts the African Charter as the benchmark, Arab individuals would be designated as 'youth' for more than half their lifetime.

Interestingly, other countries are also not helpful in resolving this problem. For example, the *National Youth Policy* outlined in 2014 defines the Indian youth as those within 'the age group of 15-29 years' who make up 27.5 per cent of the total population (Ministry of Youth Affairs and Sports, India, 2014, p. 3). Likewise, due to its ageing population, the Japanese demographic statics commonly have three categories of people; 0-14 years; 15-64 years; and 65 years and above.[4] On the other hand, Israel, which does not have an official definition, considers those within the 13-18 age bracket as youth (Brakel, Jaschinski and Jaschinski, 2009, p. 6).

Conclusions

While education, employment and marriage complicate the definition of the Arab youth, there is no consensus regarding the more tangible age criteria. For statistical purposes of its policy, the Kingdom of Jordan includes those at 12 and above as youth. However, the pervasiveness of legalised and illegal child marriages (that is, females under 18) complicates the lower age definition. The upper age is also equally troublesome. Most Arab and UN definitions set a limit of 24 years for the Arab youth, but others stretch to 26, 29, 30 and even 35. The higher age limit expands 'the youth bulge' and enables these countries to claim that they have a younger population; but expanding the age limit also increases the size of the youth unemployment, thereby undermining the success of the 'younger' population. While there is a general agreement for 18-24, the problems which forced popular protests resulted in AHDR and other agencies to push the canvas and expand the definition of the Arab youth. The increased youth bulge only added to a higher rate of unemployment figures for the educated Arab youth. Hence, a narrower and clearer age-based definition is necessary if the Arab countries were to address problems facing the Arab youth and work towards their mitigation.

Notes

1. The Dubai based Middle East Youth Initiative was launched in 2006 in collaboration with Wolfensohn Center for Development at Brookings and the Dubai School of Government. More details can be found at its homepage, https://www.meyi.org/about.html
2. "Legal voting age by country", *World Atlas*, https://www.worldatlas.com/articles/legal-voting-age-by-country.html, accessed on 4 November 2021.
3. "Life expectancy at birth", The World Bank, https://data.worldbank.org/indicator/SP.DYN.LE00.MA.IN, accessed on 4 November 2021.
4. "Japan: Age distribution from 2010 to 2020", Statista, https://www.statista.com/statistics/270087/age-distribution-in-japan/, accessed on 4 November 2021.

References

Abusharif, Ibrahim N. (2014), "Parsing 'Arab Spring'," Occasional Paper Series, Northwestern University in Qatar.

African Union (2006), *African Youth Charter 2006*, https://au.int/sites/default/files/treaties/7789-treaty-0033_-_african_youth_charter_e.pdf, accessed on November 4, 2021.

Al-Sakkaf, Nadia (2011), "The Politicization of Yemen's Youth Revolution," April 27, https://carnegieendowment.org/sada/43735, accessed on November 4, 2021.

Bayat, Asef (2017), *Revolution Without Revolutionaries: Making Sense of the Arab Spring*, Stanford, CA: Stanford University Press.

Beaumont, Peter (2011), "Mohammed Bouazizi: The Dutiful Son Whose Death Changed Tunisia's Fate," *The Guardian*, January 20, https://www.theguardian.com/world/2011/jan/20/tunisian-fruit-seller-mohammed-bouazizi, accessed on November 4, 2021.

Brakel, Kristian, Hartl Jaschinski, and Katrin Jaschinski (2009), "Studies on Youth Policies in the Mediterranean Partner Countries: Israel," Paris: EU, Regional Capacity Building and Support Unit, https://www.youthpolicy.org/national/Israel_2009_Youth_Policy_Briefing.pdf, accessed on November 4, 2021.

Cohen, Roger (2011), "Facebook and Arab Dignity," *The New York Times*, January 24, https://www.nytimes.com/2011/01/25/opinion/25iht-edcohen25.html, accessed on November 4, 2021.

Diwakar, Amar (2019), "Vision 2040: Oman's Ambitious Strategy Towards a Post-Oil Economy," *Al Arabiya*, April 16, https://english.alaraby.co.uk/analysis/

vision-2040-omans-ambitious-strategy-towards-post-oil-economy, accessed on November 4, 2021.

Government of Abu Dhabi (2008), *The Abu Dhabi Economic Vision 2030,* Abu Dhabi: Department of Planning and Economy, https://www.actvet.gov.ae/en/Media/Lists/ELibraryLD/economic-vision-2030-full-versionEn.pdf, accessed on November 4, 2021.

Government of Egypt (2016), *Egypt Vision 2030,* Cairo: Ministry of Planning and Economic Development, https://www.greengrowthknowledge.org/sites/default/files/downloads/policy-database/Egypt%20Vision%202030%20%28English%29.pdf, accessed on November 4, 2021.

Higher Council for Youth and UNDP (2004), "National Youth Strategy for Jordan, 2005-2009," Jordan: The Hashemite Kingdom of Jordan, https://www.youthpolicy.org/national/Jordan_2005_National_Youth_Strategy.pdf, accessed on November 4, 2021.

Lynch, Marc (2011), "Obama's 'Arab Spring'?," *Foreign Policy*, January 6, https://foreignpolicy.com/2011/01/06/obamas-arab-spring/, accessed on November 4, 2021.

International Labour Organisation (2011), "Youth Unemployment in the Arab World Is a Major Cause for Rebellion," April 5, https://www.ilo.org/global/about-the-ilo/mission-and-objectives/features/WCMS_154078/lang--en/index.htm, accessed on November 4, 2021.

International Labour Organisation, *World Employment and Social Outlook, Trends 2021*, Geneva: ILO, 2021.

Kabbani, Nader (2019), "Youth Employment in the Middle East and North Africa: Revisiting and Reframing the Challenge," Policy Briefing, Brookings Doha Center, February, https://www.brookings.edu/wp-content/uploads/2019/02/Youth_Unemployment_MENA_English_Web.pdf, accessed on November 4, 2021.

Kassim, Saleem (2012), "Twitter Revolution: How the Arab Spring was Helped by Social Media," *Mic*, March 7, https://www.mic.com/articles/10642/twitter-revolution-how-the-arab-spring-was-helped-by-social-media, accessed on November 4, 2021.

Kingdom of Bahrain (2008), *Our Vision: From Regional Pioneer to Global Contender, The Economic Vision 2030 for Bahrain*, Manama: Kingdom of Bahrain, https://www.bahrain.bh/wps/wcm/connect/38f53f2f-9ad6-423d-9c96-2dbf17810c94/Vision%2B2030%2BEnglish%2B%28low%2Bresolution%29.pdf?MOD=AJPERES, accessed on November 4, 2021.

Kingdom of Saudi Arabia (2016), *Vision 2030,* Riyadh: Kingdom of Saudi Arabia, https://www.vision2030.gov.sa/media/rc0b5oy1/saudi_vision203.pdf, accessed on November 4, 2021.

Lutz, Meris (2011), "Iran's Supreme Leader Calls Uprisings an 'Islamic Awakening'," *Los Angeles Times*, February 4, https://www.latimes.com/archives/la-xpm-2011-feb-04-la-fg-khamenei-iran-egypt-20110205-story.html, accessed on November 4, 2021.

Mahdi, Khaled A. (2018), *New Kuwait 2035: Kuwait National Development Plan*, Kuwait: Supreme Council for Planning and Development.

Ministry of Youth Affairs and Sports, Government of India (2014), *National Youth Policy 2014,* New Delhi: Ministry of Youth Affairs and Sports, https://yas.nic.in/sites/default/files/National-Youth-Policy-Document.pdf, accessed November 4, 2021.

Prashad, Vijay (2016), *The Death of the Nation and the Future of the Arab Revolution*, Oakland, CA: University of California Press.

Pollack, Kenneth M. and Byman, Daniel L. (2011), *The Arab Awakening: America and the Transformation of the Middle East*, Washington, DC: Brookings.

OHCHR (1990), "Convention on the Rights of the Child, 1989," https://www.ohchr.org/en/professionalinterest/pages/crc.aspx, accessed on November 4, 2021.

State of Qatar (2008), *Qatar National Vision 2030,* Doha: General Secretariat for Development Planning.

Sultanate of Oman (2020), *Oman Vision 2040: Moving Forward With Confidence*, Manama: Implementation Support and Follow-up Unit, https://isfu.gov.om/2040/Vision_Documents_En.pdf, accessed on November 4, 2021.

UNDP (2002), *Arab Human Development Report 2002: Creating Opportunities for Future Generations,* New York, http://hdr.undp.org/sites/default/files/rbas_ahdr2002_en.pdf, accessed on November 4, 2021.

UNDP (2003), *Arab Human Development Report 2003: Building a Knowledge Society,* New York, http://hdr.undp.org/sites/default/files/rbas_ahdr2003_en.pdf, accessed on November 4, 2021.

UNDP (2004), *Arab Human Development Report 2004: Towards Freedom in the Arab World,* New York, http://hdr.undp.org/sites/default/files/rbas_ahdr2004_en.pdf, accessed on November 4, 2021.

UNDP (2005), *Arab Human Development Report 2005: Towards the Rise of Women in the Arab World,* New York, http://hdr.undp.org/sites/default/files/rbas_ahdr2005_en.pdf, accessed on November 4, 2021.

UNDP (2009), *Arab Human Development Report 2009: Challenges to Human Security in the Arab Countries,* New York, https://arab-hdr.org/wp-content/uploads/2010/12/ahdr-report_2009-en-full.pdf, accessed on November 4, 2021.

UNDP (2016), *Arab Human Development Report 2016: Youth and the Prospects for Human Development in a Changing Reality,* New York, http://hdr.undp.org/sites/default/files/reports/2699/ahdr2016en.pdf, accessed on November 4, 2021.

UNGA (2001), *Report of the Secretary-General : Implementation of the World Programme of Action for Youth to the Year 2000 and Beyond*, United Nations, https://www.youthpolicy.org/basics/2001_WPAY_Implementation_Report.pdf, accessed on November 4, 2021.

UNHCR (1992), *Handbook on Procedures and Criteria for Determining Refugee Status under the 1951 Convention and the 1967 Protocol Relating to the Status of Refugees (Re-edited 1979)*, Geneva: UNHCR.

UNICEF (2019), "A Profile of Child Marriage in the Middle East and North Africa," New York, NY: UNICEF, https://www.google.com/url?sa=t&rct=j&q=&esrc=s&source=web&cd=&ved=2ahUKEwj7jJHZvunzAhUT4jgGHT_PAqcQFnoECBcQAQ&url=https%3A%2F%2Fdata.unicef.org%2Fwp-content%2Fuploads%2F2019%2F04%2FA-Profile-of-Child-Marriage-in-MENA.pdf&usg=AOvVaw3GWtz8Z6OIJuyt3QOauUcM, accessed on November 4, 2021.

United Nations (n.d.), "Definition of Youth," UNDESA, https://www.un.org/esa/socdev/documents/youth/fact-sheets/youth-definition.pdf, accessed on November 4, 2021.

3. Demography, Governance and Reforms in Saudi Arabia: An Assessment of the Vision 2030

Md. Muddassir Quamar

Introduction

Since the oil boom of the 1970s, the Kingdom of Saudi Arabia witnessed a rapid population growth with 'baby boom' and 'youth bulge' in the 1980s and 1990s. According to the Saudi General Authority for Statistics, in 2020, nearly 67 per cent of the Saudi national population was below 35 years and a majority, estimated at 36.7 per cent, were in the age group of 15-34 years (General Authority for Statistics, Kingdom of Saudi Arabia [GAS, KSA], 2020). Simultaneously, Saudi Arabia witnessed a fast and massive expansion of its education system at school and higher levels. From just eight universities in 2000, the number of universities and higher education institutions reached 50 in 2020. An estimated 250,000 students graduate from these universities and higher education institutions annually (Quamar, 2021, pp. 133-147). Logistically, Saudi Arabia is well connected and has a high internet penetration and social media usage. This means that in the 21st century, Saudi Arabia has a young, educated and globally connected population.

The 'youth bulge' is a major feature of the Saudi demographic transition (Chaaban, 2009), and this has had a profound impact on the process of governance and reforms. A young population is regarded as an engine of economic growth and social progress, but it also challenges expanding educational and economic opportunities to keep pace with rapid demographic transition. In Saudi Arabia, the challenge became multipronged because of the rentier nature of the economy and the market's preference for the cost-effective expatriate workforce, partly due to the skill mismatch between Saudi citizens and the market requirement and partly due to the preference among the nationals for high-paying managerial positions (Alsahlawi and Gardener, 2004; Achoui, 2009). These resulted in a high rate of unemployment, especially among the educated youth.

In 2010, for instance, the overall rate of unemployment among Saudi citizens was 11.2 per cent but was much higher among youth at 30 per cent (The World Bank, 2021b). According to a survey conducted by the Ministry of Economy and Planning, in the first six months of 2015, the rate of unemployment among Saudis of 20-35 years had touched the alarming level of 45 per cent (Ministry of Economy and Planning, Kingdom of Saudi Arabia [MoEP, KSA], 2015). The problem of job opportunities for women was even severe. In 2010, nearly 30 per cent of educated Saudi women were out of jobs, and as of 2015, the rate of unemployment among Saudi women had reached 33 per cent (MoEP, KSA, 2015). However, with effective reforms and a focus on creating economic opportunities, the situation has slightly improved, and as of 2019, the rate of youth unemployment among the 15-24 years age group was 22.5 per cent (GAS, KSA, 2020, p. 27).

Nonetheless, the prospect of the demographic anomaly of an educated, young and globally-connected national population with limited economic opportunities posed a probing question for the Kingdom's rulers. Resultantly, the past mantra of an incremental approach was shed by King Salman to adopt fast-paced economic and social reforms. A youthful Crown Prince Mohammed Bin-Salman is the architect of the reform measures with a focus on meeting the aspiration of the young population in terms of educational and economic opportunities and creating a conducive environment for sports, recreation and cultural activities.

One of the key initiatives to realise the fast and comprehensive socio-economic reforms is the *Vision 2030*, launched in April 2016. It focuses on two aspects—social opening and economic prosperity—that concerns the aspirational middle class, especially the youth. The foreword of the vision document states that "We [the Kingdom of Saudi Arabia] are determined to build a thriving country in which all citizens can fulfil their dreams, hopes and ambitions" (Saudi Vision 2030, Kingdom of Saudi Arabia [SV2030, KSA], 2016, p. 7). It further notes that "We [the Kingdom of Saudi Arabia] are determined to reinforce and diversify the capabilities of our economy, turning our key strengths into enabling tools for a fully diversified future." It states: "Our [Saudi] vision is a strong, thriving, and stable Saudi Arabia that provides opportunity for all. Our [Saudi] Vision is a tolerant country with Islam as its constitution and moderation as its method" (SV2030, KSA, 2016).

This chapter delineates *Vision 2030* within the context of the young demography and interlinked questions of governance and reforms. It argues that although the reform process has significantly reoriented itself both in terms of its speed and scope, it does not alter the foundation of the social contract between the monarchy and the population. Finally, the chapter explains the policy priorities of Crown Prince Mohammed within the context of *Vision 2030*, examines the compulsions for reforms juxtaposing it with the question of demography, and offers some analysis on the achievements and challenges.

A New Blueprint for Reform?

The *Vision 2030* envisions comprehensive socio-economic reforms. The vision document envisages 'a vibrant society', 'a thriving economy' and 'an ambitious nation.' It argues that to realise this ambition, the Kingdom depends on the three pillars; (i) Islam and the custodianship of the Two Holy Mosques; (ii) the potential for the Kingdom to become a global investment hub; and (iii) its unique strategic location providing connectivity to Asia, Europe and Africa. These, according to the vision document, provide Saudi Arabia with the opportunity to expand the sources of government revenues and generate opportunities for non-oil sectors to grow. Towards realising this, *Vision 2030* identifies areas such as manufacturing, information technology, mining of non-oil natural resources, tourism, leisure, recreation and sports with significant potentials for expansion. Simultaneously, it envisages expanding Saudi investments in the petroleum and gas sectors in emerging global markets.

The broader goal for *Vision 2030* is to take away the economy from the volatility of the global oil market and forge partnerships with private businesses to enhance economic capacity. The first step for this is to generate revenues for the government to invest in the identified sectors. This is to be achieved through the privatisation of national oil companies, including Aramco. This, according to the vision document, will generate funds for expansion of the earmarked areas and investments in other fields and help to achieve diversification.

Broadly, there are three components of *Vision 2030*. First, it envisages achieving transparency and efficiency in governance by eradicating corruption, improving bureaucracy and attracting global investments. As part of this objective, the Kingdom has undertaken a comprehensive restructuring of the public administration. For example, in 2015, soon after ascending to power, King Salman replaced all existing supreme councils with two empowered councils; the Council of Political and Security Affairs and the Council for Economic and Development Affairs, both functioning under MbS. The idea was to cut bureaucratic hurdles in decision-making and make it swift. Similarly, the National Anti-Corruption Commission was empowered to take action against anybody, including members of the royal family, found to be involved in financial misappropriation. The November 2017 arrests of several prominent princes, ministers, and business people were part of this anti-corruption drive (Arab News, 2017).

Second, *Vision 2030* envisions transforming the economy among the top 15 global economies. The idea is to make the Saudi economy more dynamic and responsive to global economic changes and the demands from within. To achieve this, the vision document outlines a few measures. It argues that Aramco, the world's biggest oil company, would be transformed into a global conglomerate and proposed to offer its shares as IPO on the Saudi stock exchange, Tadawul. Aramco's shares were first listed in December 2019 and within weeks, the company raised US$ 29.4 billion (Reuters, 2020). The Kingdom also plans to make the Public Investment Fund (PIF) into the world's largest sovereign wealth fund (SWF) to invest in attractive sectors globally. This has to be followed by the global expansion of Saudi corporations, including Aramco and investments in oil and gas sectors in emerging markets, including India and China (Chakraborty et al., 2017). The plan also includes improving Saudi Arabia's global ranking in ease of doing business and transparency.

Additionally, there are plans to develop non-oil sectors to withstand the vulnerability in the global oil market and meet the growing demands for employment among the Saudi youth. One of the areas identified for this has been manufacturing, including defence manufacturing. The Saudi manufacturing sector is narrow-based and the Kingdom largely depends on imports to meet domestic demands for several consumer and industrial goods. Therefore, the vision document underlines the need for developing manufacturing capacity to reduce import bills and increase employment. In this wake, the focus is two-pronged. At one level, the Kingdom is investing in mega-projects in transportation and infrastructure sectors and developing industrial cities, manufacturing hubs, special economic zones and high-tech cities like NEOM. At another level, the plan is to promote small and medium enterprises (SMEs) by increasing their share in the GDP to 35 per cent by 2030.

Other important areas emphasised in *Vision 2030* are tourism, recreational activities and sports. The Kingdom recognises the potential in its tourism sector, both religious and non-religious and aims to promote areas with potential for attracting tourists for pilgrimage and leisure. Currently, Saudi tourists prefer to go abroad for leisure activities, but developing tourist destinations within the Kingdom can offer lucrative and competitive alternatives to Saudi and non-Saudi tourists and generate micro-level economic activities and employment opportunities (Al-Dawood, 2019; Radwan, 2021). The plan includes developing infrastructure and public transport, promoting historical and cultural sites, such as Mada'in Saleh, Najran, Red Sea coast and so on, as tourist destinations.

The *Vision 2030* targets to increase umrah pilgrims from eight million annually (as of 2015) to 15 million by 2020 and 30 million by 2030 (SAV2030, KSA, 2016). Although the plan has been disrupted due to the COVID-19 pandemic, it remains an important area for non-oil economic growth. Further, the vision envisages doubling the number of UNESCO world heritage sites from four as of 2015.[1] The Kingdom also plans to get three Saudi cities recognised in top-100 global cities, increase the average Saudi household expenditure on entertainment from 2.5 per cent in 2015 to 6 per cent by 2030 and develop a culture of sports to increase participation in sports activities from 13 per cent of the population to 40 per cent. Apart from expanding the sources of revenue and diversification of the economy, the objective is to reduce the rate of unemployment among Saudis to less than 10 per cent.

The third component is the social transformation focusing on education, healthcare, housing, entertainment, sports and women empowerment. The vision document emphasises developing primary and secondary education and demand-based professional training to enhance employability. The National Labour Gateway (TAQAT) program has been developed as a digital employment exchange where job seekers can find employment while companies and businesses choose from a pool of trained and skilled labour. It emphasises digitalisation and efficiency for making the process smooth, swift and monitorable. Further, the emphasis is on enhancing the quality of higher education and reducing gaps between educational output and market needs. The government aims to have at least five Saudi universities in the top 200 global universities by 2030. The *Vision 2030* also aims to improve the preventive healthcare system and expand primary health centres to reach all Saudi citizens and residents. It also plans to make housing available for all citizens.

The vision documents tapped into newer and unprecedented areas of entertainment. The vision document noted that the current cultural and entertainment scene in the Kingdom is not up to the mark, and there is scope for better recreational opportunities for both citizens and residents. Hence, unprecedented steps such as opening cinemas, promoting cultural performances, allowing mixed audiences for live shows and sports events have been taken. Nevertheless, such endeavours also called for significant social transformations from the Kingdom's traditional religious orthodoxy to which the Vision document responded. The promotion of moderate Islam was underscored in the vision document and was underscored by the Crown Prince on several occasions. The foreword of the vision document states, "Our [Saudi] Vision is a tolerant country with Islam as its constitution and moderation as its method" (SV2030, KSA 2016, p. 7).

Concerning the condition of women, the vision document talks about both the ability of women to aspire and achieve their dreams. It aims to increase Saudi women's participation in the workforce from 12 per cent in 2015 to 30 per cent by 2030. It notes that "Saudi women are yet another great asset. With over 50 per cent of our [Saudi] university graduates being female, we [the Kingdom] will continue to develop their talents, invest in their productive capabilities and enable them to strengthen their future and contribute to the development of our society and economy" (SV2030, KSA, 2016, p. 37).

These are some of the blueprints for unprecedented changes, which seeks to make the reform process youth-centric while putting a conducive social ecosystem in place. Both the elements of continuity and change are discernible.

Change and Continuity

Historically, Saudi Arabia has promoted economic changes to adjust to market needs (Hertog, 2010). The striving for economic transformation has been a part of the Saudi evolution from a desert Kingdom to a modern oil-based economy. While initially, the wealth generated from oil led to an increase in trading and services activities, it was about building infrastructure and handling migration and urbanisation (Niblock, 1982). Therefore, the need in the 1990s was to train human resources and build capacity for a more dynamic economy with investments in the financial sector, information technology and so on (Bahgat, 1999). The focus then shifted to nationalising jobs and providing employment opportunities for the newly graduated Saudis in the 2000s (Bosbait and Wilson, 2005). In this context, *Vision 2030* is a continuation of an economy-oriented developmental plan.

Similarly, Saudi Arabia focused on education reforms in the 1980s and 1990s (Al-Eisa, 2009; Quamar, 2021) and worked to reduce extremism after 2001 (Kéchichian, 2013). King Abdullah had unveiled several reform measures for women empowerment, especially in higher education and the economy (Quamar, 2013). The national dialogue and inter-faith dialogue programs, Nitaqat, upgradation and expansion of universities, nomination of women in the *Majlis al-Shura* and voting rights in municipal elections were important initiatives during Abdullah's reign (Kumaraswamy and Quamar, 2016). Measures were also taken during his time to curb the powers of the religious police and promote moderation (Al-Alawi and Schwartz, 2012). Though dissent was not accepted, measures for making the society amenable to dialogue were made, with some degree of success (Thompson, 2014).

Nonetheless, there is a mark of freshness and break from the past in *Vision 2030.* First, there is a novelty in the approach towards reforms. Earlier, the idea of reforms was accommodated as something that is needed but not desirable. Hence, there was hesitation, a degree of sheepishness in articulating the need for it. It was conceived as a bitter pill. The *Vision 2030* changes that and articulates that reforms are desirable; it is what the society wants, and this is what the monarchy will do as part of its social contract with the citizens. It does not hesitate in admitting that Saudi Arabia's desire for moderation in social life is a break from the past. In one of his interviews, the Crown Prince pointed to the impacts of the Islamic revolution in Iran on Islamisation in the Kingdom (Chulov, 2017). Though he was not forthcoming in admitting the inherent doctrinal nature of revivalist Islam followed in the Kingdom, he was also not dismissive of the idea that moderation needs to be cultivated from within.

Second, the focus on developing the entertainment industry with film screening, theatre, cinema, cultural performances, literary activities, non-religious tourism is a clear break from the past. Under *Vision 2030*, social opening and promoting cultural activities is one of the primary goals and in the years since its launch, the Kingdom has made strides in this area. Third, it recognises the need for connecting with the youth who are the primary audience for the Crown Prince. The generational shift is the most prominent component of *Vision 2030,* which is reflected in the areas that have been prioritised. Historically, Saudi Arabia has had a problem of slow bureaucracy that was found lacking in responding to the changing aspirations of the youth. Focusing on infusing fresh blood without necessarily discarding experience, the message is that the youth are the focus of governance and reforms.

The Demographic Context

Demographic transition is the most important causal factor for bringing reforms in Saudi Arabia. More than 85 per cent of the Saudi citizens live in urban areas (The World Bank, 2016), and about 30 per cent of the population are under the age of 15 years, and nearly 67 per cent are below 35 years (GAS, KSA, 2021, p. 5). In addition, a vast majority of the Saudi youth are university graduates and a significant number have studied abroad, mostly funded through government scholarships. Hence, every year the monarchy witnesses an increase in graduates entering the job market and looking for employment. Seen together with a slowdown in economic growth due to various factors, including the global recession in 2008-09 and the meltdown in the international oil market in 2014-16, the situation in 2015-16 was alarming regarding the rising number of unemployed youths.

Hence, the idea behind *Vision 2030* was to respond to the challenge of bringing reforms to rejuvenate the historical, social contract between the monarchy and citizens. Further, the reforms were needed to respond to the demographic transition in the context of the Arab Spring protests that underlined the latent anger among the Arab youth against their non-responsive governments. Though Arab Spring protests were not strong inside Saudi Arabia, there were calls for protests, and they did resonate among the marginalised Shi'a population in the Eastern Province (Al-Matter, 2016). This forced the monarchy to find new ways to connect with the urban middle classes, especially the educated and globally-connected youth (Alnuaim, 2013). The *Vision 2030* is, therefore, the new blueprint for reforms and a response to the demographic transition to bridge the gap between the monarchy and the aspirations of the young middle-class population.

Achievements and Challenges

One of the primary objectives of *Vision 2030* is to improve the pace and effectiveness of economic diversification and improve job opportunities for Saudi citizens. Until 2020, the Kingdom has made some strides in this regard. Despite the disruptions caused by COVID-19 since early 2020, Saudi Arabia's non-oil sector has done well in growth and expansion. According to the Saudi government sources, the non-oil revenues had witnessed a growth over the five years since 2015, when it was US$ 45 billion to US$ 98 billion in 2020 (SV2030, KSA, 2021). However, since 2016, the non-oil sector has grown gingerly in terms of its contribution to GDP. In 2016, the year-on-year growth of the non-oil sector was 2.4 per cent, it dipped slightly to 1.5 per cent in 2017, rebound to 2.6 per cent in 2018 but dipped again to 0.3 per cent in 2019 and due to the impact of coronavirus, registered negative growth in 2020 (The World Bank, 2021a). Although not substantial in real terms, these are significant growth in relation to the flow of oil revenues in terms of value. In the first quarter of 2021, however, the non-oil sector has shown signs of revival with 3.3 per cent growth, though the oil sector has continued to contract due to lower demand in the international market (Kane, 2021).

The newer sectors of the economy developed under *Vision 2030*, such as tourism, entertainment, sports, and SMEs, are the driving force behind the growth in the non-oil sector. Between 2016 and 2020, the SMEs contribution to the GDP has increased from 20 per cent to 29 per cent (SV2030, KSA, 2021). With increased efforts for promoting private industries and foreign investments, in 2020, Saudi Arabia improved its global ease of doing business, ranking to 62 and topped the chart to improve the local business environment (The World Bank, 2020). As a result, the Kingdom's ranking in the global competitive index has also improved significantly between 2016 and 2020. This improvement has led to a rise in foreign investments and the private sector contribution to the economy. The FDI inflow has also improved from US$ 150 million in 2015 to US$ 4.5 billion in 2020 (SV2030, KSA, 2021).

As a result of improvement in the business environment, spurt in non-oil growth and private investments, and the development of new sectors such as tourism and recreation, there is a significant uptick in employment opportunities for youth. The share of Saudis between 15 and 34 years of age in the labour force has increased from 21.3 per cent in 2016 to 27.6 per cent in 2019, and of the total Saudis employed in the market, nearly 47 per cent are in this age group (GAS, KSA, 2020, pp. 22-30). In addition, the rate of female participation in the workforce had substantially increased to 33.2 per cent in 2020. Significantly, nearly 31 per cent of the young Saudis joining the workforce since 2016 are female. More employment opportunities have led to a decrease in the unemployment rate among Saudi women from almost 40 per cent in 2016 to 29 per cent in 2020 (GAS, KSA, 2020, pp. 22-30).

Besides the progress in economic diversification and employment generation, the Kingdom has made strides towards the social opening. In addition to easing the restrictions on recreational activities such as public screening of cinema (Arab News, 2018), there are live performances by local and international artists (BBC News, 2019). The cultural and art scene in Saudi Arabia has transformed beyond recognition at an unrealistic pace since 2015 (Foley, 2021). Many restrictions on women such as driving, visiting hospitals, travelling abroad without male guardians, gender intermixing in public places, and even restrictions on co-habitation have been gradually lifted. The change in the Kingdom's attitude towards women and religious practices has been rapid and monumental. With programs for the development of sports, cinema, health infrastructure, environment and gradual removal of social restrictions, the Kingdom has achieved some success in improving the overall social environment for its national population.

The implementation of *Vision 2030* and its various programs has led to improvement in governance and delivery of services with a focus on meeting the requirements of the bulging young population and matching their socio-economic aspirations. The launch and implementation of *Vision 2030* are interlinked with the social contract the monarchy has with the citizens. The al-Saud monarchy has historically survived the internal and external challenges due to its strong bonds with the population and its ability to undertake top-down economic and social reforms. When King Salman took over in January 2015, he was aware of the need to rejuvenate the bonds between the monarchy and the population, given the gap between them due to the demographic transition and the established governance structure and service delivery system. The King was also mindful of the context of the Arab Spring protests and its root causes, namely unemployment, corruption and a feeling of alienation among the citizens, which were also present in the Kingdom.

One of the primary targets of *Vision 2030* has been to renew the social contract between the state and the population and gain popular legitimacy for the new leaders, especially Crown Prince Mohammed. In this regard, the efficacy of the reform agenda under *Vision 2030* is significant in enhancing the popularity of the young Crown Prince among Saudi citizens, especially the youth (Cao, 2018). However, this does not mean that the process of social reforms is irreversible, especially given the history of the ulema opposing social opening and the way the Kingdom has in the past backtracked on the reform agenda in response to domestic and regional developments such as in 1979 after the Iranian revolution and the siege of Ka'ba. There have been other instances in the past, such as after the 1990-91 Kuwait crisis and the September 11 attacks, when the Kingdom took steps for reforms but gradually slowed down the process or backtracked due to opposition from the clergy or the religious sections of the society. Therefore, the Kingdom will need to be careful and dedicated to continuously working for reforms and delivering better governance, including the religious sector, to successfully deliver the agenda outlined in *Vision 2030*. Without political opening, which remains out of the question under current circumstances, the only way for the monarchy, especially the Crown Prince, to remain popular and enjoy legitimacy is to showcase an unbridled commitment towards socio-economic reforms, and thus far, *Vision 2030* has delivered on this agenda.

Undoubtedly, despite the early successes, challenges remain galore in delivering on the promises of *Vision 2030* and not entirely alienating those sections of the population that are either marginalised or remain opposed to the kind of social opening envisaged in the reform agenda. The *Vision 2030* is an ambitious plan, and it is not going to be easy to achieve all of its goals. There are several challenges at the micro level emerging from lack of proper implementation and deliverability from the bureaucracy. On the other hand, there are challenges because of financial limits, especially as the oil revenues continue to decline. Despite all the efforts, the Saudi economy remains driven by the state and petroleum revenues, and the new sectors of the economy with possibilities for private and foreign investments are also crucially dependent on state support and investments. This would pose a serious challenge in the medium-to-long term for the private sector to thrive autonomously and produce jobs for the Saudi youths.

The other challenge is the fear of backlash from those sections of the society that remains opposed to reforms, especially on the religious and gender issues. While there is a significant constituency for change, many Saudis scoff at the proposed plans for developing the entertainment industry, allowing leisure activities and do not want to see women taking part in public life. For them, upholding religious morality by maintaining a gender-segregated public space free from any 'western' influence is more important than an inclusive and flourishing economy. Finally, there are political challenges, and though the demand for political reforms remains limited, the tendency to crush dissent by force can potentially undo the popular legitimacy gained through implementing reforms.

Conclusion

The *Vision 2030* is an ambitious blueprint for social and economic transformation. It seeks to address the aspirations of a young Saudi population envisaging economic diversification and social rejuvenation. The challenge of dealing with the young Saudi population's educational, economic, and cultural aspirations is the driving force behind the new orientation in governance and reforms reflected in the launch of *Vision 2030*. The Kingdom has achieved partial successes thus far in promoting privatisation, improving the business environment and developing new sectors such as recreation and tourism. In addition, some progress has been made in creating greater employment opportunities for young Saudi men and women. However, despite the early success, there are numerous challenges in the monarchy's ability to deliver the promised outcomes. The most important being steering the economy away from its over-dependence on the petroleum industry. Besides, there are challenges regarding shortcomings in governance and service delivery system.

The *Vision 2030* reform agenda is interlinked with the demographic transition and question of governance within the existing foundations of the social contract between the Saudi monarchy and citizens. At the ideational level, *Vision 2030* responds to the challenges posed by demographic transition and adopts a populist approach seeking to reinvent the social contract without changing its foundations. Undoubtedly, there is a degree of novelty in the reforms agenda, but it also has elements of continuity for the historical evolution of modernisation and economy-oriented developmental approach. The challenge at the ideational level is to overcome the conventional social ideals of religiosity and Islamisation, which Crown Prince Mohammed wishes to leave behind.

Note

1. Among the UNESCO world heritage sites in Saudi Arabia are Al-Hijr Archaeological Site (Mada'in Salih) (2008), At-Turaif District of Dir'iyah (2010) (the capital of first Saudi state), Historic City of Jeddah (2014) and Rock Art of the Hail Region (2015).

Al-Ahsa Oasis in Eastern Province got the status in 2018 and Hima Cultural Area in Najran in 2021. In addition to these six, there are 10 other sites which the Kingdom intends to nominate for recognition as world heritage sites including Hejaz railways (United Nations Educational Scientific and Cultural Organisation, World Heritage Centre [UNESCO, WHC], 2021).

References

Achoui, Mustapha M. (2009), "Human Resource Development in Gulf Countries: An Analysis of the Trends and Challenges Facing Saudi Arabia," *Human Resource Development International*, vol. 12, no. 1, pp. 35-46.

Al-Alawi, Irfan and Schwartz, Stephen (2012), "Saudi Arabia's Religious Police Reforms," *The Weekly Standard*, October 9, http://www.weeklystandard.com/blogs/saudi-arabia-s-religious-police-reforms_654065.html, accessed on September 18, 2018.

Al-Dawood, Abdullah (2019), "Saudi Arabia Is the World's Fastest-Growing Tourism Destination, Says Group CEO of Seera Group," *Arabian Business*, November 28, https://www.arabianbusiness.com/travel-hospitality/434585-saudi-arabia-is-the-worlds-fastest-growing-tourism-destination-says-group-ceo-of-seera-group, accessed on July 8, 2021.

Al-Eisa, Ahmed (2009), *Islah Al-T'alim Fi Al-Saudia: Bain Ghiyab Al-Ru'ya Al-Siyasiya Wa Tawajjus Al-Thaqafa Al-Diniya Was 'Ajz Al-Idara Al-Tarbawiya* (Educational Reform in Saudi Arabia: Between Lack of Political Vision, Religious-Cultural Apprehension and Incompetence of Educational Administration), [Arabic], Beirut: Dar al-Saqi.

Al-Matter, Talal (2016), "Saudi Arabia and the Arab Spring: Five Year of Influence and Action," *Conference Proceedings*, Third Asia Pacific Conference on Advanced Research, Melbourne, July, pp. 448-454.

Alnuaim, Mishary (2013), "The Composition of the Saudi Middle Class: A Preliminary Study," *GRC Gulf Paper*, Jeddah, Gulf Research Center, October, https://www.files.ethz.ch/isn/171150/Middle_Class_8157.pdf0.pdf, accessed on July 8, 2021.

Alsahlawi, Khalid Abdulaziz and Gardener, Edward P. M. (2004), "Human Resources and Economic Development: The Case of Saudi Arabia," *Journal of Third World Studies*, vol. 21, no. 1, pp.175-189.

Arab News (2017), "Cabinet Reshuffle, Crackdown on Corruption in Saudi Arabia," November 5, http://www.arabnews.com/node/1188521/saudi-arabia, accessed on September 18, 2018.

Arab News (2018), "Licensing Opens for Cinema in Saudi Arabia, Says Ministry," March 1, http://www.arabnews.com/node/1257201/saudi-arabia, accessed on July 8, 2021.

Bahgat, Gawdat (1999), "Education in Gulf Monarchies: Retrospect and Prospect," *International Review of Education*, vol. 45, no. 2, pp. 127-136.

BBC News (2019), "BTS: K-Pop Band Perform in Saudi Arabia Despite Criticism," October 11, https://www.bbc.com/news/world-middle-east-50022766, accessed on July 8, 2021.

Bosbait, Mohammed and Wilson, Rodney (2005), "Education, School to Work Transitions and Unemployment in Saudi Arabia," *Middle East Studies*, vol. 41, no. 4, pp. 533-545.

Cao, Sissi (2018), "Saudi Arabia's Crown Prince is Wildly Popular Among (His Own) Youth," *Observer*, May 10, https://observer.com/2018/05/saudi-arabias-crown-prince-is-wildly-popular-among-his-own-youth/, accessed on July 8, 2021.

Chaaban, Jad, "Youth and Development in the Arab Countries: The Need for a Different Approach," *Middle Eastern Studies*, January 2009, vol. 45, no. 1, pp. 33-55.

Chakraborty, Debjit, Pandya, Dhwani and Sundria, Saket (2017), "Saudi Aramco Plans 'Mega Investment' in World's Top Oil Guzzler," *Bloomberg*, October 9, https://www.bloomberg.com/news/articles/2017-10-09/saudi-aramco-plans-mega-investment-in-world-s-top-oil-guzzler, accessed on September 18, 2018.

Chulov, Martin (2017), "I Will Return Saudi Arabia to Moderate Islam, Says Crown Prince," *The Guardian*, October 24, https://www.theguardian.com/world/2017/oct/24/i-will-return-saudi-arabia-moderate-islam-crown-prince?CMP=share_btn_tw, accessed on September 18, 2018.

Foley, Sean (2021), *Changing Saudi Arabia: Art, Culture, and Society in the Kingdom*, Boulder, CO: Lynn Reinner.

General Authority for Statistics, Kingdom of Saudi Arabia [GAS, KSA] (2020), *Saudi Youth in Numbers: A Report for International Youth Day 2020*, https://www.stats.gov.sa/sites/default/files/saudi_youth_in_numbers_report_2020en.pdf, accessed on July 8, 2021.

Hertog, Steffen (2010), *Princes, Brokers, and Bureaucrats: Oil and the State in Saudi Arabia*, New York: Cornell University Press.

Kane, Frank (2021), "Saudi Non-Oil Economy Climbs Back to Growth," *Arab News*, May 10, https://www.arabnews.com/node/1856691/business-economy, accessed on July 8, 2021.

Kéchichian, Joseph A. (2013), *Legal and Political Reforms in Saudi Arabia*, New York: Routledge.

Kumaraswamy, P. R. and Quamar, Md. Muddassir (2016), "More Effective as Regent Than as Monarch: Abdullah's Reform Legacy," *Contemporary Arab Affairs*, vol. 9, no. 3, pp. 445-460.

Ministry of Economy and Planning, Kingdom of Saudi Arabia [MoEP, KSA] (2015), *Labour Force Survey, 2015 (First Half)*, Riyadh: Central Department of Statistics and Information.

Niblock, Tim (ed.) (1982), *State, Society and Economy in Saudi Arabia*, London: Croom Helm.

Quamar, Md. Muddassir (2013), "Education as a Ladder for Saudi Women: An Overview," *Journal of Arabian Studies*, vol. 3, no. 2, pp. 265-277.

Quamar, Md. Muddassir (2021), *Education System in Saudi Arabia: Of Change and Reforms*, Singapore: Palgrave Macmillan.

Radwan, Rawan (2021), "Entrepreneurs in Saudi Arabia's Tourism Sector Get New Boost," *Arab News*, March 15, 2021, https://www.arabnews.com/node/1826011/saudi-arabia, accessed on July 8, 2021.

Reuters (2020), "Saudi Aramco Raises IPO to Record $29.4 Billion by Over-Allotment of Shares," January 12, https://www.reuters.com/article/us-saudi-aramco-stocks-idUSKBN1ZB03D, accessed on July 8, 2021.

Saudi Vision 2030, Kingdom of Saudi Arabia [SV2030, KSA] (2016), *Vision 2030 Documents*, https://www.vision2030.gov.sa/v2030/achievements/, accessed on September 18, 2018.

Saudi Vision 2030, Kingdom of Saudi Arabia [SV2030, KSA] (2021), "Progress & Achievements," https://www.vision2030.gov.sa/v2030/achievements/, accessed on July 8, 2021.

The World Bank (2016), "Percent of Urban Population in Saudi Arabia," https://data.worldbank.org/indicator/SP.URB.TOTL.IN.ZS?locations=SA, accessed on September 18, 2018.

The World Bank (2020), *Doing Business 2020: Comparing Business Regulation in 190 Economies*, https://documents1.worldbank.org/curated/en/688761571934946384/pdf/Doing-Business-2020-Comparing-Business-Regulation-in-190-Economies.pdf, accessed on July 8, 2021.

The World Bank (2021a), "Saudi Arabia" *Economic Outlook*, https://thedocs.worldbank.org/en/doc/cfe892579f0c3ec9f329e40f3a93c21d-0280012021/original/15-mpo-sm21-saudi-arabia-sau-kcm2.pdf, accessed on July 8, 2021.

The World Bank (2021b), "Unemployment, Youth Total (% of Total Labour Force Ages 15-24) (National Estimate)—Saudi Arabia," https://data.worldbank.org/indicator/SL.UEM.1524.NE.ZS?locations=SA, accessed on July 8, 2021.

Thompson, Mark (2014), *Saudi Arabia and the Path to Political Change: National Dialogue and Civil Society*, London: I. B. Tauris.

United Nations Educational Scientific and Cultural Organization, World Heritage Centre [UNESCO, WHC] (2021), "Saudi Arabia," https://whc.unesco.org/en/statesparties/sa, accessed on October 21, 2021.

4. Digital Transformation and Governance in Bahrain

Rhea Abraham

Introduction

Until the introduction of the internet and the widespread use of personal computers, the main objective of technology use in governmental services worldwide was to enhance the capacity of public administration. Technology was seen to manage the limitations and provide the infrastructure within the bureaucratic workforce. Since the 1990s, digital technology has become a pervasive entity, permitting every aspect of society, organisation, and public services. However, the promise of significant efficiencies with the emergence of information, technology and communication (ICT), in governmental services, time constraints and the more involved citizenry have significantly fuelled the growth and interest in e-services worldwide.

Since the outbreak of the COVID-19 pandemic, governments around the world have been confronted with various social and economic challenges and the increasing digitalisation of services. One of the immediate consequences of the COVID-19 pandemic has been the restrictions on the movement of people and selective closures of business and government offices. This has resulted in a sudden surge in demand for online services such as working from home, online banking services, and e-health initiatives. Online educational services have provided greater connectivity for people to collaborate and share ideas and manage knowledge production. The World Digital Competitiveness Index by the Institute for Management Development Switzerland (IMD) emphasises that governments around the world are investing heavily in the advancement of digital economy initiatives to enhance value creation, national prosperity and growth in overall per capita Gross Domestic Product (GDP) (Al-Khouri, 2020).

A digital economy characterised by the pervasive use of ICT helps accelerate opportunities for economic growth and improve public delivery of social services (UN-ESCWA, 2017). The concept of Digital Economy was first introduced in 1995 by Don Trapscott in his book *The Digital Economy: Rethinking Promise and Peril in the Age of Networked Intelligence.* It further aims to diversify the national economy by generating value-added services and products that cater to local, regional, and international markets. It is expected to shape future trends allowing individuals and organisations to share information and manage knowledge in effective methods for policy construction. This allows greater access to newer markets (Al Roubaie, 2018), increasing productivity, promoting innovation and sustainable development, and engaging local entrepreneurs in global trade.

The Government of Bahrain is a pioneer in deploying advanced technologies for citizens, residents, and businesses in the Arab Gulf region and has been actively developing its infrastructure to increase its readiness for a digital economy. Currently, the digital economy accounts for 8 per cent of Bahrain's total economy but has increased steadily over the years (Bahrain Economic Development Board [EDB], 2019). The small state of Bahrain has been consistently ranked among the top in the region in its ICT preparedness and ICT development and has a long track record as a regional forerunner in the adoption of business-friendly regulations to support the development of the digital economy. Bahrain has limited proven hydrocarbon reserves and understands the need to diversify revenues. It has been pursuing various initiatives to promote growth in non-oil sectors by introducing necessary regulatory frameworks and infrastructure to conduct a smooth transition. This also includes initiatives in education as vital to achieving long-term diversification plans, which prioritise ICT development and transition to a knowledge economy.

In 2020, the Bahrain government adopted integrated pandemic planning to create a more progressive and robust economy, including testing for COVID-19, contact tracing, quarantine, and healthcare technologies to strengthen digital transition. In addition, the government's organisational and operational resources were restructured to strengthen conventional disaster and pandemic management capabilities while ensuring business continuity in the public and private sectors. However, a digital transformation could cause several challenges for Bahrain, including the need to create a digitally skilled workforce and increasing the employment of nationals in the private sector. This is mainly due to the lack of digital skillset of the nationals vs. the expatriates, which may require sustained strategies and skill development to overcome existing labour market problems and pave the way for effective digitisation. Therefore, this paper is an attempt to understand the rise of the digital economy in the Gulf countries, particularly in Bahrain, the digital strategy employed by the government, studying its impact on the youth of Bahrain, and the labour market, and highlighting the opportunities and challenges for the post-COVID-19 era in the region. The chapter has taken primary data on digital or e-government from the official website of the Government of Bahrain to understand the process of digital transformation and the current developments.

Digitalisation in the Gulf

Digital government is a concept defined by the activity's objective, which is to transfer government information and services, rather than by the specific technology used and provider of the service/information (Yildis, 2007). Hence, many definitions of digital government are rather loose and stress over the multiple meanings depending on the specific context, regulatory environment, dominance of a group of actors in a given situation, and different priorities in government strategies. Digital government encompasses many characteristics such as managing human resources and access to and quality of public services (Infodev/World Bank, 2009). There are four main types of services (Evans and Yen, 2006): government to the citizen, government to business, government to government and intra-governmental.

An Overview

The Organisation for Economic Co-Operation and Development (OECD), defines digitalisation as "the use of digital technologies to bring changes to existing activities", and digital transformation as "the economic and societal effects of digitisation" (Mehrej, 2021). In the late 1990s, Arab Gulf governments invested heavily in ICT, enabling them to renew and expand their ICT infrastructures by implementing new technologies. In the early 2000s, the internet diffusion rate in Arab countries steadily increased with government's understanding of the infrastructural aspects of the internet and its contribution to economic growth and the need to bridge the digital divide (Mehrej, 2021). From 2003 to 2008, ICT expenditure on related services in the region was approximately 3.4 per cent of the countries' GDP, which increased to 5.8 per cent (The World Bank, 2010). Increased oil and gas revenues boosted the GDP of Gulf Cooperation Council (GCC) countries, and subsequently, these countries increased investment in their ICT infrastructure initially to attract foreign investors. The approach adopted by Bahrain, Kuwait, Oman, Qatar, and the United Arab Emirates involved partial privatisation of the state-owned telecommunication sector, which acted as the key catalyst for modernisation and the expansion of public telecommunications networks. In the Arab states, national network upgrades, technological improvements, enhanced national connectivity, and the gradual introduction of new internet provider delivery technologies started creating a favourable environment for the uptake of ICT (UNESCO Institute for Statistics, 2013).

In turn, there was a revolutionary change in the amount of information available due to its effect on the development of the economy, exposing the youth to a far greater diversity of ideas, including political and social, than ever before. The compromise was to allow internet access but with a large government body dedicated to filtering and censoring the contents. In terms of mobile phone penetration, the Arab Gulf countries became the top consumers globally, circumventing some of the traditional restrictions on information and entertainment. Currently, the younger generation in the Arab Gulf are increasingly bilingual and can therefore access an even wider range of global media. As some Arab countries continue their investments into digital knowledge-based economies, the regional ICT infrastructure grows exponentially. The United Nations Development Programme (UNDP) report on e-government or now termed as digital government, shows a high level of preparedness in Arab countries, which are classified as heavy users of electronic social networks with a high dependence on digital communication (UN, 2014). Growing efforts of the GCC governments to promote digital transformation and literacy have also elevated the region's readiness. The UAE, Bahrain, and Qatar are identified as the Arab digital government leaders with a single entry point National Digital Government portal to provide transaction capabilities to users of e-government services (Chatfield and Alhujran, 2009).

Effects of Digitalisation

Change in the availability of information also adds to expectations of greater transparency, freedom of expression and political participation. Digitalisation reduces discretion and enables accountability of government services by limiting human interactions and thereby controlling corruption (Santiso, 2021). Periodical auditing of system security and the use of the Cloud can help analyse huge volumes of data and help detect any fraudulent activities (Sugumaran and Al-Mutawha, 2020). The advent of digital technology has forced the scrutinisation of government actions and has allowed open government initiatives for the people in the Gulf to reach out to the public sector. Similarly, politics in the Arab Gulf monarchies have significantly transformed in the current decade with the opening up of Gulf countries to information flows largely as a by-product of economic and technological changes. Media, education, and greater connectivity have been improving the ability of Gulf citizens not just to consume and receive information, but also to participate more freely and actively in local and global discussions about politics and societies.

Despite the support for monarchies among the locals, the GCC countries are witnessing growing internal pressure for popular participation, including deliberation on representation by young people and women in the region. The Arab Gulf monarchies have been investing in digital government services to reach out to their people. Along with leadership backing and funding for modernising the existing infrastructure and demographics, the GCC countries have also invested in e-participation services to boost public confidence. This has, in turn, opened avenues for the international community to foster relations with the Gulf that were otherwise considered inward-looking. It is important, however, to know that while digital use in these countries may not be fundamentally rooted in sustaining participatory democracy, it still has a significant impact on governance interactions as it facilitates more individualised communication between citizens and officials (Tolbert and Mossberger, 2006).

Digital technology has also facilitated economic diversification in the Gulf countries, focusing on building skills, creating knowledge and sharing information (Al-Roubaie, 2018). In the GCC, the priority now has become the need to create employment opportunities by building up local capabilities and localising sectors such as agriculture, technology, and pharmaceuticals (PwC, 2021).

Bahrain's Digital Government

Despite its small wealth, Bahrain's oil and natural gas exports comprise about 80 per cent of public sector revenue, and the government has been pushing various initiatives to focus on non-oil sectors to diversify its economy (Mogielnicki, 2020). Like all Gulf countries, the Bahraini government has formulated its economic vision 2030 to focus on sustainable growth and fair competition in the international environment. Bahrain currently ranks second in the region for e-government readiness and capacity and is the first Amazon Web Services hyperscale data centre in the region. Hyperscale data centres are massive business-critical facilities designed to efficiently support robust, scalable applications and are often associated with big data-producing companies such as Google, Amazon, Facebook, IBM, and Microsoft. According to World Bank, Bahrain is the fourth most improved economy globally, the first to roll out nationwide commercial use of 5G and the first country in the region to shift its entire government services to the Cloud, including 62 per cent of all government services (Bahrain EDB, 2020). "The Cloud" refers to servers accessed over the internet and the software and databases that run on those servers. Cloud servers are located in data centres all over the world. By using cloud computing, users and companies do not have to manage physical servers or run software applications on their own machines. Bahrain's ICT infrastructure has been described as progressive, and several entrepreneurs and start-ups find Bahrain a good testing ground for ventures given its connectivity and proximity to larger markets in the Middle East.

An Overview

Bahrain has established a fully-equipped National Data Centre, followed by creating a secure National Data Network and the introduction of Smart ID Cards for citizens and residents. The government's digital transformation is headed by the Supreme Council for Information & Communication Technology (SCICT), chaired by the Deputy Prime Minister Shaikh Mohammed bin Mubarak Al Khalifa and supported by the National ICT Governance Committee, which monitors the coordination and implementation of its strategic digital initiatives. The eGovernment Authority was formed in 2007, and Bahrain's National eGovernment strategies ensure the effective delivery of e-services to all citizens, residents, and businesses under the motto "Delivering customer value through a collaborative government" (Government of Bahrain, 2021a).

The government set up *Tamkeen*, a semi-government authority, to assist government strategies towards achieving Bahrain's *Economic Vision 2030* and National Strategy through effective human capital development and the optimisation of talent among the indigenous workforces. The government has plans to adopt a 'digital marketplace' approach to government procurement, where Bahrain or the GCC-based companies can list their services to be procured by the government. Bahrain has launched 200 electronic services and four main service delivery channels, an eGovernment National Portal, Mobile Gateway, Government Services Contact Centre, and eService Centres. Bahrain's digital government has been encouraging citizens to interact with the government via digital channels, make accurate predictions for the government's functioning with greater transparency and civic engagement; and provide digital services for everyone. This includes:

- Improving participative governance services for women by increasing visibility and awareness of government initiatives among young women and encouraging them to discuss their matters through eParticipation Platform *Tawasul.*
- Involving people with special needs through various tools such as ReadSpeaker tool to support their access and usage of eServices.
- Electronic services for migrants and labourers are available in multiple languages facilitating the spread of awareness about laws

and procedures related to the Labour Market Regulatory Authority, protecting workers from human trafficking and salary payment deferrals, enabling them to apply for flexible work permits and a job portal to connect with job providers.

- Digital Aptitude initiatives include digital literacy initiatives, advanced digital education, and awareness about the government's electronic services.

E-Government Strategies

Numerous strategic projects and initiatives were conceptualised and implemented from 2007 to 2010 to achieve a range of objectives highlighted in Bahrain's e-government strategy 2010 (Government of Bahrain, 2021b). These include National eGovernment Interconnectivity projects such as the Integrated Workflow Management System *Zajel*, National Enterprise Architecture Framework, e-Investor, National Authentication Framework, and a National Gateway Infrastructure. Other initiatives launched during this time included an eGovernment Portal Infrastructure Project, Security Level Assessment of eGovernment Services, National Payment Platform, and Implementation for Quality Assurance Standards in ICT.

Bahrain later introduced the National eGovernment Strategy for 2011-2014 with a motto to 'advance', which included establishing necessary legislation and regulations to maintain a secure electronic environment. The national electronic service delivery channels, especially the eGovernment National Portal and the eGovernment App Store, enhanced communication channels with the citizens and residents. The government implemented *Tawasul*, the National Suggestions and Complaints System, which enables citizens and residents to submit suggestions and complaints to any government entity and helps involve citizens in decision making. Around 80 per cent of government entities were encouraged to engage in electronic participation and social media interactions with the beneficiaries. This goes a long way to reducing corruption in the country. Transparency International ranks Bahrain as 78th in the Corruptions Perception Index 2020 (Transparency International, 2021). Bahrain has set up a *General Directorate of Anti-corruption and Economic and Electronic Security* to deal with fraudulent activities in public transactions and cybercrimes. In 2015, a national anti-corruption committee and anti-corruption strategy were introduced (FATF-MENAFATF, 2018).

Entrepreneurship was encouraged by creating open data platforms to promote innovation and developing new applications and services for proactive engagement. The government also provided ICT training to 5,000 citizens to strengthen international and regional interactions between the public and private sectors and educational institutions by conducting study tours. From 2015 to 2018, the e-government strategy of Bahrain was refreshed to align with the macroeconomic factors prevailing in the region. There was a focus on personalised data that was nurturing active participation of citizens by raising awareness of the role of governance. The strategy focused on ensuring the security of citizens' information and on individual-centric services. The government established advanced ICT infrastructure such as the Cloud-first policy to attract foreign investment and strengthen the private sector. A national cyber security strategy was also implemented by providing training to 3,500 employees. Bahrain's Personal Data Protection Law, a key enabler of the country's digital economy, was introduced in 2018.

By the end of 2020, the Bahrain government provided 504 e-services, including social services, housing services, overseas affairs services, financial support services and services relating to labour and social development, employment, and financial support. Moreover, 44 health e-services were launched by the government to combat the COVID-19 pandemic. There has also been a continued focus on artificial intelligence (AI), in developing government services, including the judicial sector in Bahrain, which has helped streamline judicial proceedings. Citizens and residents can now file civil and commercial lawsuits online. Digital technology has also enabled Bahrain's education sector to offer remote learning by migrating the educational gateway EDUNET to the Cloud.

Digital Government Strategy 2022

Digital Government Strategy 2022 of Bahrain stipulates that government entities will stress upon the previous strategies focusing on inclusive approach and emphasise on specific needs of citizens, but also encourage government interactions with an assisted digital approach. In addition,

Bahrain aims to rebuild public eservices with digital delivery at their foundation and design procedures that supply certain types of data only to the government entity and thereby help create greater privacy and transparency. Each initiative from the previous strategies has been revisited in 2020 to study the possible impact in the context of the pandemic.

The Bahrain government created *Qudurat* under the public-private partnership between the civil society and the government to deliver training programmes for the citizens to operate basic daily IT tasks. As a result, approximately four million Bahraini dinars (approximately US$ 10 million), was granted to digital interventions in the pandemic period, including distributing response to monitoring quarantined individuals, more Cloud storage for each unit, platform for e-commerce activities, introducing new e-services, strengthening cyber security and other innovative initiatives such as the national Genome project. In addition, a dedicated health portal, a COVID-19 platform facilitating the delivery of medicines and doctor consultations and the *BeAware* Bahrain application to support contact tracing and COVID-19 test results were also introduced. In addition, advanced technologies were harnessed to support health workers with information and diagnostic services, while analytics assisted in making projections about disease outbreak management and health services.

The Private Sector

The private sector in Bahrain has also been empowering itself with the development of emerging technologies, creating opportunities for improving revenues and attracting foreign investments (Government of Bahrain, 2021a). The private sector, including business communities, has urged official recognition for remote meetings, direct learning and virtual communications to ensure the successful implementation of the digital economy in the sector (Saxena, 2020). The Business Licensing Integrated Systems *Sijilat.bh* has enabled entrepreneurs, business people, and investors to carry out all commercial registration transactions and reduce their setup time for starting a business in Bahrain. Even the banking sector has made tremendous achievements using digital technologies in the country. *Al Salam-Bank* in Bahrain rolled out virtual branches and a digital onboarding app; the National Bank of Bahrain was the first in the region to launch open banking services; the Bahrain Islamic Bank launched Bahrain's first fully digital bank branch; and *Meem* became the region's first Sharia-compliant digital banking service (*The Saudi Gazette*, 2018).

Youth and Digital economy

The small country of Bahrain has a total resident population of approximately 1.7 million, where expatriates constitute the majority. The percentage of those under the age of 19 years amounts to 25.9 per cent, those between 20-64 years to 71.1 per cent and those over the age of 65 to 2.1 per cent (Government of Bahrain, 2021c). In 2019, the share of unemployment among the youth during 2000-2019 was 4.6 per cent of the youth labour force in Bahrain (Statista, 2021).

Bahrainisation and employment

Bahrain, often hailed as the most accommodating country for migrants in the Gulf region, was the first to allow migrant workers to form trade unions (Dudley, 2018). It currently accommodates about 350,000 Indian expatriates engaged in various sectors in the country; 65 per cent of the Indian expatriate workforce is employed in the construction sector (Government of India, 2020). However, the country's changing economic fortunes spurred efforts to accelerate the Bahrainisation of the workforce. The nationalisation programme has lately extended into the retail and telecommunications sectors. By the end of 2018, employment of non-Bahraini workers had decreased by 0.9 per cent compared to the previous year (Government of Bahrain, 2018). The aftershock of the 2008 global financial crisis negatively affected business execution and increased the unemployment rate for Bahraini nationals and foreign workers (Abdelbaki, 2010). From 2010 to 2016, the number of unemployed Bahrainis increased from 5,336 to 8,485 and at a rate of 4.3 per cent (Government of Bahrain, 2016). The government responded to this by adopting a package of fiscal reforms and by attempting to accelerate the workforce nationalisation process. The government embarked on efforts to develop a workforce more capable of meeting the demands of the private sector. Recent studies show an increase in the size of the national workforce, with 66 per cent of the national workforce employed in the private sector and 34 per cent in the public sector (Bahrain News Agency, 2018).

Bahrain initiated the second generation of workforce nationalisation policies and programmes to redress its unemployment problem. The first generation of Bahrainisation policies was introduced in the early 1980s through *Project 10,000*, a training and employment scheme for young Bahrainis in private sector jobs. The government established the *Tamkeen* fund to train and educate Bahrainis to give them a competitive edge over foreign workers in the private sector (Abdulla, 2018). *Tamkeen* announced the relaunch of the redesigned *Mohasaba* scheme, a business development support programme for Bahraini entrepreneurs (Tamkeen, 2017). A national action plan has been introduced called the National Employment Programme, which aims to promote Bahrainis as the best option for employment in Bahrain (*Gulf Daily News*, 2019). This programme includes amending the unemployment insurance draft law to increase compensation fees, increasing fees for the Parallel Bahrainisation System and the Flexible Work Permit, and redesigning *Tamkeen*'s Training and Wage Support Programme (Bahrain News Agency, 2019)

The International Labour Organisation (ILO) announced that 1.5 billion jobs, of which one-sixth belong to youth, are threatened globally due to the pandemic. In Bahrain, the initial steps exercised by the government through *Tamkeen* and the BCCI have helped empower small and medium enterprises to fill the gap; yet systemic issues persist. This has been facilitated by fostering universities' roles, increasing their numbers, and increasing vocational and technical training. Moreover, Bahrain has been improving access to venture capital funding for early-stage businesses and start-ups within the sector. In addition, the government launched the technology transfer programme, which aims to increase patents in the country and embrace inventions that contribute to creating jobs for citizens. Furthermore, the programme links the educational sector with the industrial sector in building partnerships between young entrepreneurs and businesses.

Knowledge Creation

Since 2005, the Bahrain government has used ICT as a tool for learning and digital empowerment in schools across the country. The education sector has been leaning towards new areas such as STEM, programming and entrepreneurship with the introduction of several schools focusing on workshops on computer programming, web development and robotics. The government has been facilitating the development of e-learning in the education system and its transition to a knowledge economy through the King Hamad Schools of the Future project. Bahrain is also collaborating with the International Society for Technology in Education (ISTE), as a training centre to impart and improve ICT training to the teaching staff (Oxford Business Group, 2020). The government also aims to develop graduate programmes and apprenticeships to attract highly skilled local talent, which would support its National Higher Education Strategy 2024. Bahrain remains focused on broadening its local talent pool through university development programmes (funded by *Tamkeen*), to equip young Bahrainis with the skills required to work with emerging technologies.

The Ministry of Labour and Social Development launched a training programme for children to install and programme robots in schools around the country. Bahrain Polytechnic launched an Artificial Intelligence Academy in collaboration with *Tamkeen* and Microsoft as an educational platform for an integrated and specialised programme to enhance AI-related innovation. Bahrain also introduced a range of pioneering programmes at universities and educational institutions, such as the Big Data Operations Programme, Master of Environment and Sustainable Development Programme, and the Financial Technology Master Programme. The University of Bahrain currently awards certificates to its graduates through Blockchain technology, reflecting its adoption of modern technology in academic programmes. The university's Cloud Innovation Centre provides a platform for the public sector to test new ideas through Amazon's innovation process.

The Supreme Council for Youth and Sports launched an AI innovation competition for students called the Khalid bin Hamad Innovation and Artificial Intelligence Competition, allowing students to showcase their ideas and develop their capabilities. The Bahrain Institute of Banking and Finance launched its FinTech Masters Programme in collaboration with the University of Strathclyde to help nurture future leaders of digital transformation (Bahrain EDB, 2019). The Tech Valley programme, by the

Bahrain Institute of Banking and Finance and *Tamkeen*, provides students with opportunities to improve their digital literacy and innovation skills. Youth City 2030 by the government is an annual creative forum to promote tech inspire innovation among Bahraini youth.

Existing Challenges and Future of Digital Economy

One of the main challenges to any digitalisation process is the changing technology and subsequent customer experience. Successful digitalisation requires proper planning, augmentation of customer experiences and expectations and timely implementation of policies. The process requires solid integration in delivering government services and extensive coordination between various government activities to address the technical challenges involved. In addition, there is a need for support in terms of intellectual property and treatment protection and improvements in digital networks and communication infrastructure. Cybercrimes will remain a big challenge with the emerging new technologies, and it becomes important for the government to collaborate with the private sector to manage these risks.

The major challenge for the knowledge economy remains in ensuring the incorporation of emerging technologies and methodologies with the education system and ensuring that students at all levels have the skills and knowledge needed to support the country's economic diversification strategy and competitiveness. Lastly, the existing educational and professional environment in the Gulf, specifically Bahrain, does not prepare the Gulf nationals with the necessary digital skills to match the changing digital technology industry. The required technical and skill set for digital transformation remains uneven in the domestic sector. The Gulf countries remain a largely consumer-based technology within the underdeveloped ICT sector, and there is low digitalisation across various sectors and limited innovation in digital entrepreneurship in the region. Importantly there is a lack of academic and policy analysis in the development of digital domains in the Arab Gulf states. Bahrain could encourage more research in this area and concentrate on the management of cyberspace and the digital economy (Mogielnicki, 2020).

With globalisation, ideas about the new social movements, transnational identities and political demands on governments have been merged with the understandings of the universalising properties of new technologies (Murphy, 2006). ICTs allowed information to traverse borders and individuals to interact with other audiences beyond the reach of the state, accelerating and intensifying a global social transformation which threatens to make national political structures redundant. These further inspired theorists who posit that the new governance is characterised by network-based steering, weakened the role of the state, blurred state-society division, and managerialism (Makarava, 2011). ICT thereby aims to act as a catalyst for organisational transformation and change in government machinery by influencing governance in managing large volumes of data and workflow connectivity, reducing personal interface of citizens with public service providers, bureaucratic red tape, corruption and increasing speed of response (Mohanty, 2005). It also enables decentralisation in political or governmental institutions for expansion and interaction, with a procedure to deal more effectively with citizen inputs, demand, political capacity, mediation and support (Uhm and Hague, 2001). On a global scale, digital transformation has a positive impact on GDP, including GDP per capita (Al-Khouri, 2020). Therefore, it becomes imperative to understand the role of technological evolutions in building resilient economies and inclusive social systems.

Overall digital transformation has impacted the exponential growth in digital data or machine-readable information over the internet, such as artificial intelligence, data analytics, blockchain, cloud computing and other internet-based services. These have accelerated the digitalisation processes, opening the scopes of the digital economy post the pandemic (UNCTAD, 2021). In turn, this has affected the process of digital transformation and added urgency for the governments to respond. Currently, societies around the world are changing the ways people act and interact and this poses challenges related to ramping up of digital infrastructure and the building of institutional capacities to manage national disasters and pandemics.

Conclusion

Bahrain leads in the manner ICT technology has promoted e-governance with consequent drive towards more accountability and citizen participation. The rise of the digital economy and the ensuing digital transformation have necessitated the government to set up efforts towards building the digital capacities of their nationals as they compete with expatriates in the labour market. The multi-phase Bahranisation of the job market that aims to increase the Bahrainis' employment through skill development and improved access to venture capital get a further boost with digital transformation and efforts to integrate and mainstream education with the digitisation. The digital transformation is set to bring a catalytic change in governance, state-society interactions, and, more importantly, Bahrain's institutional capacities.

References

Abdulla, Ola (2018), "Gulfization: A Closer Look at Bahrainization," *Yale Review of International Studies,* September, http://yris.yira.org/comments/2631, accessed on December 26, 2021.

Al-Khouri, Ali (2020), "Building the Arab Digital Economy- A Strategy Blueprint.," *Dubai Policy Review*, February, https://dubaipolicyreview.ae/building-the-arab-digital-economy-a-strategy-blueprint/, accessed on September 26, 2021.

Al-Roubaie, Amer (2018), "Bridging the Knowledge Divide in GCC Countries: The Role of Digital Technologies," 17th Conference on e-Business, e-Services and e-Society, October, pp. 164-180, https://www.google.co.in/url?sa=t&rct=j&q=&esrc=s&source=web&cd=&cad=rja&uact=8&ved=2ahUKEwj5qOef2Yv1AhXG4jgGHZMzAO0QFnoECAIQAQ&url=https%3A%2F%2Fhal.inria.fr%2Fhal-02274197%2F&usg=AOvVaw2fVXTBm4LEZeZQYru7VoBv://, accessed on December 26, 2021.

Abdelbaki, Hisham H. (2010), "Assessing the Impact of the Global Financial Crisis on GCC Countries," *Journal of Business & Economics Research,* vol. 8, no. 2, pp. 139-152.

Bahrain Economic Development Board [EDB] (2019), *Annual Report 2019*, https://i2g4c9h4.rocketcdn.me/app/uploads/2020/08/Bahrain-EDB-Annual-Report-2019-1.pdf, accessed on September 26, 2021.

Bahrain News Agency (2018), "Bahrain Workforce Exceeds 158,000," October 6, https://www.bna.bh/en/Bahrainworkforceexceeds158000.aspx?cms=q8FmFJgisc…, accessed on December 29, 2021.

Bahrain News Agency (2019), "Bahrain Announces New National Employment Programme," February 25, https://www.bna.bh/en/BahrainannouncesnewNationalEmploymentProgram.aspx…, accessed on December 29, 2021.

Chatfield, Akemi Takeoka and Alhujran, Omar (2009), "A Cross-Country Comparative Analysis of E-Government Service Delivery among Arab Countries," *Information Technology for Development,* vol.15, no. 3, pp. 151-170.

Dudley, Dominic (2018), "Bahrain Tries to Reset Its Economy, With $10B Aid Package From Richer Neighbours," *Forbes,* October 5, https://www.forbes.com/sites/dominicdudley/2018/10/05/bahrain-reset-economy-10b-aid-package/?sh=c3f4664876be, accessed on September 30, 2021.

EDB (2020), "Bahrain's Journey to Digitisation," October 7, https://www.bahrainedb.com/bahrain-pulse/bahrains-journey-to-digitisation/, accessed on August 20, 2021.

Evans, Donna and Yen, David C.(2006), "E-Government: Evolving Relationship of Citizens and Government, Domestic, and International Development," *Government Information Quarterly*, vol. 23, pp. 207-235.

FATF-MENAFATF (2018), "Anti-money laundering and counter-terrorist financing measures—Bahrain", Fourth Round Mutual Evaluation Report, FATF, Paris, http://www.fatf-gafi.org/publications/mutualevaluations/documents/mer-bahrain-2018.html" http://www.fatf-gafi.org/publications/mutualevaluations/documents/mer-bahrain-2018.html, accessed on November 18, 2021.

Government of Bahrain (2016), "Bahrain in Figures: 2016", http://www.data.gov.bh, accessed on December 27, 2021.

Government of Bahrain (2018), "Bahrain Labour Market Indicators", Labour Market Regulatory Authority, http://lmra.bh/portal/files/cms/shared/file/Newsletter/Newsletter%20Q2_...., accessed on November 15, 2021.

Government of Bahrain (2021a), "Government of Bahrain's Digital Transformation Journey", https://www.bahrain.bh/wps/portal/!ut/p/a1/pZHNbsIwEIRfJRw4Rt7E-IdjiigtaqCC0hJfkAMmGBEnBBeVt69TVKmXNFTd20rfrGZ2kEBLJIw860xaXRh5qHdBVw9ToEHIwzHHCwzRlA5m_SEEIyAOSH4CgPGwBtgze-2HlMNtegjjQfDYc_o4Boj43ezp5X4AMMJt-jckkFgbW9odSlRWnMuisvKwUqYLB2k22mReKTN16kIqd5XU5uRtdKYd4zlaVSZXxnr74r0y6lIfK9d6gxKiOBAcMJ9wRfwelcxPt4D9PqWMhJKuIUi_zTdM1Bp-rsw1QMsLv4DffnQFmn0kzihrdOIuzP-YfHxDr3p_PIrItVMYqz4sWv6_njJfLHKOL_54uJ1MfJFEnc4nUtSOhw!!/dl5/d5/L2dBISEvZ0FBIS9nQSEh/, accessed on November 16, 2021.

Government of Bahrain (2021b), "eGovernment Strategy Summary 2007—2010", https://www.bahrain.bh/wps/wcm/connect/790f3079-7389-46b0-bb55-5d5ea5d2dccb/eGovernment+Strategy+2007-2010.pdf?MOD=AJPERES, accessed on November 18, 2021.

Government of Bahrain (2021c), *Population and Demographics,* https://www.mia.gov.bh/kingdom-of-bahrain/population-and-demographics/?lang=en, accessed November 18, 2021.

Government of India (2020), "Living Working Conditions", March, https://eoi.gov.in/bahrain/?2705?000, accessed on November 20, 2021.

Gulf Daily News (2019), "New Jobs Plan for Bahrainis Launched," February 26, https://www.bna.bh/en/BahrainannouncesnewNationalEmploymentProgram.aspx..., accessed on December 29, 2021.

Dev/World Bank (2009), "E-Government Primer", http://www.itu.int/ITU-D/cyb/app/docs/eGovernment_Primer%5B1%5D.pdf, accessed on November 21, 2021.

J Tolbert, Caroline and Mossberger, Karen (2006), "The Effects of E-Government on Trust and Confidence in Government," *Public Administration Review*, vol. 66, no. 3, pp. 354-369.

Makarava, Yuliya (2011), *Friends without benefits: Critical Assessment of the Relationship between E-governance and Democracy*, Mid Sweden University, www.diva-portal.org/smash/get/diva2:504522/FULLTEXT01.pdf, accessed on August 20, 2021.

Mehrej, Karim (2021), "Digital Transformations in the Middle East and North Africa: A Review of Egypt, Saudi Arabia and the United Arab Emirates," American University of Beirut, https://www.aub.edu.lb/ifi/Documents/publications/working_papers/2020-2021/20210401_Digital_Transformations_working_paper.pdf, accessed August 23, 2021.

Mogielnicki, Robert (2020), "Sovereign Data: The Development and Marketing of Bahrain's Digital Domain," AGSIW, 30 December, https://agsiw.org/wp-content/uploads/2020/12/Mogielnicki_Bahrain_ONLINE.pdf, accessed on August 24, 2021.

Mohanty, P. K. (2005), "Using E-Tools for Good Governance & Administrative Reforms", Centre for Good Governance, www.cgg.gov.in/workingpapers/eGovPaperARC.pdf, accessed September 25, 2021.

Murphy, Emma C. (2006), "Agency and Space: The Political Impact of Information Technologies in the Gulf Arab States," *Third World Quarterly*, vol. 27, no. 6, pp. 1059-1083.

Oxford Business Group (2020), "Bahrain to Bolster Digital Skills and Improve Connections Between Academia and Business," https://oxfordbusinessgroup.com/overview/future-ready-efforts-are-under-way-bolster-digital-skills-and-improve-connections-between-academia, accessed on December 10, 2021.

PwC (2021), "GCC Massive and Fast Transformation", April, https://www.pwc.com/m1/en/assets/document/gcc-massive-fast-transformation-online.pdf, accessed on December 10, 2021.

Santiso, Carlos (2021), "Digitalisation as an Anti-Corruption Strategy: What Are the Integrity Dividends of Going Digital?," OECD Development Matters, August 4, https://oecd-development-matters.org/2021/08/04/digitalisation-as-an-anti-corruption-strategy-what-are-the-integrity-dividends-of-going-digital/, accessed on December 30, 2021.

Saxena, Avinash (2020), "Steps Sought to Speed Up Digital Transformation", *Gulf Daily News*, August 26, http://beta2.gdnonline.com/Details/850744/Steps-sought-to-speed-up-digital-transformation, accessed on November 25, 2021.

Sugumaran, Harikrishnan and Al-Mutawha, Khalid Ahmed (2020), "Bahrain Cloud Transformation: Cloud First in eGovernment", https://www.iga.gov.bh/Media/Pdf-Section/Bahrain%20Cloud%20Transformation_Cloud%20First%20in%20eGovernment.pdf, accessed on November 18, 2021

Statista Research Department (2021), "Share of Unemployed Youth in Bahrain From 2000 to 2019," July 5, https://www.google.co.in/url?sa=t&rct=j&q=&esrc=s&source=web&cd=&cad=rja&uact=8&ved=2ahUKEwjQ5Zyw1Yv1AhXmyzgGHdI2B6cQFnoECAYQAQ&url=https%3A%2F%2Fwww.statista.com%2Fstatistics%2F688631%2Fbahrain-share-of-unemployed-youth%2F&usg=AOvVaw0m3P6ui69IgxCkw-TbUSSp/, accessed on December 30, 2021.

Tamkeen (2017), "Tamkeen relaunches 'Mohasaba' Scheme to support Bahraini enterprises," October 23, https://www.zawya.com/mena/en/press-releases/story/Tamkeen_relaunches_Mohasaba_scheme_to_support_Bahraini_enterprises-ZAWYA20171023065457/, accessed on December 24, 2021.

Transparency International (2021), "Country Data: Bahrain", https://www.transparency.org/en/countries/bahrain, accessed on November 18, 2021

The Saudi Gazette (2018), "Region's First Digital Bank Meem Launched in Bahrain," April 27, https://saudigazette.com.sa/article/533659, accessed on December 28, 2021.

The World Bank (2010), *Econstats*, econstats.com/wdi/wdiv_533.htm, accessed on December 30, 2021.

Uhm, Seung-yong and Hague, Rod (2001), "Electronic Governance, Political Participation and Virtual Community: Korea and UK Compared in Political Context," paper presented in European Consortium for Political Research Workshop, Grenoble, https://www.kdevelopedia.org/Resources/view/05201510280141726, accessed on July 30, 2021.

UNCTAD (2021), *Digital Economy Report*, https://unctad.org/system/files/official-document/der2021_en.pdf, accessed on December 30, 2021.

UNESCO Institute for Statistics (2013), "ICT Education in Five Arab States: A Comparative Analysis of ICT Integration and E-Readiness in Schools in Egypt, Jordan, Oman, Palestine and Qatar", www.uis.unesco.org/Communication/Documents/ICT-arab-states-en.pdf, accessed on July 27, 2021.

United Nations (2014), *E-Government Report 2014*, June, https://publicadministration.un.org/egovkb/en-us/reports/un-e-government-survey-2014, accessed on December 10, 2021.

United Nations-Economic and Social Commission for Western Asia [UN-ESCWA] (2017), *Perspectives of Digital Economy in the Arab Gulf*, https://www.unescwa.org/sites/default/files/pubs/pdf/perspectives-digital-economy-arab-region-english_0.pdf, accessed on December 10, 2021.

Yildis, Mete (2007), "E-Government Research: Reviewing the Literature, Limitations, and Ways Forward," *Government Information Quarterly*, vol. 24, no. 3, pp. 646-665.

5. The Youth and the Political Participation in the Gulf Cooperation Council States

Nawar Kassomeh

Introduction

The youth represent a huge portion of the citizens of the fast-growing societies of the Gulf Cooperation Council States (GCC) and were also the main driver in the Arab Awakening/uprisings in the last decade. At the beginning of this wave in 2011, the Gulf youth began to mobilise, and many voices started to demand reform in the GCC states; however, the governments were able to contain these demands with promises of reforms, except possibly in Bahrain, where the protests were sectarian and led by the Shia majority (Abraham, 2015). Anyhow, the rulers of the GCC showed remarkable resilience to political change (Mainuddin, 2016). Despite some slow and limited improvement, authoritarianism remains intact in these states. However, the protests and the mobilisation of the people showed that the rentier system does not guarantee the political passivity of citizens for good; nor should this passivity be taken for granted by rulers of these states (Tétreault, 2011). Indeed, the educational and technological progress in the GCC states has led to the rapid emergence of educated and tech-savvy youth who are aware of politics, and this has increased the youths' demands to actively participate in the political process (Abraham, 2015).

Hence, this chapter examines youth political participation and its limitations in the GCC states. Although it will mainly focus on youth participation, it is also important to consider women's participation because both groups are subject to the same traditional forces that might constrain their political participation—developments in one area can indicate issues and change for the other. Therefore, it will first present a demographic, economic and social overview of the Gulf states before reviewing political experience and new developments. Finally, it will assess youth political participation and activism and the government's efforts to empower women and youth.

Demographic, Economic, and Social Backgrounds of the GCC States

The population of the oil-rich GCC states has been considered one of the fastest-growing in the world (Scharfenort, 2020). This remarkable growth was due to the high fertility rate, massive economic transformation, and many labour migrants who have settled in this region. The World Bank and the GCC Statistical Centre data show that all the GCC countries witnessed a large growth in their populations between 1960 and 2019 (Table 5.1). However, notwithstanding this population growth, the citizens' life expectancy improved during the same period, signalling a simultaneous improvement in living conditions and health system.

Table 5.1: GCC Population and Life Expectancy During 1960-2019

Country	Population 1960	Population 2019	Life Expectancy 1960	Life Expectancy 2019
GCC	5,209,529	56,905,993	50.02	77.32
UAE	92,418	9,366,829	51.53	77.97
Bahrain	162,429	1,483,756	51.86	77.29
Saudi Arabia	4,086,534	34,218,169	45.63	75.13
Oman	551,735	4,617,927	42.67	77.86
Qatar	47,384	2,799,202	61.09	80.22
Kuwait	269,029	4,420,110	59.34	75.48

Sources: The World Bank Group: Kuwait, https://data.worldbank.org/country/kuwait; Qatar, https://data.worldbank.org/country/qatar; UAE, https://data.worldbank.org/country/united-arab-emirates; Saudi Arabia, https://data.worldbank.org/country/saudi-arabia; Oman, https://data.worldbank.org/country/oman; Bahrain, https://data.worldbank.org/country/bahrain, retrieved on 3 July 2021. SCC-STAT. (2019). GCC Statistical Center. https://www.gccstat.org/en/statistic/statistics/population. Retrieved on 3 July 2021.

Some scholars have attributed the persistence of authoritarian systems in Gulf states and the slow political change to the domination of the rentier system economy, which helps the rulers to avoid serious political concessions. This rentier economy is defined by Beblawi (1990, p. 51) as "an economy where the creation of wealth is centred around a small fraction of the society; the rest of the society is only engaged in the distribution and utilisation of this wealth." This applies to the Gulf states because they are highly dependent on oil income, which represents in some states more than 95 per cent of their exports and finances more than 90 per cent of their budget. However, only about 2-3 per cent of their citizens work in the oil industry and the governments directly control the rents in this sector (Beblawi, 1990; Herb, 2003).

Based on their GDP and GNI per capita (Table 5.2), the GCC states can be divided into two categories: the super-rentier states, which include Qatar, UAE and Kuwait; and the less wealthy rentier states, which include Saudi Arabia, Oman, and Bahrain. The super-rentier states can mobilise more resources to buy the loyalty of their citizens (Freer, 2018). Qatar is a clear example of a super-rentier state, and it is the only state in the GCC to see an outstanding improvement in GNI per capita in a relatively short period; according to the World Bank, it was US$ 28,400 in 2002 and US$ 61,180 in 2019, one of the highest in the world. Hence, the difference between a rentier and a super-rentier state is that, in the latter, the rulers have more resources to fulfil their social contract of providing citizens high-paid jobs and good social services. On the other hand, the fast growing populations, especially in the less wealthy rentier states,

Table 5.2: GNI per capita and GDP of the GCC States, 2019

Country	GNI per capita 2019 (US$)	GDP 2019 (billion US$)
UAE	43,470	421.142
Bahrain	22,170	38,475
Saudi Arabia	22,840	792,967
Oman	14,150	76,332
Qatar	61,180	175,838
Kuwait	36,290	136,197

Source: The World Bank Group.

are putting more pressure on the limited economic capabilities of the rulers who might become more vulnerable to face future challenges (Diwan, 2014). As a result, moving from a rentier economy into more diversified systems has become the main priority for all the GCC states, as implanted in their economic 'Visions' of the future (Miniaoui, 2020).

It is worth mentioning that all except Saudi Arabia and Oman have more foreigners than citizens which illuminates these states' economic and demographic situation. Foreigners represent the majority of Kuwait, Qatar, the UAE and Bahrain (Alekry, 2020); according to the International Labour Organisation, they represent more than 80 per cent of the population of Qatar and the UAE. Hence, it is worth noting that GNI per capita in these countries includes foreign workers, who represent in many of these cases the majority of the population and are usually paid lower wages than the citizens. As a result, GNI per capita for citizens would be double or even triple the given figures. The gap between locals and foreigners has increased the value of citizenship in these states (Hertog, 2010).

The UN defines youths as those between 15 and 25 of age (Al Munajjed and Sabbagh, 2011); however, in some cases, this classification is extended to include people of up to 35 years (Elekry, 2020). It is estimated that approximately 54 per cent of the GCC states' population is made up of people under 25 (Diwan, 2014). The high level of unemployment for young citizens is a critical issue occupying the GCC governments' attention (Scharfenort, 2020). Most GCC states suffer from high youth unemployment (Khatib, 2021), which is considered a major problem (Hanieh, 2011). Not only do younger populations have a higher unemployment rate, but the rate is also higher for young women of the same age (Alekry, 2020) and as much as three times higher than young males in the GCC states (El-Darwiche et al., 2021). In addition, it is noteworthy that the GCC youths do not usually accept lower wages and long hours of private-sector jobs (Scharfenort, 2020). Table 5.3 gives the national youth percentage of the GCC population and their unemployment rates.

Table 5.3: National Youth Percentage of the GCC Population (2015) and their Unemployment Rate (2016)

Country	Youth Nationals Population <25 years (in %)	Unemployment rate of total GCC Youth Nationals (in %)
UAE	No Data Available	No Data Available
Bahrain	51	6
Saudi Arabia	49	32.6
Oman	56	48.7
Qatar	57	1.1
Kuwait	56	12.9

Sources: GLMM, 2017, GLMM, 2018 (employment); Statista, 2020 (unemployment) in Scharfenort, 2020.

The majority of the population of these states are Sunni Muslims, except in Bahrain, where the majority is Shia, and in Oman, the majority follows Ibadism, a sect that predates the Sunnis-Shia division (Winder, 2020). The Omani Sunnis are concentrated mainly in Dhofar. Although there has been some tension between the two communities (Ibadis and Sunnis), it has not reached a serious sectarian level (Mainuddin, 2016).

All these states have similar power structures: they have hereditary rulers whose families control the state apparatus; they all have income based on abundant natural resources, which has made them rentier economies where the ruler has the absolute power; and repression, media monitoring, imprisonment, and forcing dissidents into exile are widespread (Hanieh, 2011). Accountability is absent in the GCC political systems, and any critique of the ruler results in imprisonment (Diwan, 2014). Additionally, the resident population has significant diversity but they are extremely segregated by class, gender, religion, citizenship status as native or foreigner. Lastly, the Gulf societies have an even more consumerist lifestyle than most wealthy Western states (Ouis, 2002).

It is also important to mention that Islam and Islamic culture are highly consolidated in the GCC societies (Ouis, 2002). They share the Bedouin social structure centred on the tribe, clan and family. In the past, most of the GCC rulers states were strategically claiming that elections and democracy were Western and un-Islamic while warning of *fitna* (sedition) to delegitimise political dissidents (Mainuddin, 2016). Islam relies on interpretation that leaves space for negotiation to legitimise or delegitimise certain practices, which means religion can be tactically mobilised for political ends (Ouis, 2002). For instance, in March 2011, the Omani Grand Mufti severely criticised the protests in Sohar. In Saudi Arabia, the ulama issued a fatwa to ban the protests that were *fitna* and un-Islamic because it would lead to social divisions (Diwan, 2014). Additionally, Shia ulama in the Al-Ahsa region in Saudi Arabia also called for an end to the protests; yet a Shia clerk Sheikh Nimr Baqir al-Nimr, endorsed the protests (Mainuddin, 2016), and this led to his arrest and execution in January 2016 (BBC, 2016).

Finally, Bedouin tribal culture is deeply rooted in the GCC societies, despite decades of economic and urban development. In that culture, loyalty and obedience to clan and tribal leaders are important; and Gulf rulers are clan leaders. As an example of the importance of tribal ties, in 1900, the Al Thani, the royal family in Qatar, represented almost half of Qatar's indigenous population (Hanieh, 2011).

The Immature Political Experience

Except for Kuwait, the political experience started late in the Gulf states. Although the GCC states have existed as a political unit for some time, experience in modern state politics began with their independence in the second half of the 20th century. The constitution of Kuwait adopted in 1962 is the oldest among the GCC countries (Das, 2017), and the parliamentary experience in Kuwait started in the same year. Afterwards, the Kuwaiti parliament has witnessed the rise of Islamism since 1986. Nonetheless, the role of the Kuwaiti parliament was insignificant until the American invasion of Iraq, when the rulers began to empower the parliament through political reforms. Still, the rulers did not give the right to vote to the *Bidoon* (people who live in Kuwait and have no other nationality, yet are not considered citizens). Besides, the Shia minority represents another problem for the government. Although their situation in Kuwait is better than that of Shia in other Gulf states, they still face discrimination (Kéchichian, 2004).

Despite these limitations, the Kuwaiti parliamentary election in 2003 was seen as a positive sign of democratic change. However, the Islamists' victory was considered an indicator of the weakness of the so-called liberal groups. These Islamist groups are considered conservative forces that oppose openness in Gulf societies, probably slowing the reform process (Kéchichian, 2004).

Anyhow, Kuwait is viewed as the most democratically advanced country among the Gulf states, and Kuwaiti parliament members exercise their power to question ministers and even force them to resign (Nonneman, 2006). Like in other GCC states, political parties are not yet allowed in Kuwait; however, there are many openly political blocs that are involved in the parliament and politics. These blocs usually complain that the electoral system of one-person-one-vote limits their chance to win a listing (Al-Atiqi, 2013). In addition, though the Kuwaiti parliament has a greater role than councils in the other Gulf states, the emir can dissolve or suspend parliament (Hanieh, 2011). For instance, in 2016, the Emir, Sheikh Sabah Al-Ahmad Al-Sabah, dissolved parliament and set the country towards an early election (*Al Jazeera*, 2016).

Furthermore, the current Emir, Sheikh Nawaf Al Ahmed Al Sabah, issued a decree on 18 February 2021 suspending the Kuwaiti National Assembly for one month, because of tensions between the parliament and the government (Al Mulla, 2021). In the last Kuwaiti National Council election in 2020, fifty members were elected; yet no woman could win a seat (*Al Qabas*, 2020). Nonetheless, in the new Kuwaiti Parliament, 35 out of 50 members are under the age of 45 (*Alroeya*, 2020).

Unlike Kuwait, Qatar has no organised opposition; furthermore, political parties are not allowed (Nonneman, 2006). Nonetheless, Qatar started political reform in 1999, when the first municipal election was held, and women were allowed to both vote and run, though no women were elected (Nonneman, 2006). Qatari citizens, including women, voted in 2003 in a referendum to approve a new constitution that called for creating a parliament (*Shura* Council) composed of 55 members, thirty to be elected and fifteen to be appointed (Kéchichian, 2004). Yet the elections of this S*hura* (consultative) council could not take place, and it was only on 3 November 2020 that Emir Tamim bin Hamad announced that Qatar would witness the first free elections for the Consultative Council in October 2021 (Al-Shafi, 2021). Eventually, On 2 October 2021, Qatar's first legislative polls for two-thirds of the advisory Shura Council was held and Qataris elected 30 members of the 45-seat body (Reuters, 2021).

In neighbouring Bahrain, political reform began in 2002, when people elected their first Council of Representatives (Husain et al., 2016). This and the Omani Advisory Council (Shura Council) are the only two lower chambers of the GCC where all their members are elected, while all the members of the Shura council in Saudi Arabia and the State Council members in Oman are appointed (Mainuddin, 2016).

Meanwhile, the UAE and Saudi Arabia are considered the least open of all the Gulf states regarding political participation. In the Political Participation Index in the Gulf Cooperation Council Countries, Kuwait ranked first with 535 out of 1,000 points, followed by Bahrain (451 points), Oman (440 points), Qatar (405 points), the UAE (316 points), and Saudi Arabia (192 points) (Gulf House, 2020).

The federal system of the UAE gives each of its seven emirates' sheikhs absolute power within his own emirate. Nonetheless, some emirates, such as Sharjah, have introduced appointed consultation councils. At the national level, the state has *majlis al-Itihad al-Watani* (Federal National Council FNC), but it has limited power and cannot pass or block bills, a power that still resides with the rulers. All FNC members used to be appointed; however, in 2004, the president of the UAE, Sheikh Khalifa bin Zayed Al Nahyan, announced that half of the members would be elected by the council of each emirate, and promised that the power of these councils would be expanded (Nonneman, 2006). Consequently, the UAE saw the first FNC election in 2006 and involved an electoral college composed of 6,000 members. This number increased to 224,279 in 2015 and 337,738 in 2019.

However, candidates are only allowed to run as independents. Besides, the current FNC has forty members, half of whom are appointed. According to the recommendation of the President of the UAE, Sheikh Khalifa bin Zayed, women—both elected and appointed—should occupy half of the council seats (The UAE Government Website (U.ae), 2021). The FNC still has limited power, but the rulers have promised that this power will increase gradually in future. However, in the UAE, the law also severely punished any political activity; those who organised these political activities were subject to harassment and repression by the government, including imprisonment, deportation, or their citizenship revoked (Reuters, 2012).

This mirrors Saudi Arabia, where forming a political organisation or participating in its activities is considered a crime (Ottaway, 2021). Likewise, creating any political organisation in Oman is prohibited and is a criminal offence. While in Oman, the Basic Law grants the right of peaceful assembly and the right to express an opinion, and the Omani people have the right to address the authorities, there are no laws yet that govern these proposed rights (Freedom House, 2020).

In sum, most of the councils in the GCC are still partially or completely appointed, and the rulers have the final say in these states, while political organisations and parties are restricted or severely punished. Nonetheless, the degree of freedom varies. In sum, the political experience of these states is still limited and immature.

Youth and Political Participation

Although the GCC states are taking some concrete measures to ensure the political participation of youths and women, they are characterised by under-institutionalised political systems that do not allow for political organisation and limit political participation (Freer, 2018). Political participation is usually defined as citizens' activities that influence politics, including voting, protesting, contacting politicians, internet actions and posts, signing petitions, lobbying, volunteering, boycotting (van Deth, 2016). Without exception, such political participation exists in every political system; yet it represents a valued part of a healthy democracy (van Deth, 2016). Surely, voting is considered the clearest form of political participation (Myers, 2020).

The GCC states lack a concrete channel to link the decision-makers with the people. The youth usually regard the traditional way of transmitting demands and messages through the councils as ceremonial and ineffective and do not permit citizens to influence decision-making (Thompson and Quilliam, 2018). Hence, citizens in the GCC countries use non-institutionalised means to voice their political demands (Freer, 2018). Besides, many restrictions are imposed in the GCC states on youth to establish their own organisation, association, or even a club. Freedom of gathering is restricted, and public events require permission (Alekry, 2020).

Additionally, except in Kuwait and Bahrain, youth political activism in the GCC states is still weak and unorganised, lacking sufficient resources and mechanisms to advocate a political agenda; besides, they cannot challenge the traditional religious and tribal establishment (Wardany, 2014).

Undeniably, despite all political and social restrictions, youth in the GCC states want to influence culture, politics, education, and all other aspects of their societies; their active involvement is crucial to bring about the sufficient energy necessary for progress (Al Munajjed and Sabbagh, 2011). Yet, according to Moutaz Salama of Al-Ahram Center for Political and Strategic Studies, 56 per cent of Saudi youth are not interested in political participation and have a negative impression of politics due to the warning of family and friends; nonetheless, Salama believes that the Saudi government would work in the future to reinforce the role of youths (Sarhan, 2015). Nevertheless, this discouraging percentage is driven mainly by fear, social constraints, and political restrictions rather than belief. For instance, a survey conducted in 2010 by Booze & Company in Saudi Arabia, Qatar, and the UAE, which included 415 youth respondents, found that 58 per cent of the participants want their governments to create youth councils that guarantee their active participation. This indicates that these youths want to make their voices heard by the leadership of their countries (Al Munajjed and Sabbagh, 2011).

Voices for change come from some secular or liberal activists and the Muslim Brotherhood (MB) in the UAE, which is influential in professional organisations. Both liberal and Islamists signed a petition in March 2011 addressed to the president to call the Emirati rulers to grant citizens the right of political participation (Freer, 2018). Certainly, the Islamists are considered a critical threat to some of these regimes, such as the UAE, which opposes the MB; by contrast, Qatar has openly supported them (Roberts, 2017; Freer, 2018). In 1999, the Qatari MB dissolved itself; yet MB figures continue to be influential in Qatar at the social level (Watkins, 2020).

The youth of UAE and Bahrain have positive views about Islamist movements, while Kuwaiti and Saudis youth have a more negative view about them (Al-Naqeeb et al., 2006, p. 82). After the death of pro-MB Emir of Ras al-Khaimah Saqr bin Muhammad in 2010, the UAE launched a war against the Emirati MB affiliated group the Islah (reform) and has declared both Islah and MB as terrorist groups (Roberts, 2017). Hence, the rulers of the Gulf recognised the weight and influence of the Islamists, and some of them, like the rulers of the UAE, decided to crack down on their activities; yet they underestimated the ability of these Islamists to resist and to remain present in the social sphere. Hence, Islamists will have their social base intact, and the crackdown strategy might not be the most sustainable solution. In the long run, these states might need a different strategy that includes proper political reform and dialogue to permit people to operate within the sphere of the state (Freer, 2018). A new strategy would require an openness of political life regulated by the state's laws. Meanwhile, the restriction of politics in these states moves the political life to the social sphere. The same thing can be seen in Qatar: although the Brotherhood is dissolved, it exists in the social sphere, and, in Kuwait, MB plays a role in the electoral outcome (Freer, 2018).

Another way to examine political and social developments in these states, and the involvement and participation of their citizens, is indeed to look at the situation of civil societies. Bahrain represents an exception in the Gulf states because its citizens are allowed to establish political societies. These political societies are regulated by a law that allows them to work in politics parallel to political parties but without participating in the government. This system allows these political societies to participate in the election and have their own electoral lists; nonetheless, some of these societies were dissolved by court decisions resulting in many operating undergrounds, while some of the leaders of these groups being forced into exile or arrested (Gulf House, 2020). Nonetheless, Bahrain has 700 registered NGOs in the Ministry of Social Development (Gulf House, 2020). While The law regulates NGOs in Kuwait, some were dissolved for committing violations (*Arab Times*, 2016). Likewise, NGOs are regulated by the law in Oman, and the Ministry of Social Development supervises their activities (Gulf House, 2020).

In Saudi Arabia, the country that depends on the Basic Law of Governance of 1992 and includes the Shura council and the council of regions, political participation is still unclear or well defined (Gulf House, 2020). In the last few years, the young Crown Prince Mohammed bin Salman (MbS) has been leading the reforms in Saudi Arabia, and he seems to enjoy public support, including from the youth (Husain et al., 2016). MbS presents himself as the youth leader who represents the largest portion of the Saudi population and whose unemployment rate is between 35 per cent and 60 per cent (Grand and Wolff, 2020). According to the International Monetary Fund, the increase of job offers in the Saudi market would not be able to match this growth of the youth population. Based on this problem, the Crown Prince attempts to attract the youth through his *Vision 2030* strategic and economic framework and his campaign against corruption (Ghafar, 2017). Equally important, Saudi Arabia recently allowed the creation of NGOs after a royal decree in 2015 giving the Ministry of Interior the right to accept or to reject the formation of NGOs. Almost 700 NGOs are operating in the kingdom (Gulf House, 2020). Hence, all the GCC states permit the establishment of NGOs under certain conditions and limitations. In most cases, the NGOs in the GCC states are linked to governments and dependent on their financial support; consequently, they cannot participate in politics or influence decision-making (Al-Tarrah, 2002).

According to the Qatari law, the Ministry of Interior has the right to accept or reject civil organisation formation. Nonetheless, it was reported that some of these NGOs were rejected without explanation (Gulf House, 2020). Furthermore, in UAE, over 200 NGOs are regulated by a law that gives the Ministry of Community Development the power to approve the formation of these NGOs. Some of these NGOs were dissolved for participating in politics or for issues related to their funding (Gulf House, 2020). Hence, any political activity would consequently result in the termination of the NGO in the GCC states; besides, there is an absence in these states of advocacy NGOs that campaign for human rights or the rights of minorities, women, animals and workers (Al-Tarrah, 2002). Consequently, civil society in these states is growing but with strict limitations, regulations, and restrictions imposed by the governments.

Shy Governments Efforts to Empower Women and Youth

According to Rola Dashti, a Kuwaiti intellectual and politician, there is a perpetual conflict between two trends in the GCC states. The first is the progressive trend, which promotes equality between men and women; the second is the traditional religious and tribal trend which aims to keep the *status quo* of male domination in the Gulf society. This conflict is not yet settled, and the governments' position is ambiguous—seemingly, one day they side the first trend, then the next day they side the other (Dunne, 2008). And indeed, youth also are confronting the same traditional patriarchal, tribal, and religious values whereby young people are always expected to obey and be subordinate to the elders. Most of these states are improving the situation, and some states have achieved noticeable progress regarding the empowerment of both women and youths. For instance, the 2002 Bahraini constitution granted women the right to vote and run in an election (*The New York Times*, 2002). However, regarding youth participation, the age to run as a candidate in the Bahraini House of Representatives is at least 30 years, and the age to vote is 21 years. Hence, a huge portion of youth is excluded from running or voting. Despite the national strategy to empower Bahraini youth, there is no clear policy for that; nonetheless, youths are becoming more visible in key positions (Gulf House, 2020).

Kuwaiti women have the right to vote and run for office in the National Assembly or the municipal councils. Voting in Kuwait is for citizens 21 years of age or older (Das, 2017), and to run for office, the candidate should be at least 30. Unfortunately, the Kuwaiti government has no clear policy to empower youths, who are still not visible in the government (Gulf House, 2020). Likewise, women in Oman can also vote and run for office; yet in the 2015 election, only one woman was elected out of the 20 female candidates (Kumar, 2016). The voting age in Oman is 21, and to run for office, a candidate should be at least 30 years old. Following the protests in 2011, the Sultanate formed the National Youth Commission; however, apart from this symbolic measure, the Omani government has no clear strategy or policy to include and empower youth (Gulf House, 2020).

Qatari women have the right to vote and run for office; however, the state lacks laws or customs that balance the two genders. The voting age in Qatar is more inclusive and is set at 18; however, it is 30 years old to run as a candidate. There is a lack of clear policy to engage youth in politics, but many youths are beginning to hold key positions in the state (Gulf House, 2020). In September 2021, the Qatari Ministry of Culture and Sports announced that it was drafting the Qatar National Youth Document to achieve the government's strategies in the youth sector and engage youth in decision-making processes (*The Peninsula*, 2021).

In 2015, the Saudi government gave women the right to vote and be a member of the municipal councils, where women secured 20 seats. In 2018, the Saudi government finally granted women the right to drive a car (BBC, 2018). However, laws that ensure gender balance are absent in Saudi Arabia. Here the voting age is 18, and for candidacy is 25 (GOV. SA, 2021a). Since the rise of Prince Mohammed bin Salman as crown prince, the kingdom has been focusing more efforts on youths. As a result, many young princes have started to hold key positions (Gillon, 2021); however, this empowerment does not trickle down to include youth from other social ranks. Hence, Saudi Arabia has no clear policy to empower youths in the political decision-making process, and its *Vision 2030* aims to empower Saudi youth only at the social level (GOV.SA, 2021b).

Women in the UAE have the right to vote, and it is the only country in the GCC that has adopted a progressive policy to guarantee gender balance: in 2015, it established the UAE gender Balance Council which works to ensure the representation of women in all fields. In 2019, the Federal Supreme Council issued a decree to imply that half of the seats in the Federal National Council should be allocated to women. The age to run for office is 25, and there is no specification for the voting age. According to (UAE National Electoral Committee, 2019), only citizens listed in the constituencies of their emirate have the right to vote. The UAE achieved good progress in 2016 by creating a youth council to act as an advisory in issues that concern youths. There are several young ministers in the new Emirati federal government, and many projects aim to provide support for male and female youths. And in 2016, the UAE appointed a 22-year-old Shamma bint Suhail Al Mazrui as the minister of state for youth affairs (Ministry of Cabinet Affairs, UAE, 2021), making her the youngest government minister in the world (Simmons, 2017).

Youth Political Activism in the GCC

Political awakening and activism in the GCC largely go back to the 1950s and 1960s when the migrant labour workforce settled in the Gulf states and posed a new problem for the rulers. Many of these Arab migrants began to spread new political ideas of Nasserism, pan-Arabism, communism and socialism to Gulf citizens (Forstenlechner and Rutledge, 2011). Indeed, some of these migrants also spread MB ideology.

Before the Arab Spring in 2011, there were some political activities from the youth which began to be seen through internet forums and blogs, especially in Bahrain, Kuwait, and Oman. For example, the Kuwaiti youth was behind the electoral reforms of 2006, while Saudi youth voiced criticism after the Jeddah floods in 2009 (Freitag, 2020). These early actions point to the cracks in the rentier state system and the importance of the internet and the new media tools (Diwan, 2014).

The youth of the GCC states want to reform systems but differ in their priorities. In the early 2000s, Al-Naqeeb et al. (2006) found that the demands for political reforms varied in the GCC states. For instance, Saudi, Omani and Bahraini youth want more political reform than their UAE counterparts; demands for democracy come first for the Saudi and Bahraini youth, followed by Omani and the UAE, who were the least concerned about democracy (Al-Naqeeb et al., 2006). Indeed, Saudi youth, like other GCC youth, were not always politically passive; for instance, the youth organisations which came into place after the Jeddah floods in 2009 were quickly confronted by Islamists. Despite that, these youths tried to run a candidate for the municipal council, but the government rejected their candidate (Diwan, 2014).

Additionally, after the Arab Spring in 2011, the GCC youth represented the backbone of the protesters and activists who called for political change. As a result, the governments of the GCC states, especially Kuwait, Bahrain, the UAE, and Oman, targeted many youth bloggers and activists on social media for expressing their political demands; although they typically focused on political and social reforms rather than on radical political change, except in Bahrain. Anyhow, the political activism of youths is relatively more advanced in Bahrain and Kuwait, and it is limited in Saudi Arabia, Oman, Qatar, and the UAE (Boghardt, 2013). The Youth Coalition also played a major role in Bahrain's large 14 February uprising (Moore-Gilbert, 2018). Although the Bahraini rulers were keen to initiate political reforms, this quickly ended after the Saudi troops entered the island to support the ruling family, which reinforced the position of hardliners within the Bahraini regime that relies on Saudi

Arabia for its economic and political survival in a sectarian divided state (Diwan, 2014).

As mentioned above, Kuwait has the most advanced political system, and it is also considered the most experienced in youth activism in the GCC. Compared to other states, Kuwaitis enjoy more political freedom, and they have a relatively good margin of freedom of expression so long as it is not directed at the Emir who is deemed above criticism. Apart from this taboo, the constitution guarantees Kuwaitis the right to participate in politics and voice their concerns regarding political issues (Winder, 2020). Moreover, the Kuwaiti constitution grants a relatively good level of government accountability, and the margin of freedom permits youth activists to work to reinforce the democratic experience in Kuwait further. After the Arab Spring, the Kuwaiti youth allied themselves with liberal forces (Das, 2017), and their activists marked a remarkable development in the GCC state when they were able to form in 2012 the first youth political party called the Civil Democratic Movement (CDM), which was democratic in its elected leadership and political agenda. The party included roughly 100 active members. Following this success, the emir was forced to dissolve the parliament and change the election law, which led to many protests. As a result, many protesters were charged with offending the emir and Kuwait, which was the best GCC state regarding freedom of expression, became one of the top countries that persecute people for their posts on social media (Diwan, 2014).

Lastly, many young citizens in the Gulf states studied abroad in Western universities; most GCC residents, especially the elites, spend their vacations in Europe and the United States (Ouis, 2002). As a result, an increasing number of the GCC young people become Westernised, well-travelled, and live and think differently than the older generation who followed traditional Gulf values. These youths confront their traditional parents and grandparents (Winder, 2020). Moreover, many young Gulf women and men are now studying in Western universities, which started to open branches in most GCC states except Saudi Arabia. These universities, which follow Western models, tend to emphasise the student's independence and encourage critical thinking. Thus, many of these youths are now exposed to Western ideas and will surely develop more liberal democratic thinking, and therefore will call for more gender equality, human rights, and the freedom of speech (Alekry, 2020). This is a new reality; though change will take time, it will come. The newly emerging, highly-educated youth will certainly improve the situation of youth political organisation and participation while also undoubtedly contributing to the development of their country economically, socially, and politically.

Conclusion

Islamism and tribalism are solid in Gulf societies, and they represent the traditional forces that oppose or resist modernisation and change. At the same time, youth citizens represent the largest proportion of the population and suffer from a high unemployment rate in most GCC states. In addition, the political choice is almost non-existent in the GCC states because they do not allow political parties, and political activities are strictly limited. It is clear that reform in these Gulf states is not seriously on the agenda or is at least slow and limited; the rulers continue to have the last say regarding political issues. Equally significant, most GCC countries lack a clear policy to empower their youth.

However, undeniable improvements deserve both mention and applause, despite the slow-motion that characterises all these states' political and social change. For example, the youth are becoming more visible in key positions in many of these states. In addition, women can now vote in all the GCC, after Saudi Arabia finally granted this right to women in 2015 and allowed them to run for municipal councils. Despite the restrictions and the severe resistance of the traditional (tribal and religious) forces in the Gulf states that oppose women and youth rights, women have achieved relative and noticeable progress, even in Saudi Arabia. Moreover, the youth have not been completely passive and instead were able to mobilise and voice their demands in certain GCC countries. NGOs and civil society activities in the GCC are growing; but they are still facing strict restrictions and supervision from the governments, and are allowed neither to deal with politics nor to practice advocacy for human, animal, workers or women's rights.

With the fast-growing populations and high unemployment rate facing the younger segments, they will inevitably become increasingly aware of their situation and become more politically active. Moreover, they are an increased number of young GCC citizens enrolled in Western universities in their countries and abroad who are therefore exposed to Western culture and ethics.

Thus, youth political participation, particularly women's role in political life, is much improved compared to the past three or four decades; however, there is still a long way ahead to achieve improvements that follow the Western liberal criteria. Nonetheless, these changes and reforms are not luxuries but rather a necessity if these states face future challenges. The rentier system still provides the rulers of these states with the ability to buy loyalty and push citizens away from the political sphere; yet this state of affairs should not be taken for granted. Gradual change, which seeks to integrate the empowerment of the youth population and the equality of gender, is a more sustainable strategy to maintain the stability and prosperity of this region.

References

Abraham, Rhea (2015), "Confronting the Challenge of Political Reforms in GCC States: Domestic Transition via Regional Integration," Arab Centre for Research and Policy Studies, February 23, https://www.dohainstitute.org/en/ResearchAndStudies/Pages/Confronting_the_Challenge_of_Political_Reforms_in_GCC_States_Domestic_Transition_via_Regional_Integration.aspx, accessed on July 10, 2021.

Alekry, Abdulnabi (2020), "Youth Independence in Relation to Social Change in the Gulf," in Jennifer E. Lansford, Anis B. Brik, and Abdallah M. Badahdah (eds.), *Families and Social Change in the Gulf Region*, 1st ed., pp. 117-130, Routledge.

Al Jazeera (2016), "Emir of Kuwait Dissolves Parliament," October 17, https://www.aljazeera.com/news/2016/10/17/emir-of-kuwait-dissolves-parliament, accessed on July 21, 2021.

Al-Atiqi, Suliman (2013), "Kuwait's One Man, One Vote Law, Though the Cause of Previous Unrest, Has Fractured the Opposition and Empowered Independents," Carnegie Endowment for International Peace, September 12, https://carnegieendowment.org/sada/52947, accessed on July 28, 2021.

Al Mulla, Yasmena (2021), "Kuwait: Emir Suspends Parliament for a Month," Gulf News, February 18, https://gulfnews.com/world/gulf/kuwait/kuwait-emir-suspends-parliament-for-a-month-1.77284634, accessed on August 2, 2021.

Al Munajjed, Mona and Sabbagh, Karim (2011), *Youth in GCC countries: Meeting the Challenge*, Booz & Company Inc. https://www.youthpolicy.org/library/

documents/youth-in-gcc-countries-meeting-the-challenge/, accessed on July 27, 2021.

Al Naqeeb, Khaldoun, Sabban, Rima, Hareb, Saaid, Najjar, Baqer, Hamad, Abdel Aziz, and Bin Tofleh, Saad (2006), *Itijahat Al- Shabab Fi Duwal Majlis Altaawon Al-Khaliji*, Youths' Orientations in the Gulf Cooperation Council Countries, Kuwait: Dar Qurtas.

Al Qabas (2020), "The Results of the National Council Elections in the Five Constituencies," Al Qabas Press, December 6, https://alqabas.com/article/5822421, accessed on July 16, 2021.

Alroeya (2020), "Al-Aghlabiyah Lil Shabab Fi Barlaman Al- Kuwait Al- Jadid," Youths' Majority in the New Kuwaiti Parliament, December 6, https://bit.ly/3he7RsP, accessed on July 24, 2021.

Al-Shafi, Khalid (2021), "Strengthening Public Participation," *The Peninsula*, May 31, https://www.thepeninsulaqatar.com/editorInChief/31/05/2021/Strengthening-public-participation, accessed on July 29, 2021.

Al-Tarrah, Ali Ahmad (2002), "Globalisation, Nongovernmental Organisations and Civil Society: A Study of the Voluntary Organisations in the GCC countries," [Majalat Kiliyet Al-Insaniyat Wal ʿoloum Al-Insaniyah], *Journal of the College of Humanities and Social Sciences*, vol. 25, pp. 55–118, http://hdl.handle.net/10576/8394, accessed on July 12, 2021.

Arab Times (2016), "Govt Orders Dissolution of Three NGOs," March 11, http://www.arabtimesonline.com/news/govt-orders-dissolution-three-ngos/, accessed on July 3, 2021.

BBC (2016), "Sheikh Nimr al-Nimr: Saudi Arabia Executes Top Shia Cleric," January 2, https://www.bbc.com/news/world-middle-east-35213244, accessed on July 17, 2021.

BBC (2018), "Saudi Arabia Issues First Driving Licences To Women," June 5, https://www.bbc.com/news/world-middle-east-44367981, accessed on August 4, 2021.

Beblawi, Hazem (1990), "The Rentier State in the Arab World," in Giacomo Luciani (ed.), *The Arab State*, pp. 85-98. Routledge.

Boghardt, Lori Plotkin (2013), "Youth Activism in the Small Gulf States," The Washington Institute for Near East Policy, March 28, https://www.washingtoninstitute.org/policy-analysis/youth-activism-small-gulf-states, accessed on July 25, 2021.

Das, Hirak Jyoti (2017), "National Assembly Elections in Kuwait, 2016," *Contemporary Review of the Middle East*, vol. 4, no. 2, pp. 193-210, https://doi.org/10.1177/2347798917694758, accessed on July 27, 2021.

Diwan, Kristin (2014), "Breaking Taboos: Youth Activism in the Gulf States," Atlantic Council, March 7, https://www.atlanticcouncil.org/in-depth-research-reports/

issue-brief/breaking-taboos-youth-activism-in-the-gulf-states/, accessed on August 14, 2021.

Dunne, Michele (2008), "Women's Political Participation in the Gulf: A Conversation With Activists Fatin Bundagji (Saudi Arabia), Rola Dashti (Kuwait), Munira Fakhro (Bahrain)," Carnegie Endowment for International Peace, August 12, https://carnegieendowment.org/sada/20516, accessed on July 19, 2021.

El-Darwiche, Bahjat, Kombargi, Raed, and Anderson, Stephen (2021), "GCC Countries Should Prioritise Economies, Citizens and Innovation in a Post-Covid World," *Gulf Business*, May 21, https://gulfbusiness.com/gcc-countries-should-prioritise-economies-citizens-and-innovation-in-a-post-covid-world/, accessed on July 21, 2021.

Forstenlechner, Ingo, and Rutledge, Emilie Jane (2011), "The GCC's Demographic Imbalance: Perceptions, Realities and Policy Options," *Middle East Policy*, vol. 18, no. 4, pp. 25-43, https://doi.org/10.1111/j.1475-4967.2011.00508.x , accessed on August 16, 2021.

Freedom House (2020), "Freedom in the World 2020—Oman," https://freedomhouse.org/country/oman/freedom-world/2020, accessed on August 2, 2021.

Freer, Courtney (2018), *Rentier Islamism : The Influence of the Muslim Brotherhood in Gulf Monarchies*, Oxford University Press.

Freitag, Ulrike (2020), *A History of Jeddah : The Gate to Mecca in the Nineteenth and Twentieth Centuries*, Cambridge University Press.

Ghafar, Adel Abdel (2017), "Muhammed Bin Salman and the Push to Establish a New Saudi Political Order," Brookings, November 9, https://www.brookings.edu/blog/markaz/2017/11/09/muhammed-bin-salman-and-the-push-to-establish-a-new-saudi-political-order/, accessed on July 13, 2021.

Gillon, Jihâd (2021), "Saudi Arabia: Meet the Members of MBS's Inner and Youthful Circle," The Africa Report, April 20, https://www.theafricareport.com/81138/meet-the-young-members-of-crown-prince-mohammed-bin-salmans-inner-circle/, accessed on July 20, 2021.

GOV.SA (2021), "Elections in the Kingdom," Unified National Platform, September 29, https://www.my.gov.sa/wps/portal/snp/eParticipation/electionsInTheKingdomOfSaudiArabia, accessed on October 3, 2021.

GOV.SA (2021), "Youth Empowerment," Unified National Platform, July 11, 2021, https://www.my.gov.sa/wps/portal/snp/careaboutyou/youth, accessed on October 10, 2021.

Grand, Stephen, and Wolff, Katherine (2020), *Assessing Saudi Vision 2030: A 2020 Review*, Atlantic Council, https://www.atlanticcouncil.org/wp-content/uploads/2020/06/Assessing-Saudi-Vision-2030-A-2020-review.pdf, accessed on September 19, 2021.

Gulf House (2020), "Political Participation Index in the GCC States," Gulf House Studies & Publishing, https://gulfhouse.org/wp-content/uploads/2020/09/PPIGCC-2020-En.pdf, accessed on August 14, 2021.

Hanieh, Adam (2011), *Capitalism and Class in the Gulf Arab States*, New York: Palgrave Macmillan.

Herb, Michael (2003), "No Representation Without Taxation? Rents, Development and Democracy," Georgia State University, pp. 1-29.

Hertog, Steffen (2010), "The Sociology of the Gulf Rentier Systems: Societies of Intermediaries," *Comparative Studies in Society and History*, vol. 52, no. 2, pp. 282-318, https://doi.org/10.1017/S0010417510000058, accessed on September 20, 2021.

Husain, Aasim M., Fraker, Ford M., Burton, Edward, Young, Karen E. and Al Absi, Ausamah Abdulla (2016), "Economic Reform and Political Risk in The GCC: Implications for U.S. Government and Business," *Middle East Policy*, vol. 23, no. 3, pp. 5-29, https://doi.org/10.1111/mepo.12213, accessed on September 25, 2021.

Kéchichian, Joseph A (2004), "Democratization in Gulf Monarchies: A New Challenge to the GCC," *Middle East Policy*, vol. 11, no. 4, pp. 37-57, https://doi.org/10.1111/j.1061-1924.2004.00175.x, accessed on September 25, 2021.

Khatib, Hadi (2021), "Rising Unemployment Among Youth in the GCC: Insights on Saudi and UAE Stats," *AMEinfo*, February 17, https://www.ameinfo.com/industry/life/rising-unemployment-among-youth-in-the-gcc-insights-on-saudi-and-uae-stats, accessed on August 8, 2021.

Kumar, Jatin (2016), "Majlis Al-Shura Elections in Oman, 2015," *Contemporary Review of the Middle East*, vol. 3, no.4, pp. 455-462, https://doi.org/10.1177/2347798916664628, accessed on August 9, 2021.

Mainuddin, Rolin G (2016), "Arab Spring and Democratic Transition in the GCC: Continuity Amidst Change," *Asian Journal of Peacebuilding*, vol. 4, no. 2, pp. 161-186, https://doi.org/10.18588/201611.00a030, accessed on August 12, 2021.

Miniaoui, Héla (2020), "Introduction," in Héla Miniaoui (ed.), *Economic Development in the Gulf Cooperation Council Countries: From Rentier States to Diversified Economies*, pp. 5-10, Springer Singapore Limited.

Ministry of Cabinet Affairs UAE (2021), "Her Excellency Shamma Bint Suhail Faris Al Mazrui," https://uaecabinet.ae/en/details/cabinet-members/her-excellency-shamma-bint-suhail-faris-al-mazrui, accessed on August 17, 2021.

Moore-Gilbert, Kylie (2018), "Bahrain's 14 February Coalition: Deconstructing a Revolutionary Youth Movement," *The Middle East Journal*, vol. 72, no. 3, pp. 385-407, https://doi.org/10.3751/72.3.12, accessed on August 18, 2021.

Myers, JoAnne (2020), *The Good Citizen: The Markers of Privilege in America*, Routledge.

Nonneman, Gerd (2006), "Political Reform in the Gulf Monarchies: From Liberalization to Democratisation? A Comparative Perspective," University of Durham, Centre for Middle Eastern and Islamic Studies, pp. 137, https://dro.dur.ac.uk/472/ , accessed on July 5, 2021.

Ottaway, Marina (2021), "The Conundrum of Political Parties in the Gulf Countries: Unwanted But Inevitable," The Wilson Center, June 25, https://www.wilsoncenter.org/article/conundrum-political-parties-gulf-countries-unwanted-inevitable, accessed on August 20, 2021.

Ouis, Pernilla (2002), "Islamization As a Strategy for Reconciliation Between Modernity and Tradition: Examples From Contemporary Arab Gulf States," *Islam and Christian-Muslim Relations*, Carfax Publishing, vol. 13, no. 3, pp. 315-34, https://doi.org/10.1080/09596410220220145516, accessed on August 16, 2021.

Reuters (2012, 9 April), "UAE Detains 6 Islamists Stripped of Citizenship: Lawyer," April 9, https://www.reuters.com/article/us-emirates-activists-idUSBRE8380HR20120409, accessed on August 3, 2021.

Reuters (2021), "Qatar's First Legislative Elections See 63.5% Voter Turnout," October 3, https://www.reuters.com/world/middle-east/qatar-holds-first-legislative-elections-2021-10-02/, accessed on December 10, 2021.

Roberts, David B (2017), "Qatar and the UAE: Exploring Divergent Responses to the Arab Spring," *Middle East Journal*, vol. 71, no. 4, pp. 544-62, https://doi.org/10.3751/71.4.12, accessed on December 20, 2021.

Sarhan, Homam (2015), "Mouazam Al-Shabab Als⊠oudi Ghair haris Ala Al-Mosharka Al-Syasyeh," [Most of the Saudi Youths Are Careless About Political Participation], *Swissinfo*, December 6, https://bit.ly/3dARqEw, accessed on July 11, 2021.

Scharfenort, Nadine (2020), "Generating Jobs For Youth GCC Nationals? – Tourism Development, Demographic Change, and Labour Market Situation in GCC Countries," *Zeitschrift Für Tourismuswissenschaft*, vol. 12, no. 2, pp. 274-298, https://doi.org/10.1515/tw-2020-0017, accessed on December 28, 2021.

Simmons, Ann M. (2017), "Q&A: United Arab Emirates' 23-Year-Old Minister of Youth Affairs Has High Aspirations for Her Peers," *Los Angeles Times*, March 8, https://www.latimes.com/world/global-development/la-fg-global-uae-youth-minister-20170302-story.html, accessed on August 20, 2021.

Tétreault, Mary Ann (2011), "The Winter of the Arab Spring in the Gulf Monarchies," *Globalizations*, vol. 8, no. 5, pp. 629-637, https://doi.org/10.1080/14747731.2011.621658, accessed on August 26, 2021.

The New York Times (2002), "In Bahrain, Women Run, Women Vote, Women Lose," May 22, https://www.nytimes.com/2002/05/22/world/in-bahrain-women-run-women-vote-women-lose.html, accessed on September 1, 2021.

The Peninsula (2021), "Ministry: Work Underway to Draft Qatar National Youth Document," September 12, https://thepeninsulaqatar.com/article/12/09/2021/Ministry-Work-underway-to-draft-Qatar-National-Youth-Document, accessed on September 15, 2021.

The World Bank Group: Kuwait, https://data.worldbank.org/country/kuwait Qatar, https://data.worldbank.org/country/qatar UAE, https://data.worldbank.org/country/united-arab-emirates Saudi Arabia, https://data.worldbank.org/country/saudi-arabia Oman, https://data.worldbank.org/country/oman Bahrain, https://data.worldbank.org/country/bahrain, accessed on July 3, 2021.

Thompson, Mark C., and Quilliam, Neil (2018), "State, Citizens and Institutions: Policy Making in the GCC," *Middle East Policy*, vol. 25, no. 3, pp. 124-130, https://doi.org/10.1111/mepo.12366, accessed on September 5, 2021.

U.ae (2021), "The Federal National Council," March 11, https://u.ae/en/about-the-uae/the-uae-government/the-federal-national-council-, accessed on July 25, 2021.

UAE National Electoral Committee (2019), "Frequently Asked Questions," https://www.uaenec.ae/ar/faq, accessed on August 14, 2021.

Van Deth, Jan W. (2016), "What Is Political Participation?," *Oxford Research Encyclopaedia of Politics,* https://oxfordre.com/politics/view/10.1093/acrefore/9780190228637.001.0001/acrefore-9780190228637-e-68, accessed on July 25, 2021.

Wardany, Youssuf (2014), "Masarart Qaliqah, Al-Siyasat Al-Khalijiyeh Fil Ta'amoul Ma' al-Shabab," [Troubled Paths, the Politics of Gulf States Towards the Youth], Arabic Center for Research & Studies, November 4, http://www.acrseg.org/16350, accessed on July 2, 2021.

Watkins, Jessica (2020), "Identity Politics, Elites and Omnibalancing: Reassessing Arab Gulf State Interventions in the Uprisings From the Inside Out," *Conflict, Security & Development*, vol. 20, no.5, pp. 653-675, https://doi.org/10.1080/14678802.2020.1820162, accessed on November 30, 2021.

Winder, Bayly (2020), *GCC Youth Survey Report, Middle East Policy*, vol. 27, no. 3, pp. 61-75, https://doi.org/10.1111/mepo.12513, accessed on November 30, 2021.

6. Che-Guevara T-Shirts and Changing Idioms of Popular Politics among the Youth in the Arab Gulf Region[1]

M H Ilias

Introduction

Democracy, according to the Italian political philosopher Georgio Agamben (2011), gathers sense in two ways; first as a means of constituting the *body politic* and second as a technique of governing. Democracy in the second sense acts as a major source of legitimacy for the governments to exercise power and govern the population, while it in the first sense exists in society as a natural sentiment or an essential value for the survival of the society. In the contemporary political discourse, the term's use in the former sense seldom overpowers its apocryphal meaning as an 'administrative' practice with politico-managerial attributes. The situation in the Arab Gulf countries represents no exception to that. The scope of the discussion on democracy in the region is largely limited to the creation of partially elected councils to advise unelected monarchy, and the power of the centralised state remains unchanged (Crystal, 1996). Democratisation, being process, functions as a shock-absorber when the dynasties in the region experience serious legitimacy crises.

However, the region at present is an arena of new sorts of popular political expressions which collectively seem to contribute to the democratisation of the society in a subtle manner (Davidson, 2012). There are ample indications of the assertiveness of many hitherto side-lined social actors over the issues of gender and socio-political and citizenry status.[2] However, the multiplicity of such alternate political expressions may not directly result in serious structural transformations (Ilias, 2020).

As happens in most similar contexts, the development of popular politics revolves around people's ideas and practices rather than the institutional factors, which in the normal case of the Gulf States are projected as the major means of 'democratisation' (Kanna, 2012).

One way or another, popular politics has become the subject of intense debate in the Gulf today, in part because of the limits of political accountability and crisis of traditional legitimacy for the monarchic regimes in the region. The civil liberties and citizenry rights are in peril despite introducing new measures that resulted in hitherto unheard processes and practices like parliamentary elections (Tetreault, 2013). The notions of democratisation, both conventional and imposed by the Western allies, find the Arab Gulf States a difficult place for democracy to succeed. Questioning royal authority remains a red line not covered by procedural or institutional democracy. The elections, on their part, also offer no guarantee for yielding more certainty for state-society relations (Crystal, 1996). Manipulated amendments of electoral laws further lowered the expectations of parliamentary democracy in the minds of people. The political reforms, though offered a boost to 'procedural democracy' and institutions associated with that, have never culminated in a serious rethinking of democracy at the bottom level or brought any discernible changes to state-society relations. The emergence of various forms of popular political expressions is, thus, a key development that must be taken into consideration while discussing politics and democracy in the region.

Looking at the nature of dissent in the Gulf, one can see that there are demonstrations questioning political legitimacy of Gulf regimes, and while some others are not doing so. The latter's efforts are not fully rooted in the popular quest to democratise the state and society but to retain their rights as citizens or non-citizens (Kanna, 2012). Similarly, unlike the instances happening elsewhere in the Arab World, these issue-oriented mobilisations do not have the baggage of coherent ideology. This is because the protest movements in the region are subtle in their methods of raising demands. Likewise, the popular politics pay little attention to formal politics and do not enter direct interactions with the politics dominated by the state and its institutions.

In Bahrain and Kuwait, this popular politics is a product of a particular political situation, and the informal nature does not permit tangible institutional form. But, it is incorrect to say that there is complete dissociation in certain cases as the actors in some forms of popular politics try to accommodate the ideas and practices of institutions and politics in their scheme of thinking. Anyway, with an effort to depart clear institutionally protected relations, popular politics in the Gulf generally tends to remain either as covertly operated political associations or as formal social, cultural or community initiatives and organisations with unrevealed and subtle political agendas.

The key actors in the Gulf popular politics are youth, students, women's groups, ethnic minorities and expatriate labourers representing a wide spectrum of demands and practices. The people engaged in various popular forms may or may not be having the formal status of citizens. But they do not relate to the state or participate in the political processes in the same way that the others do. The governmental agencies also do not treat them as proper citizens possessing rights. These communities are governed not within the framework of citizenry rights but rather through contextual and unstable arrangements arrived at through political negotiations.

The new political activism, which is on the rise, especially among the young generation, has given rise to serious concern among the rulers in the Arab Gulf countries. The informal and unorganised political activities and massive uprisings take centre stage, while the process of political reforms in the GCC states has been pursued with more conventional activities and failed to catch up with popular imaginations. There is a tacit concern on the side of authorities on the rising political and social demands in the society, which they see as a result of partial opening up.

The monarchic regimes of the Gulf are struggling to hold back the new generation of nationals who appear less inclined to accept arguments appealing to religion and tribal tradition to explain why ordinary citizens should be shut out of decision-making. These developments may not seem surprising to outsiders, but the trend is towards a significant political advance, making possible avenues of expression previously precluded. Moreover, such fragmented and mostly single-issue-oriented responses have collectively left a powerful mark on the politics and democratisation in the GCC states. This general mood is equally shared by half-a-dozen new stories appearing in local dailies every day on previously untouched issues. Particularly in the post-Arab spring era, the idea of popular politics has moved to the centre stage of political discourse in the Gulf.

This chapter intends to provide accounts only of non-institutional aspects of politics and democracy. The question is how democracy as a means of constituting the body politic has acquired social roots in the region and has produced new political meanings that have energised new forms of popular politics. The role of popular politics in the democratisation of the Gulf societies is either left completely unexplored or underexplored by the more formal and macro approaches of understanding the development of democracy. How values and practices of dissent and democracy become entrenched in popular politics and thereby in the political imagination of ordinary people in a subtle manner are to be examined meticulously, taking cues from innovative popular political practices that the region witnesses present.

Analysing the experience of the Arab Spring-induced protests in the Arab world, Larbi Sadiki likes to see the whole debate as a part of "an inevitable conflict between two competing but interchangeable sets of legitimacy; democratic and revolutionary" (2015). The latter revolves mainly around romantic politics in societies, where the informal kind of politics is invalidated by a long period of autocracy (2015). The experience of popular politics in the Gulf, thus, goes obviously beyond the procedural democratic legitimacy, which often seeks formal structures, procedures and contracts that frame mainstream politics (2015). Political practices associated with it often base their strength "on the principle of popular legitimacy which is often in conflict with the conventional notions of legitimacy" (Chatterjee, 2004, p. 40). Judging them from the vantage point of institutional democratic legitimacy fails to understand the dynamics involved. Such a political imagination, thus, should not be limited by the matters of institutions and legality but be assessed by a different set of criteria.

Among the forms of popular politics, perhaps subtler but striking is alternative ways of dressing for making individual political statements through clothes. The dress and the way that the youth wear it has become a site of political struggle. This is more evident with many young *khalijis*

(Gulf nationals) who have chosen to wear Che-Guevara T-shirts with implicit political statements and found themselves unwittingly labelled as bearers of 'new politics.' Wearing Che-Guevara T-shirts is generally seen as a clear indication of youth's new radical politics all around the world, but in the GCC states, it interprets youth's not-so-open anti-imperial position, which they define as something subtly challenging the knee-jerking policies of the monarchies vis-à-vis the US.

This chapter examines how wearing Che-Guevara T-Shirts is becoming a subtle but serious political statement and how it contributes to the emergence of new mode of popular politics among the youth in the Arab Gulf countries. It also examines how the concept of democracy enters the lives of youth through informal political expressions. Analysing the relationship between popular politics and democratisation of the society in a circuitous fashion, this chapter uncovers the process through which popular politics gains legitimacy among the youth in the GCC States.

Popular Politics in the Gulf: A Brief History

The modern history of popular politics in the GCC states can be discussed in three broader stages. First, during the rise of Arab nationalism; in this period, although the governments in the Gulf states rallied around the ideology of pan-Islamism under the strong leadership of King Faisal of Saudi Arabia as against the one of Arab socialism, popular politics spawned by the latter had made deep inroads into all these states. Closely parallel to the other areas in the Arab world, democracy and political accountability became issues of serious debate though it did not lead to the demand for a regime change except in Oman (Ilias, 2020). The solidarity with the Palestinian movement was also a driving force for millions of Arab youth in the Gulf. The first generation of young people in most of the newly-independent Gulf States in the 1970s was deeply ideological committed to the cause of anti-imperialism.

The increase in popularity of the anti-imperialist position of the masses was partly a result of the massive immigration of labour from other countries. The post-oil economic development in the Persian Gulf brought a huge demand for expatriate workers from different regions. The authorities at the oil companies turned to other nationalities as the demand soon outstripped local supply (Ilias, 2010). Until the mid-1970s, the Gulf governments' major option for human resources reserve for the then-budding oil industry was the fellow Arab States, like Egypt, Jordan and Yemen.[3] However, the leftist Arab nationalist ideological orientation of a large chunk of Arab human resources exporting countries offered a great source of worry for the monarchic Gulf rulers (Ilias, 2010). As a result, the supply of migrants began to depend not just on immediate availability but reflected political preference. Indians were the major beneficiaries of this change earlier, and the demand for them grew rapidly to a level in which even 'undocumented' migrants entered not through proper channels were absorbed without many hassles (Ilias, 2010).

Second, in the early 1990s, the Gulf war and the presence of foreign forces (especially the US) in the Gulf States engendered a form of politics often manifested through street demonstrations. Underlying causes of these region-wide demonstrations were neoliberal reconfiguration of the economy and the pivotal position of the Gulf States in the US imperial expansionist political and security design. Thus, the politics of open street demonstration left a new imprint on the political culture of the Gulf. Unsurprisingly, then across the region, the street has been centre stage in discussing political issues, though not so openly (Bayat, 2003, pp. 10-17). The first instance in this line in the early 1990s was an extraordinary move by a group of forty-seven Saudi women who kicked their foreign male drivers out of their cars and drove through the streets of Riyadh, disregarding the ban on female driving. Following it, a handful of Saudi women have taken their cars to the streets on a particular day of collective protest (26 October) against the ban on female drivers every year.

Third, the recent phenomenon of Arab Spring captured the popular political imagination and ignited a consolidation in the expansion of participation of disadvantaged groups, especially women and minorities, in informal politics. Three Gulf States—Saudi Arabia, Oman and most notably Bahrain—experienced their own springs with considerably large-scale protests of various disadvantaged groups, including minorities and expatriate labourers. But unlike the 1960s and 1990s, minorities were the major social categories that activated new worries about rights and citizenship. Though the protests were met with violent state repression, they have ushered in a new era with new political dynamics (Abdulla and

Salem, 2011). The failure of reforms initiated in the early 1990s to take on the then-popular movements also energised this process.

These three phases are quite distinct in their content and action. However, the popular politics of all these stages invariably highlighted some of the dynamics of what one can call anti-imperialism. The relationship of the Gulf regimes with the US remains an overriding concern today. The growth and increasing popularity of Islamist groups in Egypt, Syria, or elsewhere could certainly impact popular politics in the Gulf (Abdulla and Salem, 2011). The performance of corrupt and despotic political regimes that claim to be secular in most Arab countries have induced a return to political Islam as the ultimate political solution. Though favourably inclined towards the modern world's material and cultural accomplishments, the new generation is more Islamic than the older ones and distanced from any other ideology, especially socialism, which was a rallying point for many in the Arab world during the 1960s and 1970s. The major factor that distinguishes the current popular political initiatives from previous ones is a crisis of 'secular' ideology inherited from movements like Arab nationalism.

A new type of political expression, largely spontaneous, unpredictable in its consequences, mobilised through the social media calls, largely self-organised and loosely tied together through a few formal organisations, was born for the first time in the Gulf. The major characteristic of this stage was the unusual freedom of gathering in the streets of the cities creating huge traffic jams and bottlenecks oblivious of the vigilant forces around. Momentary freedom in an atmosphere of general restriction of freedom of gathering and speech took the Gulf governments by surprise.

The South Asian labour unrest that happened in Dubai towards the end of the last decade illustrated the possibility of an alternative political action though there were many unprecedented developments in the political history of the region. By no means was the unrest first of its kind, but it was unparalleled in scale, visibility, reach and political consequences (Ilias, 2010). The massive open demonstrations had raised many eyebrows, and the UAE government was concerned by the demonstrations' content and popularity. But what was more significant was the way they were organised; it was previously unimaginable in a place where labour unions remain illegal, and protests of any sort can end in termination and immediate deportation.

Parallel to this, in the absence of serious structural reforms, the re-invented popularity of traditional informal social-political institutions was used by the people for a variety of purposes like political mobilisation and opinion building. *Majlis* (social gathering of men in its most basic sense) and *diwaniyya* (gathering mainly based on family or business ties) represented two major traditional social institutions with a high level of democratic awareness.

The tradition of questioning the authority through civic platforms of *majlis* and *diwaniyya* for open discussion of politics is a part of Arab culture. However, in most cases, these institutions are deemed to exist outside the formal political institutions, thus creating important forms of popular politics.[4] They take many forms, and states in the Arab Gulf comprehend the everyday experience of such spaces. The activities of these civic platforms range from reciting poetry to debating serious political issues, including the corruption of rulers. Critical voices which are otherwise unheard are spoken up in these meetings. People, sometimes, clandestinely bring debates that are otherwise sensitive to the local dynasties. Though some of the political expressions invite unfriendly and intolerant reactions from the administration, there are no laws regulating these informal set up so far.

Diwaniyya and *majlis* play a key mediatory role in expressing the voice of dissent in the Gulf societies. They occupy a significant position in polities where the reforms do not change the political domain. However, these institutions broaden the concept of citizen participation in state affairs through populist forms of politics. The situation remains conducive to the emergence of various social institutions, mostly by reinvention, regeneration or reaffirmation of tradition in archaic forms.

Traditionally, *diwaniyyas* were used to be man's realm, but in the last two decades, it has been necessary for them to be mixed-gender to remain politically and socially relevant in a changing world. Its relationship with informal politics in Kuwait makes *diwaniyya* a significant public space. Its importance revolves around the fact that it is not solely, or even primarily, a political institution—it is equally a centre of traditional culture, daily social life, and political activity. In the absence of serious institutional reforms, these spaces engender a multitude of expressions of democracy. The effectiveness of these social institutions, thus, can never be judged in terms of their role in formal politics but in terms of embodying informal and sensible experiences of people.

What is 'Political' about Che-Guevara T-Shirts?

As discussed earlier, there is an apparent schism between real democracy being manifested in an avalanche of popular expressions and democracy as a neo-liberal technique of government. Analysing the Indian experience, Chatterjee has defined popular politics as emerging in response to the neo-liberal developmental policies of government aimed at specific population groups (2004, p. 40). According to him, many of these groups transgress the strict lines of legality in struggling to live and work. Thus, violation of the law becomes a norm, and civil disobedience and unlawful associations become their normal tools to mobilise people, which the government cannot ignore as their demands contain serious political messages to the regimes (p. 40).

The popular politics in the Gulf can be seen as a result of the deep disappointment of a large stratum of the population. Frequent rejection of demands or delayed response by the authorities results in the formation of it. The deepening and widening of the apparatus of monarchic regimes, of course, have transformed the nature of expressing people's disappointment in the last two decades. When formal politics seems impossible for ordinary persons to have access to, people resort to popular means. The situation in which all the possibilities of formal politics are closed necessitates one to find new informal means. As a result, the street emerged as the major theatre of urban dissent discussing sensitive political issues, though not so overtly (Bayat, 2003, pp. 10-12). After the street, the net (new media) has become the most vital locus for audible expression of collective grievances for the last two decades (Bayat, 2003, pp. 12-15).

The inability of such politics to capture popular political imagination signals the presence of a weak civil society. Primarily, there is an issue concerning the definition of 'civil'. Who are qualified to become a part of the 'civil'? The issue becomes significant, especially with the powerful institutions of the family, clan or similar structure operating in opposition to the concept of 'civil'. In such a context, only the new middle class, an emerging group of liberal technocrats with a penchant for representative government, has the potential to form a civil society, though they are yet unorganised (Crystal, 1996).

Similarly, the civil society movements are mostly patronised by the government or sometimes, with its elite social content is restricted to a small section of politically equipped citizens. "Although these groups are not private, they could certainly break with the state at the first opportunity", notes Crystal (1996, p. 262). Associations of journalists, lawyers, and academics are the most illustrious of such state-sponsored groups. Even though a variety of civil society groups emerged or submerged for a few decades, almost all of them enjoyed the protection of the state in some way or other (Crystal, 1996, p. 283). Independent groups free from the control of the ruling dynasties are generally unimportant, and associated life is weak except in the case of families and clans.

It is to this political vacuum popular politics steps in. While dynastic sensibilities constrain formal politics, the Gulf youth are developing powerful voices through symbolic means of political expression. They are indeed serious political actions but may not be described as challenging directly or undermining the legitimacy of the states. Wearing Che-Guara T-shirt results from a political condition in which the arms of administration are reaching deeper and wider into domains of everyday life hitherto untouched by the government. When one cannot express his/her political opinions openly, he/she expresses them using some metaphorical language or symbols. Che-Guevara T-Shirt is such a symbol through which serious political communication is made possible.

Mostly embossed on casual T-shirts, the image of Che Guevara is still alive as an anti-imperial icon of popular politics in most Asian and African countries (Prasannarajan, 2017; Johny, 2012). But the revolutionary political legacy has not many direct takers in the Arab Gulf region. Therefore, the popularity of Che-Guevara T-Shirts cannot be linked directly to the new mode of political consciousness getting evolved in the region. It rather indicates a sort of resentment from the side of youth against the neoliberal reconfiguration of the economy and the pivotal position of the Gulf states in the US imperial expansionist political and security design.[5] Increasing unemployment despite various measures of nationalisation and implementation of quota system for certain nationals, such as Indians whose presence outnumber the nationals in States like Qatar, also forms a major reason for the resentment of youth in the Gulf countries (Montagu, 2915, p. 3).

Strangely enough, most of such micro-political expressions do not invite unfriendly and intolerant reactions from the state as the governments in the GCC countries are unaware of their serious political content. There is nothing about the politics of the image itself, as the picture is of a revolutionary who is probably unacceptable in the religio-political context that exists in the region. But, it turns out to be a serious political action offering new avenues of subtle expression that are otherwise considered sensitive and threatening to the local dynasties.

Alternative ways of dressing in West Asia and North Africa have always been a part of making political statements through clothes. The role of *keifaya* (Palestinian chequered head scarf) in popular politics had been of immense symbolic importance for the whole Arab society and the Gulf society in particular in the 1970s and 1980s. The question of Palestinians was then the major point for millions of Arab youth in the Gulf to rally around. The first generation of young men in most of the newly independent Gulf States in the 1970s was deeply ideologically committed to the cause of anti-Zionism and thereby to anti-imperialism. By choosing to wear *keifaya*, young *Khalijis* were reliving the life of their fellow Arabs from 'the land of Palestine.' During the Islamic revolution in Iran, women migrants from Iran in many Gulf cities were wrapped in dark blue mantles in solidarity with the revolutionaries.

Al-Qasimi, in her work "Immodest Modesty: Accommodating Dissent and the 'Abaya-as-Fashion' in the Arab Gulf States," observes how productions of 'abaya-as-fashion are now being used as a symbol of passive resistance (Al-Qasimi, 2010, p. 46). The 'abaya, normally in the Gulf context, is an institutionalised form of national dress that is socio-legally imposed by the state (Al-Qasimi, 2010, pp. 46-47). Nevertheless, women across the countries in the region wear it with a sense of belongingness and solidarity. Modern 'secular' liberal feminist debates have often been portrayed as another cycle of imposition of the patriarchal hegemonic religious and national order. But the new discourses have brought to "re-positioning of 'abaya' in new fashion models standing in opposition to the judicial nationalist and religious ones and embodying pleasure of female display" (Al-Qasimi 2010, p. 46). Simultaneous to being approved and accommodated by the Islamic order, the abaya, in its new avatars, constitutes a form of passive resistance in its reiteration of power (Kandiyoti,1988, pp. 214-216; Al-Qasimi, 2010, p. 49).

Along similar lines, wearing Che Guevara T-shirt for many in the Gulf operates as a subtle political statement; concerned with political meanings and serious political communication. What happens is, wearing a T-shirt with a message becomes a political signifier generating some meanings. With Che-Guevara T-shirts, the youth communicate to others the politics they stand for subtly. There is perhaps a little point in taking the popularity of Che Guevara T-Shirts seriously in general terms; but in micro-political terms, it profoundly transforms the ground on which the routinised or institutionalised political protests and dissents are envisioned and operated.

The takers of the Che Guevara T-Shirt are mostly urban people educated outside the region, mainly in Western Europe and North America.[6] However, the author noticed during a series of fieldwork in the UAE and Qatar in 2010 and 2015 that the Che Guevara T-Shirt is popular in places where the locals closely intermingle with the Indian migrants.[7] It, perhaps, may be seen as something spilled over from the Indian community.[8] Having come from politically active backgrounds, expatriates from South India generally carry forward the anti-imperialist political legacies of the region with them and try to create a subtle replica of their political positions through informal organisations in diasporic settings. The anti-imperialist positions of these organisations are manifested mainly through their consistent but covert criticism over American policies in the Gulf and support for the boycott call against American and Israeli products.

Conclusion

As discussed earlier, debates on democracy in the Gulf region seldom go beyond the procedural democratic legitimacy, which often seeks formal structures, procedures and contracts as frames of reference (Sadiki,

2015). Therefore, rationalising political debates in such a case always fails to understand the dynamics involved in popular politics. But, on the grassroots level, there has been a dramatic rise in support for popular politics and movements (not much organised), which present themselves as the promoters of the rights of the under-privileged. This development is very significant in the absence of organised political forces to aspire the demands of such sections.

For the unorganised marginalised groups (such as women, stateless Bedouins and minorities), change in the realm of rights is more sensible than the institutional reforms that most organised groups ask for. Thus, the popular protests being staged by such groups generally aim to achieve the citizens' rights through migrant labourers differs[9] (Kanna, 2012). Their efforts have always been rooted in the popular quest for a radical change of the structure of state and society, but to retain their rights as citizens or non-citizens (Kanna,2012; Ilias, 2020). The groups' political interest also varies as some seek only limited changes, others demand serious reforms within the existing system, and still, most of them expect no substantial change or an end to the regime through a serious political intervention like revolution (Kanna, 2012). Similarly, the groups which constitute the part of popular politics all over the region never base their strength and legitimacy on the principle of popular sovereignty or the notions of liberal democracy.

The realm of popular politics in the Gulf region also operates to introduce or resume popular agency in the public sphere rather than impose absolute sovereignty, as most Islamic political activists wish to achieve. Therefore, the Islamic political activism neither provides a conscious address to the issue raised by the groups that are a part of popular politics nor attempts to mobilise them politically. Contrary to the prevailing assumptions, the region-wide springs also lacked concern over the issues of outside groups like minority Shias, transnational labourers and stateless Bedouins.

It has also become more important than popular political activism, often targeting youth, mainly recent graduates, who are more suitable for mobilisation. The young people—who make up some 60 per cent of the population in the region—have no formal voice but are social media-savvy, often unemployed or dissatisfied with their job prospects, and wishing to have a say in their country's governance and social, domestic and foreign policy making (Montagu, 2015, p. 3). Therefore, they focus more on covert political actions through comments and messages posted on social media (Ebrahimi, 2014). Such moves carry a lot of importance when power distribution via Western-modelled parliament seems incapable of addressing present issues. As a result, the mainstream political organisations throughout the region look for alternative strategies in the post-Arab Spring period. The survival of democracy, thus, lies in how far the state can appropriate such non-traditional actors and their broader democratic practices within the rubric of 'democratisation.'

As a form of serious political protest, wearing Che Guevara T-Shirt is yet to catch up with the popular imaginations, and people do not see any serious potential to challenge the regimes' legitimacies. In certain cases, those who wear it are unaware of it or even the ideology of the political icon imprinted on the T-shirt.[10] However, most of the youth think wearing it is an alternative way of expressing politics covertly.

Notes

1. Certain portions of this chapter has already been published in two previous works of the author. See Ilias (2017) and (2015).
2. There is a frequent raise of anger in Saudi Arabia's Eastern province- a strong Shi'ite bastion-over the ill-treatment of minorities in the Kingdom. Shias in Bahrain are up in arms against the repressive minority Sunni administration for their alleged programmes of de-development in the Shia dominated pockets. Open demonstrations of stateless *Bedoon* with a strong back up of human rights groups becomes a regular feature of politics in Kuwait. The Arab Spring-induced protests of unemployed youth became a wide-spread phenomenon in in the region. The recent South Asian labour unrests in the UAE and Bahrain appears to be a different sort among the political events, though there are many unprecedented developments that go into the making of contemporary political history of the region. These initiatives (though mostly single-issue oriented) appear to offer a component for a new mode of popular politics to emerge in the GCC States (Ilias 2020).
3. Options of the GCC countries regarding the workers and their nationalities also wavered at different times with the shift in international and regional political equations. Yemen and the erstwhile Persia (including Iran and Iraq) emerged as the major suppliers of labour in the early 1930s. The increase in

number of Iranian labourers because of Shiite domination caused serious religious concerns for the local rulers by the end of 1930s. When oil price began to escalate, they turned to a cheaper labour reserve in India and Pakistan (Ilias 2011 & Ilias 2015). As a staunch Cold War ally of the US, Pakistan also had benefited from the strong anti-Soviet and anti- Arab Socialist postures of the Gulf governments.

4. But in Saudi Arabia, *majlis al-Ahiya* or neighbourhood committees are incorporated as a part of local government with the task of controlling the policies of the local government and its implementation.
5. A student of University of Sharjah shared this view in anonymity during my field research in 2010.
6. This view was expressed by many nationals and South Indian expatriates during my field visits in UAE between 2010 and 2014.
7. Che Guevara T-Shirt as an alternative way of dressing has hardly made any inroads into Oman and Saudi Arabia where the role of Indian expatriates in the cultural process in marginal.
8. In a series of interviews in 2015, some shopkeepers in Dubai dealing with Che Guevara T-Shirt agreed that wearing it shows the influence of Indian expatriates.
9. The latter seek no citizenship rights and what figures in their demands, is economic rights and a dignified life in the hosting countries. The protests demonstrations staged by them are not necessarily against the rulers, but in most cases point to the inherent anomalies in the system which can't be solved through the means of political reforms. These interventions according to Kanna, "seem to want, at most, a *limited* recognition by the state, the recognition that they are *not* citizens." See Kanna (2012).
10. In interviews certain respondents revealed that only thing they know about Che-Guevara is his ardent anti-American position.

References

Abdulla, Abdulkhaleq and Salem, Paul (2011), "The Arab Spring: A View From the Gulf," Carnegie Middle East Centre, July 28, www.carnegie-mec.org/2011/07/28/arab-spring-view-from-gulf/cuj3, accessed on December 29, 2021.

Agamben, Georgio (2011), "Introductory Note on the Concept of Democracy," in William McCuaig (ed.), *Democracy in What State*, pp. 5-27, Columbia University Press.

Al-Qasimi, Noor (2010), "Immodest Modesty: Accommodating Dissent and the Abaya-as-Fashion in the Arab Gulf States," *Journal of Middle East Women's Studies*, vol. 6, no. 1, pp. 46-74.

Bayat, Asef (2003), "The Street and the Politics of Dissent in the Arab World," *Middle East Report,* vol. 226, pp. 10-17.

Chatterjee, Partha (2004), *The Politics of the Governed: Reflections of Popular Politics in Most of the World*, Columbia University Press.

Crystal, Jill (1996), *Civil Society in the Middle East*, Brill.

Davidson, Christopher (2012), *After the Sheikhs: The Coming Collapse of the Gulf Monarchies*, Hurst Publishers.

Ebrahimi, Nabiollah (2014), "Persian Gulf Arab States Witnessing New Forms of Political Action," Iran Review, April 21, www. Iranreview.org/ content/ Documents/ Persian-Gulf-Arab-States-Witnessing-New Forms-of-Political-Action-htm, accessed on December 20, 2021.

Ilias, M H (2010), "South Asian Labour Crisis in Dubai and the Scanty Prospects of Indian Policy in the Arab Gulf Region," *Indian Journal of Politics and International Relations*, vol. 4, no.1&2, pp. 74-102.

Ilias, M H (2015), "Malayali Migrants and Translocal Kerala Politics in the Gulf: Re-conceptualising the Political," in Anthony Gorman and Sossie Kasbarian (eds.), *Diasporas of the Modern Middle East: Contextualising Communities*, Edinburgh University Press.

Ilias, M H (2017), "Che Guevara T-Shirts and Changing Idioms of Popular Politics in the Arab Gulf Region," Centre for Mellemoststudier, November, https://www.sdu.dk/-/media/files/om_sdu/centre/c_mellemoest/videncenter/artikler/2017/ilias+article+november+17.pdf, accessed on December 27, 2021.

Ilias, M H (2020), "South Asian Labour Unrests and Non-Citizenry Aspects of Popular Politics in the Gulf," in S. Irudaya Rajan and Ginu Zacharia Oommen (eds.), *Asianisation of Migrant Workers in the Gulf Countries,* pp. 55-69, Springer.

Kandiyoti, Denis (1988), "Bargaining With Patriarchy", *Gender and Society,* September 2, pp. 214-290.

Kanna, Ahmed (2012), "A Politics of Non-Recognition? Biopolitics of Arab Gulf Worker Protests in the Year of Uprising," *Interface: A Journal for and About Social Movements,* vol. 4, no. 1, pp. 146-164.

Montagu, Caroline (2015), "Civil Society in Saudi Arabia: The Power and Challenges of Association," Middle Eastern and North Africa Programme.

Prasannarajan, S. (2017), "The Redundancy of Che Guevara," *Open Magazine,* October 18,

https://openthemagazine.com/columns/locomotif/the-redundancy-of-che-guevara/, accessed on December 30, 2021.

Sadiki, Larbi (2015), "Egypt Back to Square One: Tahrir or Dictatorship," Al Jazeera, June 16, https://www.aljazeera.com/opinions/2012/6/16/egypt-back-to-square-one-tahrir-or-dictatorship, accessed on December 30, 2021.

Tetreault, Mary Ann (2013), "Dissent and Citizen's Rights in Kuwait (Part One): The Limits of Electoral Democracy, *Jadaliyya*, November 5, https://www.jadaliyya.com/Details/29752/Dissent-and-Citisens%60-Rights-in-Kuwait-Part-One-The-Limits-of-Electoral-Democracy, accessed on December 29, 2021.

7. Millennials Drive the Financial Technology in the GCC

Rohit Sharma

The COVID-19 pandemic has ushered in dramatic changes worldwide, compelling people to pursue online transactions and communications. Even though online or remote working has been in vogue before the pandemic, the nature of the pandemic amplified the reliance on ICT-enabled technology. The ongoing technological innovations across various sectors were not only immune to disruption of the pandemic but have prospered as well. Big-tech companies like Amazon, Facebook, and Apple have reportedly witnessed a surge in their earnings during the pandemic as economies worldwide contracted (King, 2020). In addition, there has been a paradigm shift in consumer behaviours as they go digital for entertainment, social connection, shopping, and learning, and the industry is adopting advanced technology to adjust to the 'new normal'.

Financial technology (fintech) has also reported rapid growth during the pandemic. Fintech is any technology that "augment, streamline, digitise or disrupt traditional financial services" (Walden, 2020). According to observers, the evolution of fintech suggests that the fusion of technology with financial services is not a new phenomenon and has a longer legacy than otherwise understood (Alt, Beck and Smits, 2018). The emergence of the telegraph, ATMs, SWIFT transfers, or internet diffusion in banking illustrates a gradual progression in fintech, unlike the emerging technologies that have accelerated and revolutionised the finance industry. These technologies are predicated on advancements in information and communications technology (ICT) like artificial intelligence (AI), big data, cloud, etc., that have resulted in "process disruption and service transformation" in the financial sector (Alt, Beck and Smits, 2018).

According to a study, the global fintech industry has been largely resilient and adaptable despite the pandemic, with an average growth of 11 per cent in transactions volume (Cambridge Centre for Alternative Finance [CCAF], 2020). In response to the crisis, fintech firms have been amending their terms, products, and service agreements while enhancing fraud and cybersecurity features (CCAF, 2020, p. 29). Regionally the emerging markets in the Middle East and North Africa (MENA) have witnessed stronger and faster growth in fintech as compared to the developed markets. These are encouraging signs, but the developments are not uniformly spread across the region and are overwhelmingly clustered in the Gulf Cooperation Council (GCC) states.

Meanwhile, the GCC is undergoing unprecedented changes where member states outline their strategic frameworks for the coming decades. These initiatives are all-encompassing in response to the changing realities and harmony with a tech-centric shift in the economies across the globe. The digitalisation of financial services and the emergence of numerous instant payment apps have significantly contributed to fintech in the GCC. The UAE has emerged as the largest fintech hub for start-ups in the MENA region, predicated on investment in digitalisation. Likewise, Bahrain has also intensified its endeavour to mark its place on the global fintech map. Similarly, the Kingdom of Saudi Arabia and the remaining GCC states are marching towards the shared goal of digitalising every aspect of financial services while competing for international investments.

With the required conducive environment to thrive, the millennials (those born between 1980 and 2000) or the youth are driving significant growth of fintech in the region. It is quite easy to adapt to new banking methods for tech-savvy youth born and raised when financial services around them were undergoing digitalisation. The ease in banking that accompanied these shifts compelled many to push for more technology-friendly solutions in financial services like wealth-tech, Invest-tech, and Insur-tech.[1] Thus, the entrepreneurial youth driven by ideas and global success stories to replicate could find digital solutions to the challenges the conventional financial services confronted. Likewise, the growth in fintech has also engendered constructive effects on the GCC youth as it is proven to be more consumer-friendly than the traditional financial services. Fintech has also facilitated the financial inclusion of the unbanked via technology, which is more likely to be adopted by youth, thereby opening new avenues of participation in the domestic and international economy.

The chapter will examine the fintech industry in the GCC, the start-up companies, and individual states' responses to these developments. It will also appraise the role of youth in driving the fintech industry while considering the opportunities that these technologies offer to the youth in the GCC. Finally, the advancements and innovations of the fintech in the last decade, both within and outside the GCC, would be examined.

Fintech Landscape in the GCC

The history of finance is as old as human civilisation and has played a significant role in human progress. As cities and civilisations grew, the nature of finance evolved from barter to currency. It is impossible to trace the origin of banking and finance, but it is believed that the first "proper bank" sprung up somewhere in Mesopotamia, but with no concept of currency in its present form (McCaffrey, 2017). Gradually, minted coins and other forms of currencies were introduced across civilisations to the extent that they essentially became an inseparable part of societies and states.

In the GCC, the first "modern" banking appeared with Western imperialism in the 19th century. The Imperial Bank of Persia (now HSBC bank) was established in 1899 and was a "leader in financial services in the states that are now referred to as the GCC opening branches in Kuwait (1942), Bahrain (1944), the area now known as UAE (1946), Oman (1948) and Saudi Arabia (1950)" (HSBC, n.d.). Later, these states came up with their national banks and other financial services to better serve their indigenous cultural and social needs. Islamic banking, a unique form of financial service, was first experimented in its modern form in Egypt, which later culminated in establishing the first Islamic commercial bank-the Dubai Islamic Bank in the UAE in 1975 (Hussain, Shahmoradi and Turk, 2015) the same year, the establishment of the Islamic Development Bank came as a watershed moment for Islamic finance. Currently, the GCC accounts for 42 per cent of total global Islamic assets, indicating GCC's centrality in Islamic banking (Ferraris and Garrido, 2020). Notably, Saudi Arabia alone holds one-fifth of total Islamic banking assets worldwide (Ferraris and Garrido, 2020).

After a long history of evolution in financing services, fintech has fundamentally transformed the way consumers interact with service providers. Unlike conventional financial services, fintech companies are introducing pathbreaking technologies that facilitate financial inclusion and other turnarounds without any need to visit a provider's office. The whole consumer experience following the fintech revolution could be encapsulated in a single catch line: *banking everywhere, never at a bank.*[2] Now, what exactly has changed in the past decade that made such a technological feat possible and scalable? How are these fintech start-ups different from the previous banking methods? How are these start-ups gaining momentum in the GCC, and how are states responding to it?

Brett King, an Australian futurist and co-founder and CEO of Moven, a New York-based mobile banking start-up, explains that it is the "first principles design thinking" that makes the fintech revolution distinct from the previous technological advancements in banking (King, 2018). "First-principles design thinking" means questioning the fundamental assumptions[3] of what we know, which is different from "design by analogy," which means finding better ways to iterate on a base design[4] (King, 2018, p. 23). Previous technological advancements, particularly in the 1990s and first decade of the 21st century, aptly fall under the category of "design by analogy" when banks took products and concepts from the branch-based system and iterated them to fit on the internet and mobile phones (King, 2018, p. 28). In contrast, the fintech revolution, in conjunction with widespread internet and smartphone access, has redefined the utility of financial services, not via branch or an ATM but data, AI, and smartphones (King, 2018, p. 31).

Internet access has been instrumental in redefining banking. According to the World Bank, in 2010, around 28.74 per cent of the world population had internet access, while in 2017, it went up to almost 49 per cent of the world population (The World Bank, n.d.). Simultaneously, the number of smartphone subscribers worldwide has surpassed six billion and is predicted to grow by several hundred million in the next few years (Dea, 2021). Internet access across the GCC states is robust and extensive, and mobile phone subscriptions cover the whole gamut of the population, as evident in Table 7.1.

Table 7.1: Internet Access, Mobile Phone Subscriptions, Estimated Number of Fintech Start-ups and Global Fintech Rank (2020)

States	Total Internet Users (% of the population)	Mobile Phone Subscriptions (per 100 people)	Estimated no. of fintech start-ups	Global Fintech Rank
Bahrain	98.6	133.3	100	153
Kuwait	99.6	178.6	28	236
Oman	80.2	133.4	5	N/A
Qatar	99.7	141.9	5	N/A
Saudi Arabia	93.3	122.6	155	232
United Arab Emirates	98.5	208.5	400+	34

Source: UNDP (2020), *Human Development Report 2020*; Fintech (2021), Middle East and Africa Report 2021; Deloitte Digital (2020).

Given a robust digital ecosystem and shifting consumer preferences, cutting-edge technologies are being introduced in the market, just a tap away in mobile applications. These applications are either created by legacy banks or by specialised fintech start-ups targeting a specific segment of financial services like wealth management (wealth-tech), investments (invest-tech), or insurance (insur-tech). Other examples of fintech solutions include robo-advice,[5] crowdfunding,[6] peer-to-peer (P2P) insurance, P2P money transfer, account aggregation, open banking, mobile wallet, enhanced KYC (know your customer) with biometrics, etc. Several factors drive the fintech boom across all financial services segments, like the lack of trust in the traditional banking industry; sharp focus of fintech firms on one product or service; agility and lower operating cost (Wiwanto, 2020). Also, the strong emphasis by fintech on consumer experience rather than on processes makes it frictionless, which, for example, means that it has become easy for consumers to open an account and keep track of it remotely (King, 2018, p. 194).

The most popular fintech solutions amongst the region's banking customers are P2P transfers,[7] account aggregation, followed by robo-advisors (Deloitte Digital, 2020). Ease and convenience are the utility that customers look for in fintech solutions, while concerns about the security of data and lack of understanding about fintech are major hindrances (Deloitte Digital, 2020). Nonetheless, the region has numerous opportunities for fintech services, both by specialised start-ups and legacy banks (that have adopted fintech in their processes), as they continue to tailor their practices as per customers.

Since the opportunities are huge and fintech solutions are the future, lack of funding is no longer an issue. The investors and venture capitalists are enthusiastic about their investments in promising ideas with unique solutions. In February 2021, fintech regional firms like Tarabut Gateway (Bahrain) and Lendo (Saudi Arabia) have successfully raised US$ 13 million and US$ 7.2 million, respectively (Harrlson, 2021). According to the Forbes Middle East, the top 20 fintech start-ups in the Middle East have raised US$ 99 million in funding and are likely to raise more in the coming years (Forbes Middle East, n.d.). A cursory look at the list indicates the dominance of the GCC countries, with twelve out of twenty start-ups in MENA being located in the GCC, most of them in the UAE.

Fintech has also made inroads into Islamic finance as it has taken into account the religious and cultural impediments to financial inclusion by allowing Islamic fintech firms to thrive and provide an alternate technology to religious individuals. In Islamic banking worldwide, at least 127 fintech firms offer Sharia-compliant financial products, with the UAE and Saudi Arabia leading in "transaction volume and ecosystem creation" (Santosdiaz, 2020; Rahal, 2021). The UAE now has the third-largest number of Sharia-compliant fintech firms after Malaysia and the UK (Santosdiaz, 2021). Moreover, fintech hub like Dubai International Financial Centre (DIFC) has witnessed a marked rise in the volume of Islamic banking assets, which shows the potential that Islamic fintech hold (Amiri, 2020). Clearly, fintech is opening new avenues for millennials, facilitating the financial inclusion of unbanked while also engendering financial literacy on issues like insurance, investment, and savings.

As illustrated in Table 7.1 and the discussion above, the UAE has demonstrated exceptionally well in the region in 2020. Similarly, the number of fintech start-ups in Bahrain and its Global Fintech Rank as estimated by Deloitte has been impressive. State-supported ecosystems under a well-regulated framework have made Bahrain, and the UAE fintech hubs reportedly received the bulk of venture capital investment in the region (Mueller and Piwowar, n.d.). The three key factors driving the emergence of Bahrain and the UAE as fintech hubs in the region are (Mueller and Piwowar, n.d., p. 3): Conducive ecosystem; Government driven ecosystem; and ecosystem particularly targeting international talent as a means to stimulate domestic innovation.

The flurry of government-led strategic plans that have facilitated the aforesaid factors includes *Bahrain Economic Vision 2030*, *UAE Centennial 2071*, *Emirates Blockchain Strategy 2021*, *Artificial Intelligence Strategy 2031*, etc. In addition, both the states have decentralised "free zones" wherein each "free zone" operates under separate regulatory and governance structures, largely autonomous of the "mainland" authorities (Mueller and Piwowar, n.d., p. 22). Yet, notwithstanding these encouraging signs, the challenges remain, warranting appropriate response from the authorities.

Overall, trends suggest that GCC states have a promising future even though western fintech firms have an overwhelming advantage in skills, ecosystems, and funding over regional fintech start-ups. However, the youth being the key driver of the fintech revolution can be a game-changer for the GCC states.

Millennials and Fintech

Currently, there are 1.2 billion young people aged 15 to 24 years, accounting for 16 per cent of the global population (Organisation for Economic Co-operation and Development [OECD], 2020). The UN defines youth as people between 15 and 24 years old (United Nations Department of Economic and Social Affairs (UNDESA, n.d.). However, this categorisation is not uniformly applied, as a definition of youth often goes beyond 24 years and varies across countries. The young cohort is also dubbed millennials, often further categorised into younger (born between 1991 and 2000) and older millennials (born between 1981 and 1990). Notwithstanding categorisation, individuals born after the 1980s have witnessed and were engaged with the internet and computers, which laid the foundation of the "fourth industrial revolution."

The young generation is the first "digitally native" generation born into a world of technology, with recurrent innovations and disruptions moulding the way they shop, learn or invest. Notably, banks and fintech services have tapped into this phenomenon and focused on providing palatable solutions to the highly digitalised generation. The youth bulge worldwide and particularly in the region has overhauled the financial services and their processes. The traditional products and channels are being replaced by innovations, tailored as per consumers' utility in an increasingly digitalised world. The millennials' choices and preferences strongly influence the industry to transform and adhere to their needs (Gagllardi, 2019).

Fintech has offered the youth their preferential way of banking. The young generation is not known to trust banks as much as the previous generation (Lulic, 2020). The tech-savvy generation with 24/7 internet access and availability of smartphones has access to instant products and services. They expect banks to work in a frictionless, real-time manner (King, 2018, p. 253). They are more likely to use robo-advisors and other applications instead of financial advisors (King, 2018). The GCC millennials are different from the global cohort as they prefer to use digital currency and other cutting-edge technologies far more than elsewhere (VISA, 2016). Barring these differences, millennials have similar expectations from fintech across the globe.

The people of the region have always been known for their entrepreneurship which begins at a young age. Much of entrepreneurship had been subverted to structures of rentier states that had a patron-client relation with the citizens, created and sustained by the flow of oil revenues. However, the tech boom has revived the entrepreneurial energy in the region. The youngsters are likely to be more entrepreneurial than the preceding generation sustained by the oil boom as they see technology as the enabler of innovations to address the needs of the time (Gulf News, 2019).

Moreover, "majority of those behind fintech start-ups are millennials themselves so they can cater to the digital experiences their generation of consumers seeks and are familiar with", noted Shahebaz Khan, the UAE's General Manager for Visa. For instance, in Saudi Arabia, the fintech sector is driven mainly by young first-generation entrepreneurs who are successfully competing with the largest financial institutions (Santosdiaz, 2021) This is in synchronisation with Saudi Arabia being the largest market in the GCC with an abundant young population. The young Saudi of the age group 15-34 years, according to the General Authority for Statistics (GASTAT) report, represent 36.7 per cent of the total population (GASTAT, 2020). Furthermore, the GCC's young generation has an overwhelming imprint over fintech start-ups, which is also evident from the list of top 20 fintech start-ups in the Middle East. Table 7.2 illustrates the fintech start-ups with youngsters as founders have also been listed among the top-performing firms in the Middle East.

Table 7.2: Young Fintech Start-up Founders in the GCC

Founders	Start-ups
Abdulazis Fahad Aljouf	PayTabs
Ambareen Musa	Souqalmal.com
Talal Bayaa, Brian Habibi	Bayzat
Shaheen Alkhudari	Ajar Online
Ali Abulhasan, Ahmed Almunayes, Mohammed Abulhasan	Tap Payments
Ibrahim Mohammed	OneGram
Moussa Beidas, Nadim Jarudi	Bridg

Source: Forbes Middle East (2018).

For many, entrepreneurship is more about social impact and making a difference than business or profit-making (Lechtenfeld, 2018). For instance, Michele Grosso founded *Democrance* to bring micro-insurance to 15 million of the region's low-income population (Kamel, 2018). "Insurance companies weren't ready from a technology and innovation point of view to enter the low-income segment with micro-finance", he noted, which prompted him to build such a platform to reach this segment (Kamel, 2018). Similarly, Shaheen Alkhudhari, founder of Kuwait-based *Anjar Online*, was encouraged to disrupt the real-estate rental payments process in the region, which he observed was "broken" and exasperated both expats and citizens (Evrington, 2017). "What banks do is provide payment solution. We're a property management solution that has a payment feature", remarked Shaheen Alkhudhari (Paracha, 2017). In both cases, the young entrepreneurs are driven by personal experience and motivation to serve a larger under-represented populace. As a result, the region is brimming with an entrepreneurial spirit (Radcliffe, 2016) and the fintech drive rides on this high tide.

It is also challenging to hire millennials unless an organisation has a culture that attracts them (King, 2018)."Profitability for shareholders isn't going to motivate these candidates", observed Brett King; on the contrary, issues like "... financial inclusion, promoting renewables, promoting lower crime, greater equality" are going to allure them to fintech firms (King, 2018, p. 299). In addition, in a recent study by PwC, there are certain traits, skills, and behaviours that millennials look for in their leaders and working environment, to lead them to "commit, thrive, and drive organisational success" (PwC, 2021). Therefore, the fintech firms are not required to focus on just consumers and their utility but also the millennials in the team.

Women millennials' participation in the fintech industry is also noteworthy. Digitalisation has unlocked the space for women entrepreneurs, which was earlier unfathomable in the social fabric of the region. As a result, today, women are at top managerial positions and founding unique fintech firms that are also scalable. Even though the number of women entrepreneurs is few, the changing cultural and office norms and government-led initiatives are promising. Moreover, the success stories of women in fintech, both local and international, underline the region's transformation. Nejoud Al Mulaik, Fintech Saudi Director, notes that she was confident and hopeful about the future of women in fintech (Santosdiaz, 2020a). For women entrepreneurs, she observed, the "... ability to juggle between career progression and personal prioritisation is key" (Santosdiaz, 2020a).

Similarly, "women consider balancing work and family life as the single most significant obstacle to their career aspirations", remarked Sandra Knight, Co-founder and the CEO of *Hayatech*, a Bahrain-based technology platform (Santosdiaz, 2020c). Further, Ambareen Musa, founder of *Souqamal*, opined that regardless of gender, sound knowledge of industry dynamics is vital to "come somewhere close to succeeding" (Santosdiaz, 2020b). Undeniably, women more than ever are in leadership roles, with immense networking and mentorship opportunities.

The role of millennials on the fintech supply chain is vital for it to take off and sustain. It is equally important to explore the millennials on the demand side. It is estimated that in the coming decades, more youngsters in the region would be part of the workforce, and it is most likely that they would opt for fintech over legacy banks for better financial services. Fintech has much value to offer to the millennials in the GCC region.

Fintech Assisting Millennials

According to the *Global Findex Database 2017*, unbanked adults are disproportionately young, and globally, 30 per cent of unbanked adults are between 15-24 (Kunt, et al., 2018, p. 38). The predominant reasons for the absence of bank accounts among these populations include too little money to use an account; cost and distance; lack of documentation, and distrust in the financial systems (Kunt, et al., 2018, p. 5). In addition, the employment status of an individual and the level of financial literacy also determines the status of financial inclusion among the youths. Moreover, the need for financial services, lack of digital infrastructure, and cultural, social, and religious norms are also key to seeking or eluding financial inclusion (OECD, 2020).

Financial inclusion is a prominent value brought in by fintech. Financial inclusion supports inclusive development, which leads to the financial empowerment of individuals and helps people escape poverty. Moreover, digitalisation has amplified the reach of financial services among the millennials as they have access through smartphones and the internet to a wide range of fintech solutions in the market (Santosdiaz, 2021).

Youth unemployment (as a per cent of total labour force ages 15-24) in the region remains a cause of concern and has been betting on their financial inclusion. Qatar is better placed than most GCC states with 0.5 per cent unemployment of total labour force, while Saudi Arabia has performed the worst with 29.6 per cent unemployment of total labour force (The World Bank, 2021). Likewise, access to finance for small and medium-sized enterprises (SMEs) and youth remain a key challenge. Undeniably, SMEs have the potential to create jobs and innovations, which is why it is equally important to incubate and sustain these enterprises.

The use of fintech can potentially help solve the existing challenges with SME lending and provide a way to boost the financial inclusion of youth in the GCC (IMF, 2018). It is already established that fintech decreases information asymmetry and the cost of lending to SMEs, making it easy for young entrepreneurs to borrow or avail of financial services (IMF, 2018, p. 21). As a result, fintech firms are emerging as an additional source of financing for the regional SMEs in the region (Alothman, 2020). Also, fintech-based "… credit scoring systems powered by big data analytics enables lenders to source information from alternative sources to quickly generate a real-time credit score on SME borrowers", which is hassle-free and less time consuming (Alothman, 2020). Furthermore, fintech firms are also facilitating raising funds through methods like crowdfunding. For instance, fintech firm *Beehive*, based in the UAE, is an SME-focused P2P lending platform that connects businesses directly with investors and thereby eliminates intermediaries and associated costs (Bridge, 2019). Furthermore, fintech companies are also reducing the cost of anti-money laundering/combating the financing of terrorism (AML/CFT) and know your customer (KYC) procedures vital for SME loans.

Notably, financial literacy amongst the millennials is less than their predecessors, although in terms of "digital literacy," it is the other way around. As a consequence of lacking financial literacy, low-income consumers are likely to be vulnerable to market risk and also the nature of insurance (Kurczyk, 2020). Fintech is increasingly aiding millennials in overcoming financial illiteracy by providing them solutions to compare banking services, credit cards, and insurance on a single platform. The emergence of AI-powered robo-advisor is assuming the role of financial advisors, and with more data and faster processing, it is likely to provide better advice for end consumers that are mostly millennials. They use algorithms to analyse customers, their pattern of choices, and preferences to tailor solutions that reflect the clients' profile. AI-based fintech is also guiding wealth and risk management and financial education to drive financial inclusion (Kurchzyk, 2020.). *Sarwa*, one of the first robo-adviser firms in the UAE, intends to "democratise the whole wealth management industry" while also maintaining the human element to financial advice by making advisers available to help over the phone or in-person (Overdahl, 2019).

Crypto-currencies are also being weighed by millennials, although not very enthusiastically, as there are myths and challenges around them. For optimists, crypto-currencies can enable financial inclusion (Moy and Carlson, 2021), while being highly costly and volatile for sceptics. Notwithstanding scepticisms and challenges, states like Bahrain, Saudi Arabia, and the UAE are taking the lead in crypto-currencies, followed by strong regulatory frameworks (Singh, 2020).

Conclusion

Financial technologies have completely transformed the way one approaches banking and other financial services. The advancement of ICTs in banking has a long history, but the opportunities and solutions that fintech offer is unparalleled in history. This is driven by the "first principle design thinking" that has challenged the mainstream understanding of financial services, unlike the previous advancements based on "design by analogy". Moreover, predicated on robust digital infrastructure and internet access in the GCC, fintech has both been introduced by specialised fintech firms and adopted by legacy banks to augment the experience of consumers that look for frictionless services. The fintech landscape in the GCC is extensive and expanding to every corner and across different segments of the society. The individual states' responses to the tech-led innovation in finance are welcoming, which is facilitating an ecosystem that has produced some unique solutions to the usual problems of consumers.

Besides a robust digital infrastructure and state-led response, millennials are central to this revolution, both on the supply and demand side. The "digital natives" are fuelling fintech usage while also directly benefiting from it. The overwhelming presence of millennials as founders and CEOs of fintech firms has helped these firms expand since these individuals have first-hand experience of limitations and advantages of technology and are better placed to respond to evolving needs of consumers, who are mostly of their age. The millennials are vital not just as founders but also as part of a team that makes up a fintech firm. For these digital natives, larger good is more essential than profit-making, an attribute that has significantly impacted the way fintech firms operate and provide solutions. Entrepreneurs like Shaheen Alkhudhari and Michele Grosso have harnessed their personal experience and tech knowledge to reach and serve a wider audience that was unbanked till recently. The extensive and burgeoning market of fintech has also opened space for women to innovate and contribute across financial services.

Fintech firms also deliver services beyond products and processes, making the "financially illiterate" millennials more aware of the nuances and opportunities ahead while facilitating their participation in the larger financial market. Fintech is helping the millennials in various issues, from simple account opening to assisting them in borrowing and kick-starting SMEs while facilitating their financial inclusion. Fintech has not only ensured the financial literacy of millennials but has also turned the tables in favour of them as they are coming up with unique solutions to the problems that their peers face regularly. Overall, the fintech landscape in the GCC is still at a nascent phase, yet it has managed to offer solutions that were missing in conventional financial services. The individual GCC states have recognised the potential in the field and have built dedicated free zones with regulatory frameworks to address the demand for fintech-based solutions. The government-led policies and start-up-led innovations have provided the millennials with the ecosystem that helps them be at the helm of the change and will go a long way to ensure the overall stability of the financial system.

Notes

1. Technology dealing with insurance.
2. Taken from the title of the book "Bank 4.0: Banking Everywhere, Never at a Bank" authored by Brett King (2018).
3. Questioning and changing the base design.
4. Without fundamentally changing the base design.
5. Digital platform that provides automated, algorithm based financial planning services with little or no human supervision. For optimists this technology offers more accurate market and financial predictions than a human, although it is yet to be an established fact.
6. Platform to raise money online from large number of people.
7. Popular fintech solution across all income brackets.

References

Alothman, Abdullah F. (2020), "How FinTech Can Help Ensure the Survival of SMEs in the Middle East," *Entrepreneur*, May 27, https://www.entrepreneur.com/article/350934, accessed on December 29, 2021.

Alt, Rainer, Beck, Roman and Smits, Martin T. (2018), "FinTech and the Transformation of the Financial Industry," *Electronic Markets*, pp. 235-243.

Amiri, Arif (2020), "FinTech Can Help the Islamic Finance Sector to Innovate and Grow," *The National*, July 9, https://www.thenationalnews.com/business/fintech-can-help-the-islamic-finance-sector-to-innovate-and-grow-1.1046089, accessed on December 26, 2021.

Bridge, Sam (2019), "Dubai's Beehive Launches Crowdfunding Platform in Bahrain," *Arabian Business,* March 23, https://www.arabianbusiness.com/banking-finance/414650-dubais-beehive-launches-crowdfunding-platform-in-bahrain, accessed on November 30, 2021.

Cambridge Centre for Alternative Finance (CCAF), World Bank, World Economic Forum (2020), *The Global Covid-19 FinTech Market Rapid Assessment Study,* https://www.jbs.cam.ac.uk/wp-content/uploads/2021/03/2020-ccaf-global-covid-fintech-market-rapid-assessment-study-v2.pdf, accessed on November 30, 2021.

O'Dea, S. (2021), "Smartphone Users Worldwide 2016-2026," Statista Research Department, June 2, https://www.statista.com/statistics/330695/number-of-smartphone-users-worldwide/, accessed on December 25, 2021.

Deloitte Digital (2020), *Middle East FinTech Study,* https://www2.deloitte.com/content/dam/Deloitte/xe/Documents/financial-services/me_fintech-study-report.pdf, accessed on December 24, 2021.

Evrington, John (2017), "How Ajar Online Is Streamlining Payments in Kuwait's Real Estate Market," *The National,* September 16, https://www.thenationalnews.com/business/technology/how-ajar-online-is-streamlining-payments-in-kuwait-s-real-estate-market-1.629092, accessed on November 20, 2021.

Ferraris, Richard, and Garrido, Francis (2020), "Here Is How the GCC's 10 Largest Islamic Banks Rank," S&P Global, March 24, https://www.spglobal.com/marketintelligence/en/news-insights/latest-news-headlines/here-is-how-the-gcc-s-10-largest-islamic-banks-rank-57687584, accessed on December 29, 2021.

Forbes Middle East (n.d.), "Top 20 FinTech Startups in the Middle East," https://www.forbesmiddleeast.com/list/top-20-fintech-startups-in-the-middle-east, accessed on December 25, 2021.

FinTech (2021), *Middle East and Africa Report 2021.*

Gagllardi, Paolo (2019), "How Millennials Are Reshaping the Financial Industry," *Khaleej Times,* 9 January, https://www.khaleejtimes.com/buzzon/jobs/banking-financial-services/how-millennials-are-reshaping-the-financial-industry, accessed on December 30, 2021.

GASTAT (2020), *The General Authority for Statistics (GASTAT) Releases "Saudi Youth in Numbers" Report for the World Youth Day 2020,* https://www.stats.gov.sa/en/news/397, accessed on December 29, 2021.

Harrlson, Polly J. (2021), "The Recent FinTech Funding Rounds in the Middle East," *The FinTech Times,* March 20, https://thefintechtimes.com/the-recent-fintech-funding-rounds-in-the-middle-east/, accessed on December 28, 2021.

HSBC (n.d.), "History of HSBC in the Middle East," https://www.about.hsbc.co.om/hsbc-in-oman/hsbc-in-the-middle-east, accessed on December 29, 2021.

Hussain, Mumtaz, Shahmoradi, Asghar, and Turk, Rima (2015), "An Overview of Islamic Finance," IMF, https://www.imf.org/external/pubs/ft/wp/2015/wp15120.pdf, accessed on December 22, 2021.

IMF (2018), "How Developed and Inclusive Are Financial Systems in the GCC," December 6, https://www.imf.org/-/media/Files/Publications/PP/2018/pp120618gcc-how-developed-and-inclusive-are-financial-systems-in-the-gcc.ashx, accessed on November 28, 2021.

Kamel, Deena (2018), "Generation Start-Up: Dubai's Democrance to Help Region's Poorest Access Insurance," *The National*, June 23, https://www.thenationalnews.com/business/technology/generation-start-up-dubai-s-democrance-to-help-region-s-poorest-access-insurance-1.743234, accessed on December 23, 2021.

King, Brett (2018), *Bank 4.0: Banking Everywhere, Never at a Bank*, Marshall Cavendish International (Asia) Private Ltd.

King, Ian (2020), "Big Tech Earnings Surge During Pandemic While Economy Slumps," *Bloomberg Quint*, August 3, https://www.bloombergquint.com/business/big-tech-is-having-a-great-pandemic-while-the-economy-slumps, accessed on October 30, 2021.

Kunt, Asli D., Klapper, Leora, Singer, Dorothe, Ansar, Saniya, and Hess, Jake (2018), *The Global Findex Database 2017: Measuring Financial Inclusion and the FinTech Revolution*, Washington, DC: World Bank Group.

Kurczyk, Tomasz (2020), "How FinTech's Are Raising Financial Literacy and Risk, Awareness to Drive Financial Inclusion," LinkedIn, August 20, https://www.linkedin.com/pulse/how-fintechs-raising-financial-literacy-risk-drive-tomasz-kurczyk, accessed on December 28, 2021.

Lechtenfeld, Tobias (2018), "Millennials Welcome! Young Women Are Revolutionising the Start-Up Scene Despite Conflicts in MENA," World Bank, March 26, https://blogs.worldbank.org/arabvoices/millennials-welcome-young-women-are-revolutionising-startup-scene-despite-conflicts-mena, accessed on December 28, 2021.

Lulic, Miron (2020), "How Millennials and FinTechs Are Disrupting The Way We Borrow and Invest," *Forbes*, April 7, https://www.forbes.com/sites/forbestechcouncil/2020/04/07/how-millennials-and-fintechs-are-disrupting-the-way-we-borrow-and-invest/?sh=5e7819792268, accessed on November 26, 2021.

McCaffrey, Paul (2017), "Finance: How It Made Civilisation Possible," CFA Institute, September 13, https://blogs.cfainstitute.org/investor/2017/09/13/finance-is-a-technology/, accessed on November 29, 2021.

Moy, Christine and Carlson, Jill (2021), "Cryptocurrencies Can Enable Financial Inclusion. Will You Participate?," World Economic Forum, June 9, https://

www.weforum.org/agenda/2021/06/cryptocurrencies-financial-inclusion-help-shape-it/, accessed on November 29, 2021.

Mueller, Jackson and Piwowar, Michael S. (n.d.), *The Rise of FinTech in the Middle East: An Analysis of the Emergence of Bahrain and the United Arab Emirates,* Santa Monica: Milken Institute.

Gulf News (2019), "Millennials to Shape Future Payments," March 4, https://gulfnews.com/business/banking/millennials-to-shape-future-payments-1.1551683373086, accessed on December 20, 2021.

OECD (2020), *Advancing the Digital Financial Inclusion of Youth*, https://www.oecd.org/daf/fin/financial-education/advancing-the-digital-financial-inclusion-of-youth.pdf, accessed on December 21, 2021.

Overdahl, Stian (2019), "The Rise of Robo-Advisers in the UAE," *The National,* January 13, https://www.thenationalnews.com/business/money/the-rise-of-robo-advisers-in-the-uae-1.812514, accessed on November 30, 2021.

Paracha, Zubair N. (2017), "Kuwait-Based 'Ajar Online' Wants to Disrupt the Real-Estate Rental Payments in MENA," *Menabytes,* September 25, https://www.menabytes.com/kuwait-ajar-online/, accessed on November 30, 2021.

PricewaterhouseCoopers (PwC) (2021), *Leaders in Demand: Understanding Leadership From the Point of View of Gen Y's and Gen Z's From the GCC Region*, https://www.pwc.com/m1/en/publications/documents/leaders-in-demand-understanding-leadership-geny-z-point-view-gcc-region.pdf, accessed on November 26, 2021.

Radcliffe, Damian (2016), "Middle East's Start-Up Leaders: Five Ways They're Leading the World," *ZDNet,* June 16, https://www.zdnet.com/article/middle-easts-startup-leaders-five-ways-theyre-leading-the-world/, accessed on November 22, 2021.

Arabian Business (2021), "Islamic FinTech Is on the Rise in Saudi Arabia, UAE and Globally," March 21, https://www.arabianbusiness.com/banking-finance/460538-how-islamic-fintech-is-on-the-rise-globally, accessed on November 29, 2021.

Santosdiaz, Richie (2020), "Islamic Finance in the Global Digital Economy," *The FinTech Times,* September 19, https://thefintechtimes.com/islamic-finance-in-the-global-digital-economy/, accessed on November 26, 2021.

Santosdiaz, Richie (2020), "MEA Women in FinTech With Ambareen Musa in Dubai, UAE," *The FinTech Times,* September 13, https://thefintechtimes.com/mea-women-in-fintech-with-ambareen-musa-in-dubai-uae/, accessed on November 29, 2021.

Santosdiaz, Richie (2020), "MEA Women in FinTech With Nejoud Al Mulaik From Saudi Arabia," *The FinTech Times,* September 20, https://thefintechtimes.com/mea-women-in-fintech-with-nejoud-al-mulaik-from-saudi-arabia/, accessed on December 29, 2021.

Santosdiaz, Richie (2020), "MEA Women in FinTech With Sandra Knight in Bahrain," *The FinTech Times,* September 20, https://thefintechtimes.com/mea-women-in-fintech-with-sandra-knight-in-bahrain/, accessed on December 29, 2021.

Santosdiaz, Richie (2021), "FinTech: Middle East & Africa 2021", *The FinTech Times.*

Singh, Sunil K. (2020), "Is There a Future for Cryptocurrencies in GCC States?," *Zawya,* October 29, https://www.zawya.com/mena/en/markets/story/Is_there_a_future_for_cryptocurrencies_in_GCC_states-ZAWYA20201029035151/, accessed on December 25, 2021.

The World Bank (n.d.). *Individuals Using the Internet (% of Population),* https://data.worldbank.org/indicator/IT.NET.USER.ZS, accessed on December 22, 2021.

The World Bank (2021), "Unemployment, Youth Total (% of Total Labour Force Ages 15-24) Modelled ILO Estimate," January 29, https://data.worldbank.org/indicator/SL.UEM.1524.ZS, accessed on December 23, 2021.

UNDESA (n.d.), "Definition of Youth," https://www.un.org/esa/socdev/documents/youth/fact-sheets/youth-definition.pdf, accessed on December 30, 2021.

UNDP (2020), *Human Development Report 2020.*

VISA (2016), *Understanding the Millennial Mindset and What It Means for Payments in the GCC.*

Walden, Stephanie (2020), "What Is FinTech And How Does It Affect How I Bank?," *Forbes,* August 3, https://www.forbes.com/advisor/banking/what-is-fintech/, accessed on December 29, 2021.

Wiwanto, Frans (2020), "Three Factors Driving The Rise of FinTech and What the Banking Industry Can Learn From Them," *Forbes,* April 2, https://www.forbes.com/sites/forbesfinancecouncil/2020/04/02/three-factors-driving-the-rise-of-fintech-and-what-the-banking-industry-can-learn-from-them/?sh=12301aaf6d76, accessed on December 30, 2021.

8. From Old Money to New Wealth: Crypto-currency in the GCC

Raahat Verma

> *As for the right of coining money, it is of the same nature as law, and only he who has the power to make law can regulate the coinage.*
>
> —Jean Bodin

Introduction

In terms of form and usage, money has evolved over time. Currency as the physical embodiment of money as paper notes, coins, plastic cards etc., has also undergone a significant transformation. The value of money depended on what the people trusted in gold, oil, government backing etc. Technological evolution has transformed both the production and transaction processes. The first industrial revolution has mechanised the production process; the second industrial revolution enabled mass production and the third one brought in information and communication technology to automate production. The Fourth Industrial Revolution, the digital one has been building since the middle of the last century (Schwab, 2016). The Fourth Industrial Revolution or Industry 4.0[1] is bringing a fusion of digital, biological and physical technologies. One of the most challenging frontiers is the usage of crypto-currency. It disrupts the way currencies are issued and regulated. Besides, there is a lack of uniformity in states' responses to crypto-currencies and there are concerns over their stability.

The GCC countries' tech-savvy youth is poised to be at the forefront in the usage of financial technology (fintech), and crypto-currency and the states' initiatives and involvement have been unique. This chapter explores the various facets of crypto-currency and the variety of issues it embodies. It also throws light on the dynamic of crypto-currency in the GCC counties and the eco-system that could make it sustainable. Finally, the chapter analyses the state responses to crypto-currency and argues that the GCC states are well poised and even accelerating the pace of the crypto revolution.

Crypto-Currency Vs. Digital Currency

The institutionalised circulation of currency is under the monopolised control of every state recognised in the international system. Crypto-currency is on its way to changing this. A crypto-currency is an encrypted form of digital currency and is an electronic version of currency. However, its issuance has not been at the hands of any government so far. Therefore, crypto-currency and digital currency are different., even though the terms have been often used interchangeably. There is also an argument that crypto-currency is a subset of digital currency. Digital currency is an electronic version of banknotes and coins stored in digital wallets that can be transformed into cash in hand if necessary, by withdrawing the same from ATMs or Banks.[2] It is, thus, a form of legal tender established by the government. Traditionally, currency was backed by gold and silver. But now, representative money in the form of paper notes and coins in combination, called fiat currency, is prevalent. The government determines the value of this currency, and its value retention is backed by the stability of the said government and the state's economy.

The origins of crypto-currency relay an averseness to any form of centralised issuance. Originally, there was no system or commodity backing crypto-currency. This has changed, and many crypto-currencies have commodities backing crypto-coins like in 'onegram', one gram of gold backs one crypto-coin. An individual gains a new set of crypto-coins by mining on a blockchain via a computerised system. The demand and supply of crypto-currency have worked with the principle that there is a market cap. That is the primary difference between the two. Digital currency can also be differentiated from crypto-currency regarding the current rate, authorisation, transaction fees, and transparency. The current rate of digital currency remains largely constant, while crypto-currency rates are highly volatile. Due to the involvement of a third party, i.e., the banking system, digital currencies can have a transaction fee involved and a certain lack of transparency. On the other hand, Crypto-currency has no such authority involved, which eliminates the transaction fee, and the blockchain technology on which the crypto-currency transactions take place provides an entire stream of conversation between the two parties while maintaining absolute confidentiality that only the sender and receiver can access these records.

The encryption that involves cryptography methods uses advanced mathematical codes to store and securely transmit data values. This ensures that only the people for whom the transaction is intended can see, receive and process it. These transactions are recorded publicly on distributed, tamper-proof ledgers known as blockchains.[3] Like the different forms of currency promulgated by the national banks, crypto-currency also has different forms, the first and the most famous is Bitcoin (BTC) and there are others like Dogecoin, Erethreum, Tether, Cardano, and so on.

The absence of a central authority for the crypto-currencies and the unregulated nature of their investments could be heralded as a democratising force. Essentially, they are taking away the power of money creation from the states and devolving it to the masses. The open-source framework that is involved means that every transaction is a file of permanently recorded data blocks that must be confirmed publicly. Imagine that one has 1 BTC, and he/she attempts to spend it twice in two separate transactions. One could attempt to do this by sending the same BTC to two separate bitcoin wallet addresses. Both transactions will then go into the pool of unconfirmed transactions. The first transaction would be approved via the confirmation mechanism and then verified into the subsequent block. However, the confirmation process would not recognise the second transaction as it is invalid and would not be verified. If both transactions are pulled from the pool for confirmation simultaneously, the transaction with the highest number of confirmations will be included in the blockchain, while the other one will be discarded (Reiff, 2021). This prevents the duplication of coins and essentially eliminates the need for a central authority.

Crypto's popularity is attributed to the ease and anonymity of its transaction. With the lack of oversight, there is no reason why the transaction could be blocked, or a fee could be charged, even if the transaction takes place across the border. In other words, it represents an automatic and encrypted form of transaction which does away with the regulatory functions of the state and the fee it would charge for regulation and authentication. It brings in an age of financial democratisation, where money and wealth will never be looked at the same way. It would not be a coin held in hand, or a gold bar kept in the locker. Crypto-currency's political intent is to create individual wealth unaccountable to his/her government.

However, the risk associated with crypto-coins can often be compared to that of the American wild west. First and foremost, the price fluctuates wildly. Unlike regulated currency, the price of Bitcoin is an example of something that changes day-to-day. Therefore, some argue that it cannot be used as a form of payment for a business since the value changes quite dramatically. However, there are cases where large businesses have adopted crypto-currency, and even in some cases, companies have created their own currencies. Examples include Air Asia, Mitsubishi UFJ Financial Group, Arias Intel Corp, etc. There is another side to the proverbial coin, which insists that crypto-currency could be compared to an asset held over time, like gold.

State Responses to Crypto-currency

Jean Bodin, in the discussion of sovereignty in the first book of the *Six livres de la republique* (The Six Books of the Republic) (1529; 30-96), made the right to administer currency one of the inseparable elements of sovereign power. However, as democratised, decentralised form of money, crypto-currency, heralds the dawn of new money, the state itself is in jeopardy to regulate or ignore it because it has no control over its production. As a result, public authorities worldwide have scrambled to find a response to it.

Barber and Hansen (2015) assembled a list of international actions and regulations taken at the time in response to virtual currencies, which included all forms of crypto and digital money. The list did not have any GCC country's response (Coie, Barber and Hansen, 2015). Jan Lansky has put forward a classification of states' approaches (based on Hansen's List) in six levels ranging from Level 0, which is ignoring the existence of crypto-currencies, to Level 5 divided into three which are: a complete ban, a ban for banking institutions but not for people to people transaction;

and integration[4] (Lansky, 2018). The two studies can be critiqued for their omissions of the GCC countries. The two studies show an obvious lack of engagement with the GCC states' responses to crypto-currency. However, there is a broader criticism as the studies also fail to recognise the state's attempts to create a favourable environment with or without directly engaging with crypto-currency. Another criticism is the lack of cognisance of the people's investments into the global crypto markets, which in turn influences the state's approach towards crypto-currency.

Crypto-currency is part of a larger environment of the FinTech.[5] According to International Monetary Fund (IMF), MENAP (Middle East, North Africa, Afghanistan and Pakistan) accounted for less than 1 per cent of total global fintech between 2013 and 2018 (IMF, 2018). Nevertheless, it does provide evidence for crypto-investments in the region. Initially, the investments had been concentrated in the United Arab Emirates (UAE), but that has progressively changed. The industry has rapidly grown in the Kingdoms of Saudi Arabia and Bahrain. The three GCC states have made a concentrated effort in the banking and financial services sector (IMF,2019) and perceivable progress on blockchain applications.

The GCC region's noticeable progress in blockchain applications has been in cross-border payments, Know Your Customer (KYC) and crypto-currencies (Al-Sebaie, 2020). In 2017, Gulf investors were estimated to account for 1.5 per cent of the total value of crypto-currencies in the world (Lukonga, 2018). The progress of crypto-currency was riding on the high tide of fintech in the region. By 2022, the global fintech market is expected to grow to US$ 310 billion, and the GCC states are striving to create a comprehensive eco-system to support all fintech enterprises. David Parker, co-chief investment officer at the Bahrain Economic Development Board (BEDB), stated, "We want to be at the forefront of the Fourth Industrial Revolution. We missed the first and second; when the third revolution took place, and we saw the emergence of Silicon Valley, we were too busy making money from oil" (Buller, 2020).

The GCC Engagement with Industry 4.0

The GCC economy is largely reliant on the export of hydrocarbons. These countries have about 40 per cent of the world's known oil reserves and

23 per cent of proven natural gas reserves. The risk of sustainability of an economy where hydrocarbon revenues are predominant has been a concern for decades as the world is set to move away from hydrocarbons. There is an inherent change across the world that indicates a substitution away from oil (Masumoto, et al., 2020). There are also long-term concerns about the fiscal sustainability of the dependence on hydrocarbon exports given the market volatility, technological progress in alternative energy and environmental concerns. Though the GCC states have been trying for two decades to diversify away from oil, the fourth industrial revolution in the region is the most significant change for leap-frogging the process. Moreover, economic diversification in the middle of a global pandemic has gained a sense of urgency.

Oil substitution not only accounts for attempts to harness alternative energy sources for the GCC countries but also for the region to divest their dependencies on the energy industry for state revenue generation. To diversify their revenue streams and build up their sovereign wealth funds, many GCC states are looking into new kinds of assets and, more specifically ones, for which their own citizens need considerably less incentive to participate. The answer to the question "What's next?" has been in the digitisation and development of financial infrastructure, especially to encourage private industry. It has also been said that developing fintech eco-systems to make financial systems more efficient is necessary for the GCC states. The level of smartphone penetration in the GCC region stands at 96 per cent. Their share in global mobile payments is growing, and the level of confidence in digital wallets in the Middle Eastern region is much higher than in Asia (Chan, et al., 2021). This is noteworthy that the digital wallet eco-system is not as mature in the region. A McKinsey report found that in the Middle East, institutions such as stand-alone wallets or tech companies have a larger piece of the pie than the banks in the payment platform (Chan, et al., 2021). These companies have better technological infrastructure, giving them a competitive advantage in the digital payments eco-system.

The GCC states are on their way to successfully exploiting the potential of this transactional industry. The blockchain, the technology on which crypto-currency has been built, is considered one of the securest and its adoption has become the leading enterprise for states like UAE and Bahrain. The UAE has taken up the mantle to develop these eco-systems, where incubators, enterprise development funds and programs, and innovation hubs support local entrepreneurs' creation and growth. It launched the *Blockchain Strategy 2021* in 2018. The strategy aims to transform 50 per cent of government transactions into a blockchain platform by 2021 (United Arab Emirates' Government Portal (U.ae), 2021). By adopting this technology, the UAE government expects to save:

- US$ 2.99 billion in transactions and documents processed routinely
- 398 million printed documents annually
- 77 million work hours annually

Bahrain and Saudi Arabia have also been active concerning fintech. For example, Bahrain's *Economic Vision 2030* is now a base for incorporating digital banking and is collaborating with fintech hubs to encourage Bahraini youth to develop digital capabilities and increase opportunities for economic growth (Bignell, 2021). Meanwhile, Saudi Arabia has envisioned reaching 70 per cent of the e-payment target by 2030 (Chan, et al., 2021).

Oman has also dipped its toe in the pond by building a sandbox[6] initiative in which participants can apply to live test fintech solutions in an environment with mitigated risk and under Omani central bank (Finextra.com, 2020). Qatar formed its fintech task force in 2017. Classified as a high-income country by the World Bank and one of the top five countries in terms of GDP per capita, Qatar has been making a bid to attract fintech investment (Ozelli, 2020) as one of its economic diversification strategies. Kuwait is also close at heals. The Global Fintech Index 2020 ranks Kuwait city as the ninth-best fintech destination in the Middle East and North Africa region and fourth-best in the GCC. The Central Bank of Kuwait has also established its own sandbox experimentation phase, and the government has stated that fintech has become one of its economic priorities (Winder, 2020). The Kuwait Investment Authority, the world's oldest and the third largest sovereign wealth fund, has made significant investments in fintech. The fintech eco-system provides the conducive infrastructure where crypto-currency is gaining traction.

For any fintech eco-system to function, there must be a sustained collaboration among governments, financial institutions, and entrepreneurs. The establishment and nurturing of a fintech eco-system are state-driven in the region. It is part of the GCC countries' national economic visions directly or indirectly. In cases of regulatory sandboxes, UAE and Bahrain have led the path to engage entrepreneurs more quickly, and they have been successful enough to widen their horizons beyond the risk-controlled settings. Saudi Arabia has also announced its own sandbox and has invited 30 fintechs. Kuwait and Oman have made similar strides. Three key factors have made the eco-system favourable for UAE to be the leading fintech hub in the MENA region: (i) The government is at the centre of efforts to drive innovation as part of a larger vision; (ii) it has an eco-system that is conducive to new financial alternatives; and (iii) continuous initiatives and policies are implemented to attract international human capital to stimulate innovation domestically through spillover effects (Bakhouche, Ghak and Zarrouk, 2021). With the success of the UAE, others in the region are more likely to follow suit more robustly.

Crypto-currency in the GCC: State and Public Opinion

The GCC has one of the most favourable environments to sustain the growth of the fourth industrial revolution and, thereby, crypto-currency. The progression of these countries in terms of adaptability to use blockchain and transforming their financial sector has been due to the welcoming regulatory environment that fintech has received. The Bahraini government is pushing to make Bahrain the Middle East headquarters for crypto-currency. In July 2018, the Bahrain-based crypto-currency trade platform—Rain reported that it had become the first completely controlled, inland cryptographic money trade platform in the Middle East and North Africa region and had finished a US$ 2.5 million subsidising round. Rain obtained a Crypto-Asset Module administrative permit from the Central Bank of Bahrain following graduation from the national bank's Regulatory Sandbox programme (Abdeldayem and Aldulaimi, 2020)

Furthermore, the UAE has its own regulation of crypto-currency. There are two parallel crypto worlds, one informal and unregulated and the other by well-regulated entities like Dubai International Financial Centre (DIFC) and Abu Dhabi Global Market (ADGM) (Gulf News, 2021).

As trading in crypto-currencies is considered high-risk by the Central Bank in UAE, all parties involved in the transaction must show strict compliance to the Anti-Money Laundering and Counter-Terrorism. The UAE is considered one of the most-friendly nations to crypto-currency trading. BitOasis, one of UAE's crypto-currency exchanges, has now been operating for six years in the country. The recent regulatory approvals in September of 2021 that allowed the exchange to start trading within its inshore markets have led to BitOasis raising US$ 30 million (Sapra, 2021). UAE has made attempts to make the high-risk venture of crypto-currency trading safer by collaborating with BitOasis to raise awareness and educate people about crypto investments.

None of the states in the GCC has rendered the trade of crypto-currencies as illegal as some other countries in the world have. As mentioned above, UAE has progressed on the crypto-currencies, and Bahrain has recognised and licensed Rain, the crypto-currency platform that trades in all GCC countries. This is indicative of the readiness of the governments to look at crypto-currency as assets for private citizens. However, there are specific bans for financial institutions from trading "Bitcoin" like in Kuwait due to its high volatility. The crypto-currency in the GCC states is not a legal tender; yet is increasingly gaining acceptance. Even though Saudi Arabia has restricted the use of crypto-currency, the existence of crypto-currency ATMs (Randeev, 2021) and the introduction of cross-border payments using blockchain and Aber[7] between Saudi Arabia and UAE (Bharathan, 2020) are illustrative cases. The partnership between Saudi Arabia and UAE is a harbinger of the region's emerging crypto-currency environment, as others would likely follow suit (Townsend 2019).

The positive outlook of the GCC states can be further gauged by their views that blockchain technology is Sharia-compliant and in conformity with Islamic finance. The GCC states and the masses are particularly sensitive to the Sharia compliance of their financial transactions. The GCC financial systems are generally bifurcated into conventional and Islamic subsectors. Crypto-currency being dominantly in private investments has invited careful consideration from the Sharia-compliant regulatory bodies. The volatility and the speculative nature of these virtual assets that have no intrinsic value are points to be made against the crypto-currency trade in these countries. Nevertheless, Bahrain and UAE have created a positive attitude towards crypto-currency and are issuing Sharia compliance certificates to platforms and currencies.

The Sharia compliance certificate accorded to Rain by Bahrain is noteworthy. The Sharia Review Bureau licensed by the Central Bank of Bahrain determined that Rain's purchase and custodian activities comply with Sharia principles (Rain, n.d.). In addition, there has been a crypto-currency called Caizcoin that has claimed to be the first official Islamic compliant blockchain and crypto-currency (CAIZCOIN, 2021). One gram crypto-currency is backed by a gram of physical gold stored in a vault and has obtained a ruling that its crypto-currency conforms with Islamic principles from Dubai-based Al Maali Consulting (*Khaleej Times*, 2018). The increasing investments in crypto-currency and blockchain transactions and their wide spectrum of usage in countries like the UAE and Bahrain would eventually generate considerable social and political influence over opinions made for their Sharia compliance.

The scope of a virtual asset like crypto-currency is essentially determined by public perception. The intrinsic value of crypto-currency is in its number of users. Anything can be a currency as long as the buyer and seller agree to it. The "value" backing crypto-currency here is public opinion or consent. The public opinion towards crypto-currency is poised to change into a favourable one, given that there has been an increased interest in the digitisation of transactions. In the face of a global shutdown, there was a disruption of business as usual and, therefore, an adverse effect on the economic development of all countries. A significant turn among the masses was the inclination towards digital payment modes. In a McKinsey consumer survey, 58 per cent of Middle East consumers strongly preferred digital payment methods, while only 10 per cent strongly preferred cash (Chan, et al., 2021). This newfound acceptance of digital payments can easily translate into an appreciation for digital money and, in turn, for digital currencies, including virtual currencies. Essentially, the concept of "cash in hand" is going out of trend.

The demography in the Gulf Arab states is going through a remarkable transition. The region's young population is transitioning into adulthood in the middle of a pandemic and during a daunting shift in the state's wealth generation structures. The unemployment rates for some of these countries have been in double digits due to the disconnect between the public and private sectors and the migrant workforces that came to work in these states. The present generation is more likely to find increasingly virtue in an asset like crypto-currency protected from inflation and can give value-added returns, especially when the state can no longer continue the traditional pattern of offering public sector jobs and other privileges. Their inclination is revealed by an exploratory study, published in 2020, the first of its kind on "Crypto-currency in the GCC economy", found that the respondents of their survey had high awareness levels in relation to crypto-currencies; 40 per cent of whom had invested in a start-up business and 8 per cent had made a "Bitcoin" investment, and 15 per cent owned different types of crypto-currency (Abdeldayem and Aldulaimi, 2020).

Recent reports have converged on showing that the younger population of age group 18-24 years are more bullish on crypto-currencies and consider them as exiting investment opportunities compared to the old age group of 45 and above (*Khaleej Times*, 2021; Gulfnews.com, 2021). The younger generation has acquired deep crypto-technology knowledge and has gained millions (Gulf News, 2021). The DMCC Crypto Centre is home to about 100 organisations operating in crypto-space, and another 900 have applied for licenses (The National News, 2021). More than 400 crypto-currency businesses are presently operating in the UAE, which is set to grow to 1,000 by 2022 (Cabral, 2021).

Navigating Challenges

Crypto-currency has a democratising influence, and it was built to give power to the masses. The public participation in authenticating transactions in a crypto-currency platform is diametrically opposed to the centralised nature of economic systems prevalent before. In general, crypto-currencies worldwide have captured significant imagination because they grant anonymity, security, and ease of access in transactions without the state being a party or an institution levying transaction fees to complete a transaction. In other words, it does away with the authorising or mediating role of any third party other than the buyer and seller. For a region where central state control is the hallmark, crypto-currency is potentially a valued virtual asset that does away with state intervention and regulation.

Non-transparency and corruption have infested the traditional financial sector in all parts of the world. The peer-to-peer nature of crypto-currency transactions which never passes through intermediaries and is recorded on a decentralised ledger, dramatically reduces the opportunity for corruption. On the perception scale for corruption, most countries in the Middle East and some in the GCC do not farewell. The discretionary power that the states' rulers wield unwittingly poses significant economic hurdles. A secure transaction done on a public ledger can mitigate much of the concerns of lack of transparency and corruption in the financial sector in the region.

Another aspect of crypto-currency is that it was built to be inclusive. Despite the high penetration of expansive smartphones in the GCC countries, the unbanked population is still very high. A 2018 report by the IMF surmised that financial inclusion indicators suggest gaps in access to financial services, particularly for women and youth, either due to institutional gaps or people's aversion to financial services. The GCC households prefer peer-to-peer financing channels especially placing them above structural bank loans (IMF, 2018). Besides, several million expatriates in the region have to shell their hard-earned money as a transaction fee and wait in long queues in hot and sultry weather to be able to remit their money back home, usually every month (*The Economic Times*, 2021). UAE is close to opening licensed crypto-currency exchanges that could boost the financial inclusion of migrants (*The Economic Times*, 2021) and reduce their time and cost of sending remittances. While the crypto-currency is gaining traction among investors and at the institutional level, it is yet to gain confidence among the expatriates and the banks (*The Economic Times*, 2021; Gulf News, 2021).

During the COVID-19 lockdown, consumers and even businesses' inability to access banks was more than just an inconvenience. Inability to access the conventional banking outlets and thus lack of options to move their funds could be redressed by the new age of fintech. Especially for migrant workers who are looking to send 90 per cent of their salary back home, eventual progression to crypto-currency rather than just digital payment systems provides an opportunity to "get their money's true worth", whether an individual mines crypto-currency, plays the currency markets or simply chooses to cut out third parties to avoid paying a service fee.

One of the most contentious aspects of crypto-currency is their mining energy consumption. "Bitcoin" has been debated relentlessly internationally by states and the media for its energy consumption. Bitcoin is essentially "mined"[8] that requires computational power, which requires large energy consumption. As a region that is surplus in energy, therefore the power that the Gulf countries can wield in the field of crypto-currency is immense.

The role of crypto-currency in the post-oil scenario comes from its opportunities for private investments and individual wealth generation. The public fascination with Bitcoin, Ethereum or others has translated to crypto-currency being termed 'virtual gold'. Bitcoin today has enough financial power to have the same hedging abilities as gold, and even though it has been called a high-risk, speculative asset; it is still an asset to be traded. Besides, it is also creating a space in the alternative energy industry as the states contemplate using crypto-currency and link it to their alternative energy industry. To prepare for a post-oil scenario, there has been significant awareness and initiative to create alternative energy industries among the GCC countries. Linking the renewable energy industries to fintech and even crypto-currency mining will be a positive incentive to their younger populace for whom these technological innovations have captured the imagination. One such example is Qatar's national solarised fintech strategy. "Qatar has committed to a National fintech strategy to diversify its economy, which will be solarised with world's second cheapest solar energy, to increase the proportion of renewable energy in its total electricity generation to 20 per cent by 2030 as part of a broader effort by the gas-exporting nation to decarbonise its electricity grid and reduce the footprint" (Ozelli, 2020).

Conclusion

The progress of fintech towards intangible assets has been gradual but today stands at a revolutionary stage. Crypto-currencies have evoked various state responses in the world from their ignorance to complete ban or partial or total integration. It takes away the state's monopoly in issuing currencies, regulating and authenticating financial transactions by facilitating end-to-end encrypted transactions on a public ledger using complex computational methods that can terminate non-authentic transactions. The GCC states' strong eco-system of financial technology has provided the young population in the region the opportunity to engage with crypto-currency, a virtual asset that is exceedingly popular among the youth across the globe. With the positive engagement of the rulers through progressive regulations and enough security to smoothen risk concerns, the GCC states may well be developing a new digitised asset framework. They have already experimented with crypto-currency as a tradable asset for private citizens, as cross-border payments between two national banks and its technology are now being used in different governance sectors.

The decentralised process of crypto-currency that gives power to the people to do their transactions at zero-intermediation cost is a paradigm shift in a region that has experienced centralised state control. The younger population has shown a greater inclination towards crypto-currency and is mastering its technique and technology. By unintentionally aligning themselves with crypto-currency, the rulers of these Gulf Arab states have bought themselves out of their "cradle to grave welfare" social contracts with their citizens, which were, anyway, fast running out of time along with their oil. The only thing that remains to be seen here is if financial democratisation will be enough for a population coming to age in the crypto era.

Notes

1. Industry 4.0 or originally Industrie 4.0, originated in 2011 from the German Government. Klaus Schwabb, executive chairman of the World Economic Forum introduced the phrase in an article titled "The Fourth Industrial Revolution" in *Foreign Affairs* in 2015 (Schwab,2015). Schwab underscores the combination of cyber-physical systems in this era. It is expected to be marked with breakthroughs in artificial technology, quantum computing, the internet of things, decentralized consensus, fully autonomous vehicles, and the like.
2. This constitutes another difference between digital currency and electronic Money. The fiat currencies like the US Dollar, the Euro, etc. have an equivalent which is electronic money. Essentially it is the money balance recorded on a value card or a server. It accounts for what is in an individual's bank and can

be reproduced via ATMs or banks to cash in hand. Digital currency has been characterised as a subset of electronic Money.

3. "Blockchain" first appeared in a paper titled "Bitcoin: A Peer-to-Peer Electronic Cash System" by a pseudonymous individual or group known as "Satoshi Nakamoto" in 2008. The term was first applied to the core component of "Bitcoin" digital currency that is discussed in that paper. Blockchain today is used in many other applications that can utilise a public ledger to enable secure and direct transactions without involving a controlling authority. This technology has been deployed in supply chain management, logistics and healthcare as well.
4. The levels mentioned in Jan Lansky's paper include six levels with subsections, the first is Level 0 which is essentially the state is ignoring cryptocurrencies, level 1 is monitoring, level 2 is the recommendation of approach by the state towards crypto for the citizens, this can be in terms of risk warnings and/or crypto potential. Level 3 is guidance for the institutions in terms of anti-money laundering directives, directives of tax considerations towards crypt-ocurrency and/or mining activities and the acceptance or non-acceptance of crypto as assets. Level 4 is regulation and Level 5 can be ban or integration of crypto-currency.
5. Fintech was initially applied to backend systems of financial institutions but has grown to include sectors and industries today which are using technology to improve the activities in finance. It consists of start-ups that are deploying artificial intelligence, introducing automation to conservative financial institutions, and using big data to predict investments, behaviours and market practices.
6. A regulatory sandbox is an environment in which live testing of new products takes place in a controlled manner under a regulator's supervision.
7. Project Aber was to create a central bank digital currency that could be used for cross-border payments among commercial banks.
8. Bitcoin mining is the process of solving complex mathematical equations to create new crypto-coins, this is also the process that verifies a transaction as legitimate. When someone sends a bitcoin anymore, it is called a transaction which has to be stored on a blockchain. The miners by solving mathematical equations clump these transactions together into blocks and add them to the blockchain.

References

Abdeldayem, Marwan M. and Aldulaimi, Saeed (2020), "Cryptocurrency in the GCC Economy," *International Journal Of Scientific & Technology Research*, vol. 9, no. 2, https://www.researchgate.net/publication/342411659_Cryptocurrency_In_The_Gcc_Economy", accessed on December 28, 2021.

Al-Sebaie, Fatima (2020), "GCC: Promoting Blockchain Technology Adoption in the Financial Services Sector: Insights From Bahrain's Experience," DERASAT, May 31, https://www.derasat.org.bh/gcc-promoting-blockchain-technology-adoption-in-the-financial-services-sector-insights-from-bahrains-experience/, accessed on December 29, 2021.

Bakhouche, Abderazak, Ghak, Teheni EL and Zarrouk, Hajer (2021), "Exploring Economic and Technological Determinants of FinTech Startups' Success and Growth in the United Arab Emirates," *Journal of Open Innovation Technology Market and Complexity*, vol. 7, no. 1, pp. 50.

Bharathan, Vipin (2020), "Digitizing Financial Markets: Project Aber From Saudi Arabia and the UAE Addresses Cross Border Payments With Digital Currencies," *Forbes*, December 29, https://www.forbes.com/sites/vipinbharathan/2021/12/29/digitizing-financial-markets-project-aber-from-saudi-arabia-and-the-uae-addresses-cross-border-interoperability-of-digital-currencies/?sh=7cba814d13dd, accessed on December 28, 2021.

Bignell, Francis (2021), "As a Part of Bahrain's Vision 2030, the NBB Launches Its Digital Banking Challenge," *The Fintech Times*, August 19, https://thefintechtimes.com/as-a-part-of-bahrains-vision-2030-the-nbb-launches-its-digital-banking-challenge/, accessed on December 28, 2021.

Buller, Alicia (2020), "How the Gulf States Bet Big on Cryptocurrency," *WIRED*, October 11, https://wired.me/business/cryptocurrency/gulf-states-cryptocurrency/, accessed on December 28, 2021.

Cabral, Alvin R. (2021), "Dubai Expects to Have More Than 1000 Cryptocurrency Business by 2022," *The National News*, October 18, https://www.thenationalnews.com/business/cryptocurrencies/2021/10/18/dubai-expects-to-have-more-than-1000-cryptocurrency-businesses-by-2022/, accessed on December 20, 2021.

CAIZCOIN (2021), "Caizcoin- The First Islamic Blockchain Offering Unparalleled Anonymity & Security," *PR Newswire*, June 4, https://www.prnewswire.com/news-releases/caizcoin---the-first-islamic-blockchain-offering-unparalleled-anonymity--security-301306230.html, accessed on December 28, 2021.

Chan, Jon, Dayal, Vaibhav, Denecker, Olievier and Jain, Yash (2021), "The Future of Payments in the Middle East," McKinsey & Company, August 23, https://www.mckinsey.com/industries/financial-services/our-insights/the-future-of-payments-in-the-middle-east, accessed on December 28, 2021.

Coie, Perkins, Barber, Eric and Hansen, J. D. (2015), "Virtual Currencies: International Actions and Regulation," JDSUPRA, November 13, https://www.jdsupra.com/legalnews/virtual-currencies-international-51034/, accessed on December 28, 2021.

Finextra (2020), "Central Bank of Oman Opens Fintech Regulatory Sandbox," December 14, https://www.finextra.com/pressarticle/85467/central-bank-of-oman-opens-fintech-regulatory-sandbo, accessed on December 28, 2021.

Gulf News (2021), "What Does the Future Hold for Cryptocurrency in the UAE," June 1, https://gulfnews.com/business/what-does-the-future-hold-for-cryptocurrency-in-the-uae-1.1622547606316, accessed on December 20, 2021.

International Monetary Fund (2018), "Gulf Cooperation Council: How Developed and Inclusive Are Financial Systems in the GCC?," December 6, https://www.imf.org/en/Publications/Policy-Papers/Issues/2018/12/04/pp120618gcc-how-developed-and-inclusive-are-financial-systems-in-the-gcc, accessed on December 28, 2021.

Khaleej Times (2018), "How Cryptocurrency Traders Are Wooing Islamic Investors," April 8, https://www.khaleejtimes.com/business/banking-finance/how-cryptocurrency-traders-are-wooing-islamic-investors, accessed on December 28, 2021.

Khaleej Times (2021), "Revealed: How Many UAE Residents Wants to Invest in Cryptocurrency," May 19, https://www.khaleejtimes.com/uae/revealed-how-many-uae-residents-want-to-invest-in-cryptocurrency, accessed on December 20, 2021.

Lansky, Jan (2018), "Possible State Approaches to Cryptocurrencies". *Journal of Systems Integration*, 9(1), http://si-journal.org/index.php/JSI/article/view/335.

Lukonga, Inutu (2018), "Fintech, Inclusive Growth and Cyber Risks: Focus on the MENAP and CCA Regions," International Monetary Fund, September 1, https://www.imf.org/en/Publications/WP/Issues/2018/09/11/Fintech-Inclusive-Growth-and-Cyber-Risks-Focus-on-the-MENAP-and-CCA-Regions-46190, accessed on December 24, 2021.

Masumoto, Akito, Zhu, Ling, Zhang, Tian, et al. (2020), "The Future of Oil and Fiscal Sustainability in the GCC Region," International Monetary Fund, February 6, https://www.imf.org/en/Publications/Departmental-Papers-Policy-Papers/Issues/2020/01/31/The-Future-of-Oil-and-Fiscal-Sustainability-in-the-GCC-Region-48934, accessed on December 29, 2021.

Ozelli, Selva (2020), "Qatar's National Solarized Fintech Strategy," *PV Magazine*, August 26, https://www.pv-magazine.com/2020/08/26/qatars-national-solarized-fintech-strategy/, accessed on December 28, 2021.

RAIN (n.d.), "Sharia Compliance," https://www.rain.bh/about-rain/licenses/sharia-compliance?__cf_chl_captcha_tk__=cZbdEstRfOMmZFG8iwGGv_1KiuhkjwIahszRcw5q1dE-1635956151-0-gaNycGzNCT0, accessed on December 28, 2021.

Randev, Viraj (2021), "How to Buy Bitcoin in Saudi Arabia-Buy Bitcoin in Under 5 Minutes," Economy Watch, September 23, https://www.economywatch.com/sa/cryptocurrency/buy-bitcoin, accessed on December 28, 2021.

Reiff, Nathan (2021), "How Does a Block Chain Prevent Double-Spending of Bitcoins?," Investopedia," August 26, https://www.investopedia.com/ask/answers/061915/how-does-block-chain-prevent-doublespending-bitcoins.asp, accessed on December 28, 2021.

Sapra, Bani (2021), "UAE Cryptocurrency Exchange BitOasis Raises $30m," *WIRED*, October 6, https://wired.me/business/uae-cryptocurrency-exchange-bitoasis-raises-30m/, accessed on December 28, 2021.

Schwab, Klaus (2016), "The Fourth Industrial Revolution: What It Means, How to Respond," World Economic Forum. https://www.weforum.org/agenda/2016/01/the-fourth-industrial-revolution-what-it-means-and-how-to-respond/, accessed on December 28, 2021.

The Economic Times (2021), "Cryptocurrency Promise for UAE's Unbanked Population-But Not Yet," August 3, https://economictimes.indiatimes.com/markets/cryptocurrency/cryptocurrency-promise-for-uaes-unbanked-migrants-but-not-yet/articleshow/84996080.cms?from=mdr, accessed on December 20, 2021.

Townsend, Sarah (2019), "Saudi-UAE Cryptocurrency Pilot Could Revolutionize Cross-Border Payments," *The National News,* January 23, https://www.thenationalnews.com/business/banking/saudi-uae-cryptocurrency-pilot-could-revolutionise-cross-border-payments-1.815737 , accessed on December 23, 2021.

United Arab Emirates' Government Portal [U.ae] (2021), "Emirates Blockchain Strategy 2021," October 12, https://u.ae/en/about-the-uae/strategies-initiatives-and-awards/federal-governments-strategies-and-plans/emirates-blockchain-strategy-2021, accessed on December 28, 2021.

Winder, Bayly (2020), "Kuwait and the Fintech Industry: Aspirations and Obstacles," *Oxford Business Review*, October 13, https://oxfordbusinessreview.org/kuwait-and-the-fintech-industry-aspirations-and-obstacles/, accessed on December 28, 2021.

9. The Social and Cultural Realms of Digital Communities in the UAE

Melissa Cyrill

Introduction

The proliferation of internet-powered digital media networks in the United Arab Emirates (UAE) has reshaped the ways its people interact in society, as the lines between the virtual and real spheres have blurred. Internet users can overcome the immediate spatial and experiential limitations of the real world and create new and imagined communities of belonging. Since the UAE population is predominantly foreign and its national culture is conservative and Islamic, the proliferation of internet-enabled devices and online interactions have fostered widespread connectivity that would not have otherwise been possible.

The artificial closeness of online relationships established among disparate or even like-minded communities in one place can, in the best circumstances, negate prejudices and promote tolerance. Abundant access to information and social access to different people, albeit in the virtual realm, is bound to impact the attitudes and cultural ascriptions of the UAE's multi-ethnic and relatively young population. Nevertheless, virtual interactions are by their nature complex and layered as online users can choose to be either visible or invisible, play up certain identity markers or create whole new personalities, and wield disproportionate influence in real-time. This scope for mass mobilisation and engagement can create ripple effects in the physical world, depending on the nature of online conversations, temporal factors, and the perceived stakes. Moreover, as internet media are essentially global, online users in the UAE can track or learn of local, regional, and global events and actively participate in popular trends and help shape public opinion (*Hindustan Times*, 2021).

This is revolutionary for the UAE public due to the country's historically opaque and state-controlled media environment, which was meant to ensure the stability of the monarchy in the country.

The Emirati regime is not unaware of this dissolution of strict social and cultural boundaries facilitated by the internet. Consequently, it has actively pursued a strategy of technocracy with regulatory institutional, legal, and technical oversight to extend its policing authority to the digital realm and retain control. This is critical to its primary goal of political stability and ensures it wields ample influence through internet proxies, both state and non-state actors (Perlroth, 2016), and continues to hold relevance to the public.

Given the near-complete access to the internet in the UAE, the country has witnessed inevitable changes in its population's social behaviour and public consciousness. The rapid advancement of information and communication technologies (ICT) has created multifaceted entrepreneurial opportunities through the digital economy, tech-enabled sectors, and start-ups. Web 2.0 and voice over internet protocol (VoIP) have made possible the plurality of digital media applications by facilitating all manner of communication, media sharing and consumption, open-source access to expert knowledge, invention and innovation, and commercial enterprise. These have further transformed the UAE's scale of development, helping its transition to a post-oil era.

Economic diversification is a common goal for all the seven emirates in the UAE to future-proof against market shocks, overcome dependency on renewables, and create high-tech opportunities. The steadfast progress of ICT investments supports this agenda by facilitating the capacity expansion of the UAE's services sector, such as banking and financial services, education, tourism, trade, and start-ups. These developments are likely to motivate Emirati youth to move away from complete dependence on state welfare or at least exercise entrepreneurial talents (Van Horne, Yi Zhang and Dutot, 2016) and/or work their way up in private sector jobs or start their business ventures (Tesorero, 2019).

While the UAE state has struggled with its workforce nationalisation goals, more young nationals are now willing to participate productively in the economy. As a result, in September 2021, the UAE government announced spending plans worth US$ 6.5 billion to make private-sector jobs more attractive to Emiratis and to absorb 75,000 citizens in the private sector workforce over five years (Fattah, 2021). Here, the internet—its connectivity and informational ecosystem—can act as a driver of social and cultural change and foster entrepreneurial possibility. Moreover, restrictions on physical mobility and traditional commerce during the pandemic have expanded the use of digital applications, such as e-commerce. While before the breakout of COVID-19, locals were more hesitant due to emphasis on cash usage and preference for building in-person relationships, this is now changing (Radcliffe, 2021).

Given the breadth of activity that people engage in through internet platforms, this chapter will first profile online behaviour among people in the UAE and the government's digital efforts to co-opt the country's youth as key stakeholders. It is important to note that the UAE has a native minority population who enjoy preferential access to subsidies and welfare schemes provided by the state. In addition, the country is a traditionally patriarchal and tribe-based society governed by a hereditary monarchy (both at the federal and emirate levels). The chapter will highlight how traditional controls of authority in the UAE have been both diffused and strengthened by the expanding internet access and track its impact on the country's youth. The analysis will also touch on the cosmopolitanism of UAE society and its linkage to ICT developments, which have introduced the public to newer cultures and have been tapped into by the government's soft power agenda. Finally, a digital survey of the Emirates provides insights into how long-term cultural shifts may have been permanently triggered by increasing internet consumption, which is essentially an individual activity linked to a virtual community.

Digital Society in the UAE

Internet spread within most Arab Gulf states reached near-universal levels by the early 2010s. According to Kemp (2021), internet penetration in the UAE stood at 99 per cent in January 2021, or close to 10 million internet users. The country observed a 1.6 per cent increase in its internet users between 2020 and 2021—adding about 158,000 new internet users. The number of social media users in the UAE was 99 per cent of the total population in 2020. The UAE leads other countries based on internet connectivity, followed by other developed countries like Denmark, South Korea, Sweden, Switzerland, and the UK (The Media Lab, 2020).

According to 'The UAE Digital Transformation Report 2020', issued by the Telecommunications Digital Government Regulatory Authority, the country ranked first in the following indices in 2020: mobile broadband internet subscriptions, mobile broadband subscriptions, mobile network coverage per population, wireless broadband, and entrepreneurship. The report also noted the UAE's digital achievements in 10 main sectors, including education (e-learning platforms and artificial intelligence research), healthcare (online information system, telemedicine, robotic pharmacy), human and societal development (digital governance initiatives like the Inclusive Initiative, which electronically links ministerial authorities to provide bureaucratic services, and BAYANATI, which is a Human Resource (HR) information management system for government entities), smart city initiatives, etc. (Government of UAE, 2021) (World Economic Forum, 2017).

Previously, the International Telecommunication Union (ITU) ranked the UAE 40th in the 2017 ITU ICT Development Index (24th in the access sub-index) and noted the country's interest in international ICT and big data initiatives. In terms of telecom regulation, the country's nodal authority is the Telecommunications Regulatory Authority (TRA), and the UAE has two main telecommunication providers: Emirates Telecommunications Group Company (Etisalat) and Emirates Integrated Telecommunications Company (EITC) or 'du'. There were 229.8 mobile subscriptions per 100 inhabitants (ITU, 2017).

Open source tracking data show that UAE online users between the ages of 16-64 spent an average of about seven or more hours daily on internet platforms (The Media Lab, 2020). Out of this, social media use accounted for about three hours, music streaming for about an hour and a half, and console gaming for about an hour and a half. In addition, daily television consumption was recorded at an average of about three hours (The Media Lab, 2020). The overall consumption data indicates that virtual entertainment and communication are central to the UAE's social and cultural lives. This is supported by another set of figures that track device usage derived through survey data. It shows that 92 per cent of the UAE population use smartphones while only 11 per cent use basic mobile handsets; 66 per cent own a laptop and/or desktop; 36 per cent own a tablet device; 19 per cent use a smartwatch; 9.3 per cent stream television via the internet through a facilitating device; 19 per cent own a gaming console; 8.1 per cent own a smart home device; and 4.8 per cent have a virtual reality (VR) device. In terms of websites frequented, Alexa rankings indicate Google, YouTube, Facebook, and Manorama to be the most visited in the UAE (The Media Lab, 2020).

Further, social media usage per day in the UAE is dominated by Facebook (8.10 million user accounts; 73.8 per cent male/26.3 per cent female), LinkedIn (4.30 million user accounts; 70.8 per cent male/29.2 per cent female), and Instagram (3.80 million; 63.2 per cent male/36.8 per cent female). Other popular social media platforms are Twitter (3.3 million user accounts; 63.6 per cent male/36.4 female) and Snapchat (2.35 million; 44.2 per cent male/55.2 per cent female) (The Media Lab, 2020).

Except for Snapchat, the top frequented social media platforms are male-dominated in the UAE. This may be easily explained because the country's total population has a high degree of gender imbalance. As per data reported by Statista for 2018, out of a total resident population of 9.37 million, 6.3 million were male and 3.1 million were female. The UAE's demography is dominated by male immigrants as most jobs are male-dominated (Statista Research Department, 2021a). Previously, the imbalance was due to the structure of labour sourcing for industries like construction; now, the gender bias has spilled over to other areas of the private sector due to a mix of recruiting challenges and socio-cultural norms affecting female mobility (Goby, 2020).

Moreover, immigration to the UAE is tightly regulated around economic opportunities and the needs of the Emirati state—like infrastructure development. The UAE does not provide citizenship to the migrant worker population, who are essentially hired on short-term contracts (Weidmann, 2020). The practice is in place to protect the socio-cultural sensitivities of its small native population and preserve the demographic balance. This results in transient populations whose presence in the UAE is functional and time-bound by contractual obligations.

Further, according to a July 2021 report by Global Media Insight, the UAE's expatriate population is around 8.84 million out of 9.99 million, which is about 89 per cent of the total resident populace (GMI Blogger, 2021). South Asians are the largest expat cohort, led by Indians (2.75 million), Pakistanis (1.27 million), and Bangladeshis (0.74 million), followed by those from the Philippines (0.56 million), Iran (0.48 million), and Egypt (0.42 mil-lion) (GMI Blogger, 2021). Most expatriate workers come at a young age to work or move to the country without their families (World Population Review, 2021). According to Emirati official statistics, the UAE labour force was about 7.4 million in 2018, out of which 7.2 million people were employed (Government of UAE, [n.d.]a). The UAE government defines 'youth' as those aged between 15 and 30 years of age—who, as per its estimates, constitute 40 per cent of the country's population (Emirates Youth Council). It may thus be inferred that the total UAE population is both dynamic and relatively young.

The Internet and the Public Sphere

Rauchfleisch and Kovic (2016) have studied whether the internet can impact certain generalised functions of the public sphere. For example, the network structure of the internet and two-way or many-to-many communication platforms under Web 2.0 like social media technically enable users via their user-generated content to function as active agents than passive bystanders consuming mass media. Ultimately, the authors proposed a functionalist model using a systems theory approach. This did "not operate with *a priori* beliefs [about] what the public sphere should do", like Habermas' normative conviction, but instead focused on what the public sphere does. Based on this approach, Rauchfleisch and Kovic proposed a hierarchical order of generalised functions of the public sphere:

- Level 1 is identity building, which requires access to communication. Its effect is the creation of a collective identity, upon which the internet impact is designated as 'medium'.
- Level 2 is agenda-setting, which requires the participation of a critical mass of people. Its effect is receptivity, for which the internet can be 'highly impactful'.
- Level 3 is control and criticism, or in other words—accountability—which requires freedom of speech and impacts policymaking. As an intermediary, the internet can have a 'medium' impact.

- Level 4 is deliberation, which requires access and participation and can achieve rational consensus, although the role of the internet has been deemed 'low' in this regard by the authors.

Upon testing their model, the authors described the internet's contribution to the public sphere functions as "a diminishing marginal utility", where the greatest impact they observed was in agenda-setting.

Interestingly, in the intervening years since their publication in 2016, the internet's networked information ecosystem—particularly social media platforms like Facebook and Twitter—have acquired newfound notoriety. Through sudden mass mobilisation tactics by troll farms (MIT Technology Review, 2021) and bots, deliberate misinformation campaigns, and the virality of internet content, the unpredictable and universal impact of the internet on creating collective identities, agenda-setting, discourse shaping, and decision-making cannot be minimised. Moreover, in value terms, the role of the internet, though immensely significant, is no longer viewed as positive.

State Control of the UAE Internet Sphere

It is interesting to understand how the UAE 'public sphere' functions in the background of the aforementioned theoretical discussion. The country has so far implemented vaguely formulated laws with wide-ranging legislative and coercive powers, which ensure that self-censorship is rampant. This is more so among the foreign population who can be expelled at any time or be subjected to inscrutable legal procedures (Freedom House, 2020). Ostensibly to prevent cybercrimes, religious defamation, terrorism, or denial of the absolute authority of the ruling regime—the UAE's technology and internet regulations have established an online environment that provides clear limits to free speech with severe consequences for those found to be in violation (Freedom House, 2020).

Moreover, the UAE regime has combined blocking access to key platforms and websites with surveillance and infiltration tactics to achieve panoptic control of individual users (Perlroth, 2016). This strategy repurposes the mobilisation potential of internet-based media, which previously broke down the complete media control wielded by ruling authorities. Its adoption became more pronounced after the Arab

Uprisings erupted across the Middle East and North Africa (MENA) in 2012 and considering the UAE's increasingly aggressive foreign policy ambitions in the region.

Analysing the online public sphere in the Arab Gulf countries, Leber and Abrahams (2019) make an important observation on the impact of online government mobilisation using research on China's online censorship:

> When social media serves as a yardstick for the prevailing views of "society" or other reference groups, these interventions can have the effect of encouraging citizens to believe that official statements or narratives enjoy widespread popular support due to the volume of perceived online engagement. (Leber and Abrahams, 2019, p. 244)

The authors also cite the "three F's" of censorship by Roberts, M.E. (2018):

> Striking fear into individual users through threats of offline sanctions, slowing the spread of critical information by generating higher friction in users' efforts to access certain sites or posts and flooding online platforms with distracting information or preferred narratives. (Leber and Abrahams, 2019, p. 244)

The Emirati Youth Cohort and State Efforts at Technocratic Inclusion

While controlling the online environment is a clear security goal for the UAE, it serves as a useful medium for ruling authorities to engage with the country's youth on the other end of the spectrum. To this end, in 2016, Sheikh Mohammed bin Rashid Al Maktoum, Prime Minister and Vice President of the UAE and Ruler of Dubai, created a dedicated government position—the Minister of State for Youth. The position is presently occupied by Shamma bint Suhail bin Faris Al Mazrui, who was appointed in 2020. Al Mazrui was previously appointed as the Minister of State for Youth Affairs in February 2016. Her inclusion in the UAE Cabinet is indicative of efforts to more visibly include women in the government and participate in the agenda-setting process (UAE Cabinet, n.d.). The UAE government has also implemented policies that focus on youth participation in governance, which it regards as being at "the core of the country's development strategy". Among its policy initiatives, the UAE Cabinet mandated federal entities to include Emiratis under the age of 30 as members of the Board of Directors of their respective entities. A digital platform was subsequently launched for youth candidates to register and apply. As per official records dating 3 February 2020, there were 33 youth applicants appointed as members of the Boards of Directors for key federal entities (Government of UAE, [n.d.]a).

The intended impact of these initiatives is to promote the creation of empowered youth who embody the culture of the UAE and its identity besides fulfilling productive and entrepreneurial goals. The digital governance platforms and public diplomacy via social media become essential to mainstreaming the government's youth agenda and ensuring an equivalence between their prosperity and national success. All the emirates and prominent ruling figures have dedicated social media channels and sponsor youth programmes. A popular instance of the government's online youth outreach was "#TheNationalDialogueOnYouth", which launched a federal digital campaign under the Dubai ruler Sheikh Mohammed bin Rashid Al Maktoum to enable the youth to share their "dreams, aspirations, and concerns". A two-day youth retreat also accompanied this; while announcing the initiative, the Dubai ruler tweeted: "What do we want from the young, and what do the young want from us? How can we support them and enable them to do their part towards the country?" (UAE Cabinet News, 2016).

This type of internet-based outreach is a well-calibrated effort by the government; aware of how youths spend their time online, officials can establish direct lines of communication with them. Meanwhile, Emirati youths feel convinced they have much to gain by participating and propagating the government's aspirations. It is useful to understand that Emirati society is traditionally tribal, and the affiliation of locals with leading tribe members, not to say the Emirati rulers, via ostensibly two-way communication channels online, is exceedingly attractive. Moreover, as a relatively young nation, completing fifty years in 2021, the native population of the UAE is still appreciative of the shift to modernity experienced by recent successive generations in their own families. Nevertheless, with each new decade, more Emiratis will become less conscious of their country's leap to modernity from a desert community and nomadic existence. This is why the UAE's ruling authorities carefully and consistently promote their patron identity on all digital platforms.

Impact of the Internet in the Cultural Realm

Over the five decades since its independence, the UAE has emerged as a highly cosmopolitan and urbanised hub in the Arab Gulf region. This has been made possible by constructing modern cities by the labour-power of a vast, albeit transient, immigrant population and the government's soft power approaches to brand its national identity as unique in the region. Meanwhile, widespread internet access has fostered openness to other cultures that can be seen in food, linguistic, and entertainment preferences. In addition, visibility on social media platforms and sharing content through audio-visual platforms have spawned huge fandoms and awareness of global trends among the country's youth that depart from traditional preferences for regional Arabic media, English language exports, or the local heritage of Emiratis. This is because online platforms host spaces and facilitate individuals accumulating cross-cultural encounters within their everyday lived experience with considerable ease (Marc, 2017). Moreover, the familiarity with foreign cultures has been followed by an active interest in foreign cultural expressions and cultural consumerism.

An interesting case-in-point is the reach of South Korea's Hallyu wave to the country since the early 2010s. In a 2019 survey conducted by Statista in the UAE, about 35 per cent of the respondents considered K-Pop (or Korean music) to be very popular within the country, and a further 27.3 per cent of the respondents acknowledged K-Pop to be quite popular (Statista Research Department, 2021b). News media frequently report how the UAE youth actively listen to K-Pop, is part of global fandoms, and buy tickets to their favourite K-Pop concerts held in the country (Andrews, 2019). Popular UAE destinations in Dubai and Abu Dhabi already provide the film sets for high-budget music videos and are now seeking to tap into the K-Pop frenzy (Samar and Bindu, 2019). Finally, the country regularly hosts cultural events to cater to the fandom communities across the MENA region (Korea.net, 2021).

Such widespread appeal of Korean music and cultural contents in the UAE may appear as bewildering to external observers; it is unlike Western pop culture exports (which are globally popular) or Indian cultural exports (linked to the large Indian expat population in the region) or other Arab media from MENA countries. On a superficial front, this popularity can be put down to the proliferation of short-form content platforms and streaming applications, which have removed technical and physical barriers to culture sharing and influence. Connected to this online presence is the widening scope of South Korean influence—beyond music and TV to beauty products, fashion trends, and foods—resulting in franchise deals targeting the regional market (Choi, 2015). The music streaming giant Spotify has noted that UAE and Saudi Arabia are its top K-Pop markets in the Arab market, while Netflix attributes its overall success in the UAE to its K-drama contents, which feature consistently among its top 10 viewed shows (Saberi, 2020). In her analysis of the global cultural and consumer reach of Hallyu and the "solidarity-fostering function of social media", Choi (2015) references the experience of a UAE-based respondent who explains that through Facebook and Twitter, they could connect with K-Pop fans from around the world and at any time unlike the one-way-at-a-time communicative limitations of TV and radio.

These trends indicate a watershed moment for cosmopolitanism in the UAE and its long-desired appeal as a global destination. The UAE's young generation of online users is also internet savvy, having been borne into an ICT-enabled society and economy. It is likely that cultural trends from different geographies will similarly find appeal in the country in the internet's flattened ecosystem unless new variables enter into the mix, like top-down interference. Moreover, the appeal of Korean content in the UAE can be understood instrumentally as tapping into the internet public's desire for new cultural products. K-Pop and South Korean television sustain their appeal as huge amount of contents are constantly produced by online creators and consumed by UAE internet users in the long hours they spend on their internet-enabled devices. Globally, internet users flock to any form of content that has quality or caters to niche tastes or has a unique entertainment proposition value. The virality of social media trends is most illustrative of the internet's multiplier effect—whereby whole communities are found around topics and audio-visual contents—and shape public opinion in real-time. This influences social behaviour, such as the acceptance of new ideas and cultural phenomena, and economic choice, such as fashion, food, technology, and aesthetic preferences. It would appear that South Korea's long-term focus on expanding its soft power exports has capitalised on this ability of online media to boost its culture and tourism industries.

Analysing the popularity of South Korean media contents via the social media domain, Jung, Eun-Young (2015) writes:

> Contemporary transnational popular cultural flows constitute an increasingly fluid terrain as boundaries between nations, regions, and cultures are rapidly imploding. With the ubiquity of the internet and the recent explosion of "social media," the global cultural environment is constantly being reconfigured by flows that are instant, momentary, pervasive, and unremitting. It is this environment in which Korean popular culture is spreading in ways unimaginable only a decade ago. (p. 73)

Similarly, the UAE, too, is keen to build up its image and glamour online. It considers this to be an investment parallel to the towering estates that populate its modern cities—promoting a national identity that is modern and sophisticated, where multicultural communities are welcome, and immense prospects are available for businesses and entrepreneurs (Kathiravelu, 2016, pp. 28-53). An example of this intersection of culture and consumption is the UAE's internet-influenced economy. Social media patrons from the region and worldwide indirectly and directly advertise the UAE's lavish and distinctive appeal—to benefit local tourism and associated industries. As a renowned business hub, Dubai has cemented its appeal as a widely popular destination for influencer marketers, who also appreciate the country's tax breaks and duty-free commerce.

Meanwhile, the UAE government has introduced a new license for influencers based in the country or abroad, which they must secure to advertise on their social media or collaborate with brands. Without this license, influencers are not entitled to get paid (Sila, 2021). The move reveals the cultural and social power of internet platforms. Regulating the influencer industry directly through a license regime enables UAE authorities to gain some sense of control over the type of UAE exposure being broadcast online via images and videos of the country (Ruth, 2021). While influencers can promote a whole range of products and services, from travel destinations and itineraries to cosmetic surgery, government authorities also routinely approach local professionals to work on public campaigns. For example, Emirati influencers were asked to promote handwashing or support families in need during the pandemic as officials knew their reach on online media surpassed any offline public campaign. On their part, Emirati influencers are reluctant to decline these requests as their business depends on the state's patronage via license approvals, at the very least (Ruth, 2021).

At this juncture, it is interesting to read Breslow and Allagui (2019), who write on the perceived stress to Emirati culture and polity from expanding internet consumption (pp. 21-29). Their insights are based on findings from the Emirates Internet Project (EIP), longitudinal surveys of the internet usage patterns among the UAE's residents. The project is associated with the World Internet Project (WIP), a consortium of institutions researching internet usage in 22 countries. According to the authors, who are faculty at the Department of Mass Communication, American University of Sharjah—widespread internet usage has impacted language and social networks in the UAE. They premise their argument that fundamental to a national community is its shared language. In the UAE, Arabic is the historical language spoken by the Emirati peoples and is intrinsic to their identity. While private education emphasises English as the lingua franca, online communication reinforces this. The authors note that data from the EIP survey show younger respondents are more likely to frequent English language websites. A majority of Emirati respondents under the age of 41, including a large majority of Emirati respondents aged 18-25 and every Emirati respondent under the age of 18, visited English language websites. However, only 3 per cent of the EIP survey respondents stayed within the Arabic language web universe.

Another "pressure" is brought upon by the proliferation of internet-based media that affect traditional patterns of social networks. Breslow and Allagui note in their survey study that the social construction of families in the Arabian Peninsula, including the UAE, is based on clan and tribe. Families are primary social units and central to how social relationships are formed in the region. Entertainment and media consumption, such as radio and television, are thus communal activities. However, digital consumption has shifted the individual, based on their usage preferences, from the physical community to the virtual community. A new equilibrium emerges, engendering new relationships and displacing the family at the centre of the Arab individual's social life. Technology determinists like Rheingold have long advocated that virtual communities can take the place of traditional communities as they decline (Jones, 1997), though sociologists argue that the multipronged effects of technology on society are not always positive or linear.

Results from the EIP survey also showed that over 50 per cent of the respondents spent the same time with their friends since using the internet, while about 40 per cent of the respondents spent the same time with their families. About 40 per cent of the respondents said they spent less time with family since adopting the internet. In the age cohort below 18 years, 66.7 per cent of the Emirati respondents stated they spent less time with family after adopting the internet. Among UAE expatriate respondents, 66 per cent reported that the quality of their relationship with their family either "somewhat" or "greatly increased" after using the internet—as it likely saved communication costs. Other observations derived from the EIP survey tracked political impact and utility. Since the bulk of the UAE population consists of expatriates and labour migrants on temporary residence visas linked to job contracts—they expressed a distinct lack of interest in local political affairs, understandable in the absence of their ability to participate in any political process in the country. Lastly, and most interesting, about 83 per cent of the EIP respondents said that the internet was the most important source of information in the UAE, supplanting mass media.

Conclusion

The UAE has, since its creation, strived to distinguish its national identity in the Arab world as a progressive and modern state. Key to this image building is its curated 'openness'—favouring finance capitalism and liberal market access but stopping short of free speech and free internet. Patronage activities by prominent royal family members and state agencies also support this strategy on online media. A deeper look into the UAE's state priorities thus reveals the importance of the growing digital economy and technocratic governance. The widening internet access has, however, not created any vulnerabilities for the UAE state as the regime controls communication flows online discreetly—through constant monitoring and regulation of internet use on the one hand, and political socialisation on popular social media networks, on the other. The country's youth also take centre stage for the UAE's ruling authorities, who are looking to gradually steer Emirati society away from traditional dependence on state benefits.

The UAE state's end goal is to establish ways to transform locals into self-motivated, future-minded citizens capable of creating value-added economic opportunities to sustain their wealth, including on social media platforms, and in doing so, propel national progress. Beyond this, the UAE's extreme digitisation and hyper-connectivity have also opened avenues for greater cross-cultural interactions in young people's everyday lives in the country. This could even affect the youths' familiarity with their Emirati customs and traditional norms in the long term. Nevertheless, the youth of the UAE—just as elsewhere in the world—are all online, in pursuit of entertainment, socialisation, business and entrepreneurship, education, and other forms of consumption. While this internet usage will not decrease, the UAE state has demonstrated that it can direct its adoption to productive outcomes and meet regime aspirations.

References

Andrews, Farah (2019), "UAE Fans Among the Biggest K-pop Lovers in the Mena Region," The National News, October 10, https://www.thenationalnews.com/arts-culture/music/uae-fans-among-the-biggest-k-pop-lovers-in-the-mena-region-1.920886, accessed on August 14, 2021.

ANI (2021), "Indian Diaspora Immensely Contributed Towards UAE's Growth: Piyush Goyal," October 3, https://www.aninews.in/news/world/asia/indian-diaspora-immensely-contributed-towards-uaes-growth-piyush-goyal20211003204417/, accessed on November 1, 2021.

Hindustan Times (2021), "No Longer Silent, Gulf Arab Citizens Express Anger at Israel," May 19, https://www.hindustantimes.com/world-news/no-longer-silent-gulf-arab-citizens-express-anger-at-israel-101621413516014.html, accessed on December 12, 2021.

Bin Bishr, Aisha (2017), "How Digital Technology Is Transforming Dubai," World Economic Forum, May 16, https://www.weforum.org/agenda/2017/05/how-digital-technology-is-transforming-dubai/, accessed on August 15, 2021.

Breslow, Harris and Allagui, Ilhem (2019), "Stresses Upon an Emergent Imagined Community: Results and Insights From the Emirates Internet Project," in Aris Mousoutzanis and Daniel Riha (eds.), *New Media and the Politics of Online Communities*, pp. 22-28, Brill.

Choi, JungBong (2015), "Hallyu versus Hallyu-hwa: Cultural Phenomenon Versus Institutional Campaign," in S.J. Lee and M.N. Abe (eds.), *Hallyu 2.0: The Korean Wave in the Age of Social Media*, pp. 34-36, University of Michigan Press.

Ekşioğlu, Sila (2021), "The Rise of Dubai: How Dubai Influencers Affect the Destination's Economy," Inflow Network, February 23, https://inflownetwork.com/the-rise-of-dubai-how-influencers-affect-the-destinations-economy/, accessed on August 15, 2021.

Emirates Youth Council (n.d.), "National Youth Agenda" https://councils.youth.gov.ae/en/download-file/183#:~:text=Youth%2C%20which%20is%20defined%20as,of%20economic%20and%20social%20life, accessed on October 2, 2021.

Fattah, Zainab (2021), "UAE to Spend $6.5 Billion to Boost Private-Sector Jobs," Bloomberg, September 12, https://www.bloomberg.com/news/articles/2021-09-12/uae-to-spend-6-5-billion-luring-citizens-to-private-sector-jobs, accessed on November 1, 2021.

Freedom House (2020), "Freedom on the Net 2020: United Arab Emirates," https://freedomhouse.org/country/united-arab-emirates/freedom-net/2020, accessed on August 15, 2021.

Freer, Courtney (2018), "National Identity and the Emirati State," LSE, December 11, https://blogs.lse.ac.uk/mec/2018/12/11/national-identity-and-the-emirati-state/, accessed on August 15, 2021.

GMI Blogger (2021), "United Arab Emirates Population Statistics 2021," GMI Blogger, July 1, https://www.globalmediainsight.com/blog/uae-population-statistics/, accessed on August 14, 2021.

Goby, Valerie Priscilla (2020), "Emirati Women's Professional Legitimacy: Synergy of the Political and the Personal Amid Constraint and Self-Determination," *International Journal of Organizational Analysis*, vol. 29, no. 1, pp. 1-15.

Government of UAE (n.d.)a, "Information and Services", March 29, https://u.ae/en/information-and-services/jobs/uae-workforce, accessed on August 15, 2021.

Government of UAE (n.d.)b, "Youth", August 15, https://u.ae/en/about-the-uae/the-uae-government/government-of-future/youth, accessed on November 1, 2021.

ITU (2017), "Big Data for Measuring the Information Society, Country Report—United Arab Emirates," https://www.itu.int/en/ITU-D/Statistics/Documents/bigdata/United%20Arab%20Emirates.pdf, accessed on October 29, 2021.

Jones, Quentin (1997), "Virtual-Communities, Virtual Settlements & Cyber-Archaeology: A Theoretical Out-line," *Journal of Computer-Mediated Communication*, vol. 3, no. 3.

Jung, Eun Young (2015), "New Wave Formations: K-Pop Idols, Social Media, and the Remaking of the Korean Wave," in S.J. Lee and M.N. Abe (eds.), *Hallyu 2.0: The Korean Wave in the Age of Social Media*, pp. 34-36, University of Michigan Press.

Kathiravelu, Laavanya (2016), *Migrant Dubai: Low Wage Workers and the Construction of a Global City*, pp. 28-53, Palgrave Macmillan.

Kemp, Simon (2021), "Digital 2021: The United Arab Emirates," DATAREPORTAL, February 10, https://datareportal.com/reports/digital-2021-united-arab-emirates, accessed on June 5, 2021.

Khouri, Samar and Rai, Bindu (2019), "Inside K-Pop Group SuperM's UAE Music Video," Gulf News, October 5, https://gulfnews.com/entertainment/music/watch-inside-k-pop-group-superms-uae-music-video-1.66909996, accessed on October 30, 2021.

Leber, Andrew and Abrahams, Alexei (2019), "A Storm of Tweets: Social Media Manipulation During the Gulf Crisis," *Review of Middle East Studies*, vol. 53, no. 2, pp. 241-258.

Korea.net (2021), "KPOP in UAE: Korea-UAE Cultural Exchange Through the Years," July 1, https://www.korea.net/TalkTalkKorea/French/community/community/CMN0000009531, accessed on August 15, 2021.

MADRASA, Digital Teaching Platform. https://madrasa.org/, accessed on August 15, 2021.

Michaelson, Ruth (2021), "In This World, Social Media Is Everything: How Dubai Became the Planet's Influ-encer Capital," *The Guardian*, April 17, https://www.theguardian.com/world/2021/apr/17/in-this-world-social-media-is-everything-how-dubai-became-the-planets-influencer-capital, accessed on August 15, 2021.

NYU Abu Dhabi (2021), "StartAD Invites UAE's Young Innovators to Join Fourth Edition of Flagship Entrepreneurship Program," April 1, https://nyuad.nyu.edu/en/news/latest-news/science-and-technology/2021/april/startad-youth-entrepreneurship-program.html, accessed on August 15, 2021.

OECD (2020), "Teaching in the United Arab Emirates: 10 Lessons From TALIS," https://www.oecd.org/education/talis/Teaching_in_the_UAE-10_Lessons_from_TALIS.pdf, accessed on August 15, 2021.

Perlroth, Nicole (2016), "Governments Turn to Commercial Spyware to Intimidate Dissidents," *New York Times*, May 29, https://www.nytimes.com/2016/05/30/technology/governments-turn-to-commercial-spyware-to-intimidate-dissidents.html, accessed on August 15, 2021.

Radcliffe, Damien (2021), "Online Shopping Hasn't Been a Hit in One Part of the World. But Things Are Start-ing to Change," ZDNet, September 8, https://www.zdnet.com/article/how-covid-accelerated-e-commerce-adoption-in-the-middle-east/, accessed on October 30, 2021.

Rauchfleisch, Adrian and Kovic, Marko (2016), "The Internet and Generalized Functions of the Public Sphere: Transformative Potentials From a Comparative Perspective," Social Media + Society, vol. 2, no. 2, pp. 1-15

Roberts, Margaret E. (2018), *Censored: Distraction and Diversion Inside China's Great Firewall*, Princeton University Press.

Saberi, Donya (2020), "The Korean Wave Rises in the UAE," *The Diplomat*, October 5, https://thediplomat.com/2020/10/the-korean-wave-rises-in-the-uae/, accessed on October 30, 2021.

Statista Research Department (2021a), "Total Population of the UAE 2018, by Gender," March 26, https://www.statista.com/statistics/976236/uae-population-by-gender/, accessed on October 30, 2021.

Statista Research Department (2021b), "K-Pop Popularity in the UAE 2019," August 12, https://www.statista.com/statistics/956113/south-korea-kpop-popularity-in-the-uae/, accessed on October 30, 2021.

Tesorero, Angel (2019), "Young Emiratis Willing to Start From the Bottom to Gain Work Experience," *The Khaleej Times*, February 6, https://www.khaleejtimes.com/news/general/young-emiratis-willing-to-start-from-the-bottom-to-gain-work-experience, accessed on October 30, 2021.

Government of UAE (2021), "The Digital Transformation in the UAE Report 2020," October 13, https://u.ae/en/about-the-uae/digital-uae/digital-transformation-in-the-uae, accessed on October 30, 2021.

UAE, The Cabinet (n.d.), "Shaikh Mohammed Announces Youth Retreat to Discuss Ideas," Media Centre, https://www.uaecabinet.ae/en/details/news/shaikh-mohammed-announces-youth-retreat-to-discuss-ideas, accessed on October 30, 2021.

UAE Digital Media Statistics 2020, The Media Lab, https://www.themedialab.me/uae-digital-media-statistics-2020/, accessed on November 1, 2021.

Van Horne, Constance, Yi Zhang, and Dutot, Vincent (2016), "Young Entrepreneurs and the Digital Space: Case Studies From the UAE," *International Journal of Business and Management Studies*, vol. 5, no. 2, pp. 293-300.

Verboord, Marc (2017), "Internet Usage and Cosmopolitanism in Europe: A Multilevel Analysis," *Information, Communication & Society*, vol. 20, no. 3, pp. 460-481.

Weidmann, Florian (2020), "Migrant Urbanism in Gulf Cities: A Reality Without Vision?," in Mehran Kamrava (ed.), *Routledge Handbook of Persian Gulf Politics*, pp. 99-112, Routledge.

10. Fractured Narratives of Gender: State, Space and Visibility in the Gulf

Priyanka Chandra

Introduction

The talk of change in West Asia remains a constant. Yet, three emerging factors seem to potentially create real change in the Gulf at a much faster pace. First, the precipitous fall of the oil economy during COVID-19 as oil prices dropped to the lowest in Wall Street history, brought the realities of the oil-dependent economies to the forefront. The emerging young leaders, including Crown Prince Mohammed bin Salman and his politics, could not have pre-empted this development but have certainly foreseen it; hence, the urgent drive towards consolidating a post-oil economy. This drive has gained momentum, in turn, because of the rapid digitisation necessitated by the pandemic. Digitisation has opened a plethora of new economic opportunities and possibilities for greater assimilation of people, especially the more tech-savvy youth and, in particular, women into the workforce, in accordance with the strictures observed in places like Saudi Arabia and Qatar. Third, the young leadership itself is a manifestation of this change, it's push to open up the economy and simultaneously project a more progressive image of the regime.

On the other hand, mandates of Wahhabism and male guardianship law[1] indicate the continued pervasiveness of old patriarchal and authoritarian politico-legal and social structures. According to Human Rights Watch, the guardianship law remains "the most serious impediment to realising women's rights in Saudi Arabia, rendering adult women legal minors who cannot make key decisions for themselves" (Human Rights Watch, 2016). This is evident in multiple issues including the limited nature of elected legislative, restrictions on traditional and new media, attacks on journalists, monitoring of women's movement and performative gender, continued ban on homosexuality, etc.

Women have been the most visible manifestations of adherence to religion in the Gulf. Thus, women's bodies, status and rights have been closely controlled and monitored by the state. With the recent shift in leadership and a move towards a post-oil economy, countries like Saudi Arabia seek to project a new image, and social reforms for women are especially important to this project, as evident from initiatives like the Saudi *Vision 2030*. Combined with opportunities accruing to digitisation, this could potentially redefine women's social realities. However, when juxtaposed against continued state control over political spaces and performative gender as well as other socio-political factors, there are gaps in these state-driven narratives.

In this context, how have the lives of the youth changed? What have the changes meant for young women? How has the digital space as a space of the public sphere affected their perception of citizenship and political participation/activism post-2011? To what extent do economic opportunities alter social realities in the seemingly closed (public) spaces in the Gulf? Most importantly, how do these altering socio-economic landscapes reflect in the lived experiences of young women? And to what extent do some of these redoubtably cosmetic changes gouge insecurities about the future?

This chapter presents a hermeneutical analysis of the narratives of change pertaining to women and sexuality in the Gulf. It explores these changes by contextualising them within the broader political, social and cultural landscapes in the region, their limits and concerns regarding them. It examines social and cultural narratives of change emanating from lived experiences juxtaposed against hegemonic regime discourse and state-sponsored narratives of change. State-sponsored narratives of change and reform present an additional layer, or a veil in engagement with social transformations pertaining to women and gender in the region, and require urgent critical examination. Reviews of journalistic accounts are combined with critical theoretical perspectives and discourse analysis to examine whether contemporary developments in the Gulf are creating new spaces within old structures. The chapter argues that the changes reflected in state narratives remain cosmetic at large, and further narratives of change are partial and continue to be rooted in a predominantly Oriental gaze. State narratives and control over visibility obfuscate actual social transformations that have been underway emerging organically from within Gulf societies. Further, they ellipse people not belonging to the mainstream gender.

Mainstream Narratives on Women and the Oriental Gaze

In March 2001, *Princess: A True Story of Life Behind the Veil in Saudi Arabia* by Jean Sasson was published to wide reception. It received significant acclaim as well as attention for bringing out barely known secrets of members of the Saudi royal family, and Saudi society at large. Written as a first-person account of a Saudi princess under the alias Sultana, it revealed in detail the unknown intricacies of the Saudi royal family, and the Saudi society. Noticed for the mostly scandalous revelations it brought out, consumed widely by the American and subsequently global readership. It remained a *The New York Times* bestseller for thirteen weeks, and along with the following books that comprise the Princess series, remains a popular reading choice for those not quite well acquainted with the region.

Sasson's works are not representative of gender narratives at large, but they do highlight the problem of looking at such narratives. They present extremes in terms of the class component under scrutiny and the notions of extreme depravity and decadence that are typically associated with wealth being interwoven into narratives of the lives of women. The telling of these stories is further complicated by the additional layer of narration about the 'other', bordering on fantastical, mythical and in those extremely repugnant ones. Sex trafficking, rape and disciplining of women's bodies in the name of religion and honour are contextualised within ostentatious palaces and privilege. While this narrative is valid as an individual one, it is also symptomatic of problems regarding perceptions of women in the region. Broadly these problems are mystification of the 'Muslim' woman and sexuality as the other, and the selective class-based focus on elite segments of society, obscuring what is happening in much of it.

This hegemonic narrative perpetuates Western liberal notions of Muslim women and the presumed need to rescue them. That Muslim women do not need saving from religion per se has already been established through the works of several feminist scholars (see Abu-Lughod, 2013). However, Western liberal feminism continues to view problems of gender disparity as being rooted in religion. The case of the Gulf societies in that way is slightly different from other parts of the West Asian region in that religious doctrine has certainly been employed as the means to control and police women and the scope of their public activity, civil rights and even personal rights and safety. A detailed discussion of the role of religion and its dogmatic manifestations is not possible within the scope of this chapter, but the gaps between dogmatic doctrine and hermeneutical readings of the Islamic texts have been amply demonstrated by numerous feminist scholars such as Amina Wadud (1999).

Orthodox interpretations of a hyper-masculine clergy have been forcefully and questionably enforced through state bodies like the *Muta'wa* or the Committee for the Prevention of Vice and the Promotion of Virtue, which even the monarchy could not justify. Severe criticism from within even in a closed and monitored public sphere combined with international outrage, compelled the Saudi leadership to do away with this body. However, laws and enforcement of values which are culturally normative and subject to interpretation continued to be a problem in thinking about the rights of women as individuals and citizens. What has typically been viewed as a Western construct of the private-public distinction in this context was seen as an important local determinant further limiting the imagination of women as full citizens. The guardianship laws have been particularly contentious and a serious impediment in this process.

A majority of transnational feminist scholarship also contributes to this problem by viewing the West Asian region through the prism of cultural exceptionalism and thereby casting Muslim women in the mould of the 'Other', and seeing them primarily as victims. This view, perpetrated by mainstream internal scholarly as well as journalistic narratives eclipse the actual shifts on the ground which often occur in the form of a 'quiet encroachment', in the words of Asef Bayat (2013). According to this view, feminist movements and interventions for change in women's status need to be understood within the cultural paradigm of West Asian and Gulf societies, rather than as exceptional to them. This requires a closer look at both actual changes and voices that reflect on the impact of these changes emerging from within Gulf societies, through what has been a more organic form of gradual, often silent, movement for resistance and reform.

Narrative Shifts: State and Non-State Voices

The past decade has seen serious efforts from governments across the Gulf to bring women into the mainstream in a more holistic way, which is reflected far better in the fields of education and healthcare. More recently Gulf leadership has been focusing on bringing them into the workforce. There has been a significant improvement in the primary, secondary and higher education for women as well as other markers such as maternal mortality (Abousleiman, 2019). Yet when it comes to the workforce, the disparities in percentages of women's participation in the workforce in the Gulf as compared to the global workforce are vast.

> In 2018, 39% of the global workforce were women, but in MENA, women's share was just 20.3%, and in the GCC it is even less. Close to half of the GCC region's population are women, and their full participation in economic activities would augment their children's prosperity and the overall economic growth of their countries. (Abousleiman, 2019)

Thus, the Gulf leadership has become more focused on bringing women into the workforce in higher numbers. It is important to note that shifts in the role of women especially their expanding role and presence in the economy, political arena and by extension in the public sphere have been underway for over a decade. Contrary to postulations of current ruling dispensations, the newer changes in the role of women are not entirely a product of state or the leadership's initiatives. Rather, it is based on this preceding expansion of women's role and agency that the state is now able to claim a more progressive and modernising stance on the question of women's status and liberties. Agitations for greater political representations and economic freedoms in Saudi Arabia such as the driving law or women's representation in the Shura Council have been witnessed for over a decade. Multiple YouTube videos and individual interviews in print and online journalism attest that women have been foraying into unchartered territories of economic activities through which they have also subverted the traditional roles they have been cast in.

Significantly, the roles and strategies employed by women in countries like Saudi Arabia have been uniquely unconventional. For instance, the public statement made by women who drove before it was sanctioned by law or women who have made their presence felt through fashion, blogging, vlogging (video blogging), film making, and entrepreneurial activities have contributed to greater political mobilisation. Before the state and current leadership took a somewhat progressive stance on some of these issues, the state was in a crisis caused by deep anxieties when confronted by these unconventional methods and strategies. Consider the case of Loujain al-Hathloul, a Saudi woman whose image was seated behind a steering wheel back in 2014 led to her arrest (Regan, 2015). She was subsequently released and arrested again for her social activism in 2018 on charges of harming national security. Even as her activism along with that of several others led to the new driving laws, she remained in prison for three years (Qiblawi and Fox, 2021).

It is important to note that while Muslim women in the Gulf like majority of the Muslim women across the region do not view their challenges or place their politics within the simplified binary of East vs. West or religious vs. Western liberal secular debates, many of them have directly addressed the Orientalist perceptions that cast Muslim women perpetually in the role of victims in an exaggerated view of Muslim societies. Any number of videos titled 'A day in the life of a Muslim/ Arab/Saudi women' or some variation of the same represent both views emanating from the West that present a caricature of what they understand the lives of Muslim women to be, and counter-narratives where several of these perceptions, myths and allegations are constantly debunked.[2]

Economic Modernisation vs Gendered Spaces

Several studies have linked the oil dependency of Gulf economies to the reaffirmation of patriarchal structures owing to the focus in foreign policy on trade relations and diplomacy which excluded gender-based discussions in the past (Al Alwai, 2017). The higher level of economic development in the Gulf accruing to oil wealth was, unlike most other

Latin American and South Asian countries, linked inversely to gender parity. Traditionally oil-rich rentier economies have not provided as many opportunities for women employment as export-oriented industries. Even if the latter has provided low wage opportunities, fields like agriculture, garment and textile have played an important role in providing limited economic mobilisation for women in other countries. In the Gulf, these opportunities have been scant as the economies focused on heavy industry/trade-based economic activities with disproportionate employment opportunities for men. Women find limited opportunities in bureaucratic and other jobs in select fields in countries like Bahrain and Kuwait. But in general, the gendered nature of both women's roles and the workspace especially in the heavy industrial sector has meant that an increase in job opportunities has not reflected gender equity. Combined with the impact of a sizeable expatriate workforce, the actual opportunities for women have been severely limited.

The shift to a post-oil economy with rapid digitisation and growth of soft skills industries provides an opportunity to incorporate women in much higher proportions into the workforce. Saudi Arabia's *Vision 2030* includes the National Transformation Programme with the aim of increasing women participation in the labour workforce to 25 per cent in 2020, a target that has already been exceeded to 31 per cent (Akeel, 2021). However, providing easy access to the labour market is only part of the change required to achieve this objective. On the one hand, it needs to be supported by the change in societal norms, gendered domestic roles of women and the patriarchal control they are subjected to through traditional understanding of honour, notions of "good mothers" and "obedient wives". On the other hand, newer issues pertaining to digitisation and protection of digital identity have emerged, which are simultaneously creating their own paradoxes of resistance and presence of women vis-à-vis monitoring and surveillance, discussed below. Challenges to creating safe workspaces for women both physically and in the digital domain persist. The gendered views of workspaces are more prevalent in some sectors of economy such as heavy industry compared to others like education and healthcare. Thus, gender equity across economic verticals remains undermined.

This shows that the economic opportunities projected by the political leadership through programmes like *Vision 2030* or digitisation, even as they open many erstwhile closed professions to women, do not ensure gender equity. Gendered norms pertaining to women's roles in society continue to create obstacles to any potential change. These changes need to be substantiated with an opening up of the discursive spaces that can address women's roles in both public and private spaces as well as critically examine patriarchal attitudes to performative gender. Given that women are constantly cast in familial and caregiving roles, the performative notions of gender become merely extensions of these roles. Thus, women's dress and notions of modesty, comportment, mobility, etc., are constantly seen within the context of the "obedient wife" or "good mother" construct. This is not to say that these roles are antithetical to possibilities for economic agency, rather that the prevalent gendered norms perpetuate a reductionist view of the scope of women's roles both within and outside the family. They need to be also seen as financially independent, politically as well as socially active and as active agents of change rather than passive recipients of 'empowerment' imposed in a top-down approach by the state or agencies external to them. Unfortunately, neither the state-sponsored narratives of change nor especially the classical liberalism feminisms (emerging primarily from the West) acknowledge or reflect these roles of women (Abu-Lughod, 2013). The limitations of discursive representation arise both from the continued Oriental gaze to non-Western, particularly Muslim societies on one hand, and the limits to actual change on the other, as discussed below.

Emerging Discursive Spaces in the Gulf

A brief comparison with other societies such as Egypt, Tunisia and to a lesser degree Morocco, which has a monarchical regime, brings out interesting points to consider. First, there is greater social mobilisation among a more diverse populace in these societies compared to Saudi Arabia and Qatar. The mobilisation has been visible in countries like Egypt and Tunisia in the form of several movements ranging from social activism focusing on gender violence and women's safety, especially in the face of state repression in Egypt, to greater political representation for women in politics and in the elected legislative bodies of the state. While outcomes post-Arab Spring have varied from country to country and leave much to be desired, it is important to note that these women movements have been long-standing and have emerged organically from both within secular and religious feminist movements in Arab societies. This mobilisation has been channelled into strong resistance and opposition movements before, during and after the Arab Spring Uprisings in spite of authoritarian regimes (Chandra, 2018). Second, this change achieved through mobilisation has been sustained and often in tandem with religious influences. Much of the opposition in Egypt and Tunisia has been informed by the religious framework of political Islam both directly through organisations like the Ikhwan and Ennahda and indirectly through influences such as Islamic modernism and more recently Islamic feminism (Chandra, 2018). This confounds the notion that Gulf countries do not witness the same degree of change because of their religious orthodoxy or conservativeness.

Third, the nature of economically and socially "liberalising" forces and regimes in the Gulf need closer scrutiny as they are able to control and contain social unrest far better than military regimes. This has a few reasons, the most obvious one is the economic aspect. Countries like Saudi Arabia, Qatar and Bahrain have been able to minimise and limit resistance and protests partially on account of the legitimacy of economic deliverance, facilitated by their oil wealth. Remarkably, the little opposition that has been seen has come from marginalised segments of the population like the Shia minority community who have faced severe economic challenges owing to their status vis-à-vis the state. For the most part, the regime's role as a provider through social benefits, fine infrastructure etc. have been an important source of legitimacy and validation of their rule. However, this wealth and its benefits to the citizens, and therefore the regimes, have been waning in recent years.

What emerges in this study is the unique organisation that monarchies like Saudi Arabia have been deeply systemically entrenched in these societies. This is not to say they have roots in society, on the contrary, they are quite divorced and alienated from society. However, they are deeply entrenched in the social psyche, memory and belief based on religion (Cooke, 2014). The priorities of society and the objectives of social mobilisation are hence limited to more specific and immediate concerns such as women's right to drive, new work laws or the question of segregation in the workplace. It is important to note that these societies including the youth do not seek to overturn or undo the traditional social ethos which is quite conservative, through reform. Rather they attempt to bring about change within it. This is mostly outcome-driven policy change through an approach of negotiation. The emergence of women on the cultural scene in elite circles in museums, etc., or segregation in the workplace cited as instances of bringing more women into the labour force point to this more cautious and limited mobilisation.

Further, there is little opposition or criticism (in the limited space allowed for it) against the monarchical rulers themselves, or their right to rule. The protests for democratisation that have been witnessed in other parts of West Asia, have been marginal and successfully contained in the Gulf. Traditional kinship and religious allegiance to the tribal leader, the patriarch or the guardian of the holiest sites of Islam persist (Cooke, 2014). Notions of liberty and what it amounts to are both culturally and politically relative. They are subject to the political, economic as well as cultural landscapes within which they are engaged with, and strategies of engaging with them.

What this implies is not an absence of the understanding of political liberty or economic rights, but different and ingenious ways of engagement with political subjects and issues. The life of the civil society in the Gulf cannot be compared with other societies in the region. This is primarily because typical methods of civil society activism do not apply to the socio-political terrain of the Gulf. In comparison to other societies, fields of visibility are restricted in the way that these methods or strategies (such as physical embodiment on the public square) do not appeal to people nor do they have much space to exist. On the flip side, unconventional and unsuspected spaces of socialisation have been accessed and mobilised for a long time and quite actively so. These comprise of newer spaces opened through social media and individual voices as well as places in a more traditional social landscape where they have organically opened. Socialisation in these spaces has mostly been through the family unit and familial-kinship ties rather than outside of them. Countries like Kuwait and more recently Saudi Arabia are prime examples of this kind of social and consequently political mobilisation (Cooke 2014 and Weiner 2016). These take the shape of the traditional *majlis* which is primarily a male-dominated space, but with family gatherings, one sees off-shoots of these which are solely inhabited by women. Sasson's work partially reflects how women's gatherings in the traditional spaces often take up political subjects directly pertaining to them, however much of current socialisation occurring in traditional discursive spaces remains undocumented.

With changing times and expansion as well partial shift in women's roles, the discursive traditions in these spaces have also expanded to varying degrees. In other places, they remained closed or closely monitored in terms of what issues can be discussed. One such example is given by Muna Al Gurg when she recounts

> … for at least a decade, I'd regularly see one particular woman at these functions, usually weddings, only to later find out at a business mentoring session that not only does she run a successful women's social enterprise but she also won the region's Acumen Fund Award for Social Impact. I had no idea. (Al Gurg, 2018, p. 28)

These unique spaces and their potential for social transformations is not reflected in most mainstream narratives on women and feminist politics in the region. A key problem with the kind of narratives produced about feminist and gender politics in the Gulf is that rather than highlight, they often obfuscate the actual movements for social mobilisation in the region. This is caused by the fact that there is a severe lacuna with regard to anthropological studies that capture these ingenious and organic spaces within which social mobilisation actually occurs. Given the strong biases regarding the family unit in classical liberal feminist views, these spaces remain unexplored while they continue to play a crucial role in informing politics within the Gulf.

On the flip side, the claim to bring more radical change has come from the younger leadership, especially that of Muhammad bin Salman, striving to break free from the image of the previous leadership. The preservation of pre-Islamic heritage and attempts to redefine the identity of the Saudi nation are a part of these efforts.[3] It is questionable how much this change is felt on the ground as most of it is driven towards an international audience of major players, primarily the United States under the new Biden administration and for the diversification of the Saudi economy (Vohra, 2021).

Limits of Percolating Change

The nature of shifts at the societal level are difficult to trace because patriarchal social attitudes prevail. Different countries present their own peculiarities at the social and political levels. For instance, Qatar presents unique peculiarities in both its regional diplomacy as well as its domestic rule. Mobilisation and democratisation discourse produced through agencies like Al-Jazeera is deeply tied to the 'soft' exporting of religion through them. While Al Jazeera opened a freewheeling style of debate on numerous contentious issues in the Arab world, it has also been accused of promoting a pro-Sunni, anti-Shia Islamist discourse (Ibish, 2016). Simultaneously it has prevaricated any criticism of the Qatari leadership. On the whole, the leadership still continues to maintain tight control over the population. Gulf countries also benefit greatly from having a sizeable expatriate population. The ability to discern between the working class and its own citizenry enables the state to retain control without seeming illegitimate to its own citizens. One of the spaces where women's participation has been instrumental in Qatar and Abu-Dhabi is in the cultural renaissance and particularly art entrepreneurship with the emergence of museums that are working to curate and preserve Islamic arts in conjunction with national identities (see Cooke, 2014).

However, this is mostly limited to women from the royal family and cannot be seen as a society-wide movement for cultural and economic agency. Further, it is interesting to explore the ways in which this project for cultural renaissance ties in with the state narratives of the role of the monarchy. Simultaneously, one sees the emergence of a carefully curated, guarded kind of revival of women's role in important positions, often helmed by women members of the royal families. One area in which women's participation has notably risen has been cultural revival and the projection of these countries as a cultural hub with a renewed interest in Islamic art, etc. (Lorch, 2018).

Sample surveys conducted by online sources have shown that some of the concerns of women are common to other Muslims and non-Muslim societies such as the need to balance work and family life and the impact of marriage and childbearing on women's careers. Women have been known to make choices between child-rearing and their careers, often re-joining the labour force at a later stage after fulfilling these obligations (Nureldine, 2020). Further, while some changes may be introduced legally, they take far longer to percolate through society as social attitudes remain rooted in traditional thinking. For instance, segregation in education and employment is preferred by some women as it prevents potential social alienation and especially with regard to the 'marriageability' quotient (Salem and Yount, 2019).

Even though new laws have brought about greater representation for women and higher levels of education (still not equal to men and thus common to other countries), it is some of these social barriers which are far more difficult to traverse in the lived experience of everyday life. As stated by Al Gurg (2018),

> … (M)en's opinions still matter a great deal in a patriarchal society. Social pressures weigh on the decisions women make and therefore shape the direction in which their lives take. This reality reduces choice for women in much more powerful ways than it does for men. It's common, for example, for an academically gifted woman to study in her home country even when her less studious brother goes abroad to attend a top university.

Social media plays an important role therefore in enabling the overcoming of some of these social barriers, due to the ease of access. As certain aspects of the state are liberalised to expand economies, these spaces are opening further, providing an important platform for individual expression, creativity and entrepreneurship. Digitisation and soft skills have become an instrumental pathway to economic empowerment for women in the post-oil economy. Their public role as individuals, professionals and citizens seem to garner far more attention, representation and acknowledgement as their potential to contribute to this shifting economic context is now being explored. This in turn has created newer challenges for digital users, especially women. Women with online profiles are frequently harassed, threatened and their digital identities are frequently targeted. Those who choose to make their identities known in the digital space face the additional brunt of social attitudes that continue to view women's roles as being restricted to the domestic spheres. The states are increasingly concerned with issues of cyber-crime and harassment and are seeking newer strategies for containing it (see Al-Nusrawi, 2021). Yet the need for effective legislation and online vigilance remains an urgent one.

The segregation of sexes in the new workspaces in Saudi Arabia is another such issue that posits both challenges as well as opportunities. While the tendency of liberal feminism may be to read this approach as highly regressive, does it not present more avenues for women to be able to exercise their right to work? The possibilities presented by such solutions are also subject to the willingness of both the regime and employers to adapt to an increasingly mixed workforce and provide requisite infrastructural support for them. Yet the opportunities created by such a system cannot be denied. With the increasing digitisation of work and the current scenario of the pandemic forcing both men and women to work from home, employment opportunities for women with soft skills are much higher. At the same time, they may be able to avoid some of the challenges of navigating social and religious norms of conduct posed to those looking for economic mobility.

While religion and social framework are certainly important factors determining the spaces available to women, many of these are exclusively issues of more gendered spaces akin to other parts of the world. The casting of women in limited familial roles as wives and mothers is not unique to this region but is also seen across South Asia and parts of Southeast Asia. Rather than presenting images of 'Muslim women that need saving', they present the gendered socio-political spaces, narratives and lived experiences that pervade different cultures. There is a fine line between reading the cultural specificity of their predicaments and attributing such problems entirely to them. One has to be discerning of the economic status, educational background and individual choices as much as the religious-political climate within which women operate.

Fractured Narratives of Queer Politics

Joseph Massad's thesis on attitudes to queerness is still significant in that global forces and globalised Western liberal assertions of homosexuality have created a conflict with questions of religious permissibility in a society where homosexuality and homoeroticism have existed far more organically for centuries (Massad, 2007). This is partly the result of exotification of the other through the misrepresentation of eroticism in art, literature and other cultural productions, especially in the colonial subjectivities produced to dominate culture and knowledge production on sexuality. And partly it is also the result of the subsequent decades of the West playing the saviour in educating the exotic other about ideas of liberty and right of sexual orientation as enforceable by the modern state. This introduction of the legal-rational aspect has created a conflict as Sharia edicts do not allow the justification of homosexuality (Massad, 2007). Hence homosexuality and queerness are not new issues, rather the legal-rational conflict arising from modern law and statehood have jeopardised the place it organically inhabited in society.

In the modern era, this problem has been further exacerbated to another level. As an issue of human rights and international relations, it only serves to further polarise the current situation about the position of these societies vis-à-vis international pressure. Domestically this polarisation has translated into the rise of the police state and increasing disciplining and punishing of queer citizens as well as travellers. Human Rights Watch reported the case of Mohamed al-Bokari who travelled to Saudi Arabia on foot after being targeted and threatened in Yemen for his online activism and gender non-conformity. In Saudi Arabia, a video posted by him in support of LGBTQ rights prompted outrage from both the authorities and the public at large. He was subsequently arrested, charged with promoting homosexuality and "imitating women" and sentenced to 10 years in prison, facing deportation upon release. Held in solitary confinement for weeks, he was subjected to a forced anal examination and beatings compelling him to repeatedly confess his sexual orientation (Human Rights Watch, 2021).

The most recent example of such activities of the police state has been the crackdown on homosexual men in Gulf countries like Kuwait (Toumi, 2017). Time and again the announcement of such policies are used to re-emphasise the religious doctrine upheld by the state, and occasionally to assert independence in defiance of international pressures. But the state-level intolerance for queerness has persisted through various policies for decades since the creation of the modern borders.

The paroxysms of transcending from a traditional conservative society with closed attitudes to religion and culture to modern, modernised economic power centre (especially in softs skills and technological production) have been most keenly felt by queer citizens and non-citizens (for a detailed report see Human Rights Watch, 2018). The back and forth on questions of opening of state attitudes to women's public role which affords possibilities to push through for women have not been mirrored in the case of queer identities. In fact, intolerance to queerness and homosexuality have only become more institutionalised in the course of the socio-political flux caused by the limited orchestrated modernisation (Labanieh, 2021). This is seen in discussions on policy and legislation such as travel bans and proposed homosexuality tests in various Gulf countries (Sieczkowski, 2013). Not all of these debates have translated into new laws, but they clearly demonstrate the growing anxiety of Gulf states vis-à-vis homosexuality.

The state-enforced criminalisation of homosexuality has pushed queer identity and people further beyond the purview of public space and public sphere. Hence homosexuality exists but illegally in the private space, covered in a veil. The creates highly problematic conditions for queer people, leading to physical, psychological and emotional trauma along with a crisis of civil liberty. The forced silence produced by this veil covers up and silences narratives of these troubled lived experiences of queerness in public discourse. This in turn impedes any possibilities for the negotiation or even recognition of the rights of the queer people. Thus, in contrast to women who have some limited space for agitation, queer identities are simply not allowed to exist in the modern discursive tradition in the Gulf. Intersecting with other practices, experiences and social issues, this veil shrouds acts of violence, aggression and exploitation in a power relation between individuals where members of the affluent classes, in particular, can potentially exploit or abuse someone and get away with it through the function of privilege.[4]

The backlash extends to discursive fields with the increased use of pejorative terms like "*boyat*" which is an Arabisation of the English word 'boy' and is used to refer to transgender women or women who do not conform to the typically prescribed feminine behaviour and body language (Al-Bargi, 2014). The repression of homosexuality has been exacerbated by the perceived threat of extra-normative behaviour and has consequently seen an increased policing of bodies. Such instances include the criminalisation of "imitating members of the opposite sex" by Kuwait in 2007 which led to arbitrary arrests, detention and torture and sexual harassment at the hands of police authorities (Human Rights Watch, 2011). In 2009 Dubai introduced the "Excuse Me, I am a Girl" awareness campaign, cautioning women against the dangers of masculinisation and educating them on felinity and feminine behaviour (Human Rights Watch, 2011).

Such policing of outwardly behaviour and physical body represents deep anxieties societies which constantly impose hetero-normative familial social structures and hierarchies. The case of Saudi Arabia is pertinent.

> In fact, most arrests have been for "gay weddings" and boisterous parties. Other arrests took place when behaviour became too public, such as the case of the Saudi man who appeared in a YouTube video behaving suggestively and gender-inappropriately in 2010. This indicates that the greater fear is the perceived challenge to orthodox practices and gender roles, family structures and "cultural values" rather than homosexual behaviour *per se*. (Human Rights Watch, 2011)

The crackdown on non-conformist behaviour (also extending to the virtual world) has been a direct attack on the *visibility* of resistance and non-conformativism. As morality, debauchery and prostitution laws are employed to target any outward expression of non-conformist sexual identities or behaviours, the field of visibility becomes completely policed into subjugation. More than the direct assault on homosexuality it is the absolute control over this field of visibility which prevents any resistance or push back against orthodoxy. This reflects the anxieties of the patriarchal state in confronting any perceived threat, going far beyond concerns of religious conformity. As is evident from this discussion, they are constant enforcement of not just religious edicts, but more so the traditional hetero-normative behaviour which does not tolerate or allow for any scope of difference. This is yet another way in which the state ensures total control on the social psyche, wherein even if clandestine behaviour may find space to exist, the mainstream physical spaces and virtual spaces, and therefore the public sphere at large are completely policed.

Conclusion

With regard to changes in law pertaining to women and gender, the long struggle that has served to create awareness and a gradual albeit partial shift in attitudes promises to provide a supportive framework. Even so, the fact that decisions of the ruling dispensations across the Gulf are subject to the current political climate, poses a pertinent threat to the limited relaxation of spaces for gender debates to emerge. This can manifest at both the level of policy formulation and laws as well as at the level of the discursive spaces for organic and newer narratives to emerge.

The possibility of governments rescinding certain liberties pertaining to women in the Gulf along with the resistance and criticism to change from religious and social orthodoxy cast severe doubts over how much things are truly changing. More importantly, they raise the question of whether these changes are sustainable. The fear of rolling back of reforms as in the case of Bahrain and Kuwait (Mufarreh, 2019) is always imminent. This is subject to the political inclinations of the individual leaders like MbS as well as the willingness to appease the orthodox segments of society, especially the *ulema*.

It is important to note that in spite of all attempts by the current young leadership to veer the country away from an exclusive and primary religious identity to a more diverse and comprehensive one, the religious foundations of the Saudi state continue to remain very strong and deeply entrenched. Consequently, the *ulema* continues to hold immense power and possible sway over the ruling dispensation. If current experiments with reform do not yield projected outcomes for the economy and in terms of foreign investments and an enhanced position for Saudi Arabia vis-à-vis the international community, it can relapse into the old system of relying almost entirely on the sanction of the *ulema* for its legitimacy. In the absence of the security provided by oil wealth in the previous decades, this could assume even greater importance.

The question of narratives that truly reflect changes on the ground and their future scope, the challenges are greater. The limited space and limited voices of dissent or criticism are the most important indicators of the limits of change. Narratives are scant, and polarised in nature, reporting schizophrenic realities of life in the Gulf kingdoms. Modernisation and socio-political reform imposed by the state invariably results in the emergence of state-sponsored narratives. Further, the situation regarding the more contentious issues of trans identity and homosexuality poses peculiar problems of their own. As discussed above, it is more the outwardly appearance and expression of non-conformist bodies and sexualities that produce anxieties in the hyper-masculine patriarchal state. Subsequently, it is the *fields of visibility* that constitute an important aspect of the discursive spaces mentioned that the state is concerned with controlling. This has been the case in the past decade, where the leadership in Saudi Arabia as well as other Gulf countries has monopolised the currents of change and claimed all responsibility for them. Further, the situation regarding the more contentious issues of trans identity and homosexuality poses peculiar problems of their own.

Thus, the more local discursive shifts that emanate at the granular level of the family, the *majlis* and the informal spaces of socialisation remain obscured by these larger narratives. In the absence of socio-anthropological research at this granular level, the narratives pertaining to gender remain fractured. Further, the hermeneutical, scholarly and political biases rooted in orientalist perceptions which inform engagements with these narratives from the international community form an additional layer of obscurity as local spaces and movements and voices they contain are not sufficiently acknowledged. Unconventional mediums like social media have traversed these obstacles to a degree, however, they have also seen the rise of problems of maintaining online identities in addition to the ever-present threat of the surveillance state. This is especially problematic as the impact of this particularly for women can be felt not just in concrete disciplinary or policing measures that the state might undertake, but more so in the social marginalisation and exclusion that accrue to the patriarchal structure of society. Limited economic mobilisation without changing the social underpinnings can only partly addresses this problem.

Notes

1. The male guardianship law is still prevalent in Saudi Arabia and Qatar, and is one of the most criticised aspects of Gulf politics as a primary cause for marginalisation of and discrimination against women. Recently, there has been some relaxation in the guardianship laws in Saudi Arabia with women being allowed to drive and obtain passports and travel internationally without any male guardianship. However, social and political activists have criticised these changes as superficial and ineffective, especially as several of the activists who protested against the various aspects of this law, remained imprisoned and faced state harassment even after such reforms are introduced.
2. Vlogs or video blogs like this of Sukkari Life demonstrate this point in the way they document the everyday life and challenges of a young Saudi woman which resonate with young viewers across cultures as evidenced by reaction to videos like this: https://www.youtube.com/watch?v=IscUGIX-56Q&ab_channel=SukkariLife (accessed 30 December 2021) or that of multiple women sharing their experiences in countries like Saudi Arabia seen on BBC Trending at: https://www.youtube.com/watch?v=E8M87NnZ8vU&ab_channel=BBCTrending, accessed on 30 December 2021.
3. Under reforms pushed by MBS, the kingdom has allocated US$ 1 billion to preserve its (pre-Islamic) heritage, in a move to promote a more moderate view of Islam. See Kalin 2018.
4. This is captured in Sasson's work, which partially exposed the nature of the excesses of members of the monarchical family and regime, as well as the means and strategies they employed to get away with flouting the law and/or appeasing the *Mutaw'wa*.

References

Abousleiman, Issam (2019), "Women in the Gulf Countries: Perceptions and Realities," *Arab Voices*, World Bank Blogs, November 10, https://blogs.worldbank.org/arabvoices/women-gulf-countries-perceptions-and-reality, accessed on September 17, 2021.

Abu-Lughod, Lila (2013), *Do Muslim Women Need Saving?*, Cambridge, Massachusetts and London: Harvard University Press.

Akeel, Maha (2021), "Women Politicians on the Rise But More Must Be Done," Arab News, https://www.arabnews.com/node/1838676, accessed on November 8, 2021.

Al Alwai, Dalya (2017), "Gender Equality Over a Barrel: How the Gulf's Oil Dependence Holds Back Women," International Peace Institute: The Global Observatory, June 9, https://theglobalobservatory.org/2017/06/middle-east-gender-saudi-arabia-vision-2030/, accessed on September 23, 2021.

Al-Bargi, Abdullah (2014), "Some Gender Issues Are Pretty Complicated," Arab News, June 3, https://www.arabnews.com/node/581666, accessed on October 4, 2021.

Al Gurg, Muna (2018), "The UAE Is Making Strides in Closing the Gender Gap," *Gender (Im)Balance in Gulf Societies, Gulf Affairs*, Oxford Gulf and Arabian Peninsula Studies Forum, https://www.oxgaps.org/files/gulf_affairs_spring_2018_full_issue.pdf, accessed on September 12, 2021.

Al-Nusrawi, Sukaina (2021), "Combating Cyber Violence Against Women and Girls: An Overview of the Legislative and Policy Reforms in the Aarab Region," in Jane Bailey, Asher Flynn, and Nicola Henry (eds.), *The Emerald International Handbook of Technology-Facilitated Violence and Abuse* (Emerald Studies In Digital Crime, Technology and Social Harms), Emerald Publishing Limited, Bingley, pp. 493-512.

Bayat, Asef (2013), *Life as Politics: How Ordinary People Change the Middle East*, Stanford: Stanford University Press.

Chandra, Priyanka (2018), "Women in the Arab Spring- Participation and Outcomes: The Case of Egypt," in Bansidhar Pradhan (ed.), *West Asia in a Changing World: The Emerging Regional Architecture and India*, New Delhi: Academic Foundation Publications.

Cooke, Miriam (2014), *Tribal Modern: Branding New Nations*, California: University of California Press.

Human Rights Watch (2011), "The Gulf's Gender Anxiety: Moral Panic Over Transgender Men and Women Is Symptomatic of the Gulf's Problem With Shifting Gender Roles," https://www.hrw.org/news/2011/07/07/gulfs-gender-anxiety, accessed on October 4, 2021.

Human Rights Watch (2016), "Boxed In: Women and Saudi Arabia's Male Guardianship System," https://www.hrw.org/report/2016/07/16/boxed/women-and-saudi-arabias-male-guardianship-system#, accessed on November 2, 2021.

Human Rights Watch (2018), "Audacity in Adversity: LGBT Activism in the Middle East and North Africa," https://www.hrw.org/report/2018/04/16/audacity-adversity/lgbt-activism-middle-east-and-north-africa, accessed on December 29, 2021.

Human Rights Watch (2021), "Clean the Streets of Faggots: Digital Targeting of LGBT People by Middle East/North Africa Governments," *The Conversationalist*, https://www.hrw.org/news/2021/08/04/clean-streets-faggots, accessed on October 1, 2021.

Ibish, Hussein (2016), "Why America Turned Off Al Jazeera," The Arab Gulf States Institute in Washington, February 19, https://agsiw.org/why-america-turned-off-al-jazeera/, accessed on December 31, 2021.

Kalin, Stephen (2018), "Saudi Bid to Protect Pre-Islamic Sites Upends Religious Dictates," Reuters, July 9, https://www.reuters.com/article/us-saudi-tourism-idUSKBN1JZ1PH, accessed on November 2, 2021.

Qiblawi, Tamara and Fox, Kara (2021), "Saudi Women's Rights Activist Loujain al-Hathloul Released From Prison," CNN, February 11, https://edition.cnn.com/2021/02/10/middleeast/hathloul-saudi-released-intl/index.html, accessed on September 17, 2021.

Labanieh, Aya (2021), "Queer and Arab," *Aeon*, September 7, https://aeon.co/essays/was-there-no-room-for-the-queer-individual-in-arab-history, accessed on December 29, 2021.

Massad, Joseph (2007), *Desiring Arabs*, Chicago: University of Chicago Press.

Mufarreh, Saadia (2019), "Gulf Women Have Come a Long Way," Al Jazeera, March 8, https://www.aljazeera.com/opinions/2019/3/8/gulf-women-have-come-a-long-way, accessed on August 29, 2021.

Nureldine, Fayez (2020), "Women in Arab Countries Find Themselves Torn Between Opportunity and Tradition," *The Conversation*, February 11, https://theconversation.com/women-in-arab-countries-find-themselves-torn-between-opportunity-and-tradition-130460, accessed on September 1, 2021.

Pratt, Nicola (2013), "Women, Girls and the Arab Spring," Warwick Knowledge Centre Archive, June, https://warwick.ac.uk/newsandevents/knowledge-archive/socialscience/arab-spring/, accessed on December 30, 2021.

Regan, Helen (2015), "Two Saudi Women Who Were Detained for Driving Have Been Freed," *Time*, February 13, https://time.com/3708599/saudi-women-driving-ban/, accessed on September 15, 2021.

Salem, Rania and Yount, Kathryn M. (2019), "Structural Accommodations of Patriarchy: Women and Workplace Gender Segregation in Qatar," *Gender, Work & Organization*, vol. 26, no. 4, pp. 501-519.

Sieczkowski, Cavan (2013), "Gulf Countries Propose Test to Detect Gays, Ban Them From Entering," *Huffpost*, September 10, https://www.huffpost.com/entry/gulf-countries-detect-gays_n_4065927, accessed on December 29, 2021.

Lorch, Danna (2018), "The Women Taking Charge in the Gulf's Rising Art Scene," *The Art Newspaper*, December 12, https://www.theartnewspaper.com/2018/12/12/the-women-taking-charge-in-the-gulfs-rising-art-scene, accessed on December 29, 2021.

Toumi, Habib (2017), "Kuwait Deports 76 Gay Men in Crackdown," Gulf News, August 7, https://gulfnews.com/world/gulf/kuwait/kuwait-deports-76-gay-men-in-crackdown-1.2070054, accessed on December 29, 2021.

Vohra, Anchal (2021), "MBS Is Desperately Trying to Rehabilitate Himself Since Biden Won the Elections," Observer Research Foundation, January 31, https://www.orfonline.org/expert-speak/mbs-is-desperately-trying-to-rehabilitate-himself-since-biden-won-the-elections/, accessed on December 31, 2021.

Wadud, Amina (1999), *Quran and Woman: Rereading the Sacred Text From a Woman's Perspective*, New York and Oxford: Oxford University Press.

Weiner, Scott J. (2016), "Kinship Politics in the Gulf Arab States," The Arab Gulf States Institute in Washington, July 22, https://agsiw.org/wp-content/uploads/2016/07/Weiner_Kinship_Web.pdf, accessed on December 30, 2021.

11. Art as an Emerging Field for the Young GCC Women

Lakshmi Priya

What is so wonderful about the cultural sector is that it all boils down to talent. Talent, and not gender, is what should define you in the art world.

—Noura Al-Kaabi, the UAE Minister of Culture and Knowledge Development (Greenwald, 2018)

Introduction

Young GCC women are making careers in art and entertainment and are emerging as professionals while balancing domestic responsibilities with élan. Numerous factors have encouraged women to delve into these professions due to social and political reforms in these countries, sweeping changes at familial and societal levels and individual exposure led by access to social media. At a deeper level, the financial support provided by the state, economic and moral support of the family and demand for art and entertainment leading to a possibility of stable career provide a cushion for the GCC women daring to enter the profession.

The presence of women in art and entertainment is not a new phenomenon, even though the number of the GCC women taking this up as a full-time profession has increased in the last two decades. The Fertile Crescent region has produced several female artists over time, but this is the awakening for the GCC women. The GCC countries are implementing reforms in tandem with the changing times, and this is encouraging more young women to experiment in choosing their professions and break away from the set mould of opting for either teaching or medicine. In addition, the possibility of sharing their art with the larger society and reaching out to male and female audience through social media has acted as an enabler.

Gender reforms in GCC

The reforms led by the GCC countries have enhanced women's political and economic inclusion while improving women's access to education, health care and employment. For instance, due to the Saudi reforms, 30 women were appointed to the Saudi Shura Council in 2013, and 17 women were appointed to municipal seats in 2015 for the first time. Moreover, according to the *World Bank's Annual Report on Women, Business and Law 2020* (The World Bank, 2020), the Kingdom of Saudi Arabia (KSA) was the top reformer while UAE and Bahrain figured among the top ten reformers based on eight indicators of mobility, workplace, pay, marriage, parenthood, entrepreneurship, assets and pension. In addition, Saudi Arabia granted freedom of movement to women, invalidated the need for permission from a male guardian to travel abroad or to obtain a passport, amended the Civil Status Law and allowed a woman to choose where to live.

Riyadh introduced new legal amendments protecting women in the workforce from discrimination, prohibited employers from dismissing a woman during pregnancy and maternity leave, and equalised the retirement age for women and men at 60 years, consequently extending women's working lives, earnings and contributions. More importantly, the Kingdom also encouraged women's entrepreneurship by prohibiting gender-based discrimination in accessing financial services. The reforms are in tandem with the long-term development programme of the Saudi Crown Prince Mohammad bin Salman and are a part of *Vision 2030*'s goal of increasing women's labour force participation from 22 per cent to 30 per cent (Vision 2030, KSA, n.d.).

Similarly, the UAE allowed married women to apply for a passport without the written consent of their husbands, prohibited gender-based discrimination in employment, lifted restrictions on women from working at night, allowed women to work in agriculture, mining, manufacturing and energy that were considered as dangerous occupations for women (The World Bank Group, 2020). The gender-specific reforms were carried out by the Gender Balance Council, the federal agency responsible for implementing initiatives to enhance women's representation in the country's private and public sectors.

Saudi Arabia, UAE and Bahrain introduced the provisions for criminal penalties for perpetrators of sexual harassment in employment and allowed women to be recognised as heads of their households. In addition, Dubai hosted the Women Entrepreneurs Finance Initiative (We-Fi) MENA Regional Summit in February 2020 as part of its Global Women's Forum, while UAE and Saudi Arabia have been key partners to We-Fi, pledging US$ 100 million to the initiative. These reforms provide women with the required space to grow, prosper and make a name in the male-dominated public spaces.

Art and State Policies

The GCC countries have been engaged in promoting art, as they aim for economic diversification and boost tourism. The Saudi government has been supporting the creative endeavours of women as part of its *Vision 2030* strategy. The vision states that culture is indispensable to the quality of life and the country intends to enhance the quality and quantity of its cultural activities. Culture Minister Prince Badr bin Abdullah bin Mohammed bin Farhan Al-Saud stated that the ministry would adopt a collaborative approach with the Saudi creative artists and said they are the jewels of the Saudi cultural sphere (Saud, 2021). The ministry declared 2020 as the year of calligraphy and launched a virtual training programme for the music industry.

The Saudi film commission launched the filmmakers' programme for training amateurs and professionals in filmmaking. It organises exhibitions and promotes artists by including their creations; *From Within* is one such exhibition for contemporary art (Ministry of Culture, KSA, 2019). In addition, the Saudi government grants scholarships, grants, and awards for emerging artists and organises competitions regularly. Saudi Arabia returned to the Venice Biennale in 2019 after a gap of eight years, and in 2020, it partnered with the California-based group Desert X to organise an art show. The government fellowships enabled women to pursue their passion for art. Danya Alhamrani is a managing partner in the Saudi company *Eggdancer Productions*, which focuses on producing documentaries. She said that earlier women applied for grants and programmes internationally due to a lack of national fellowships (Tashkandi, 2020).

The Saudi government has recognised that Saudi women's skills and expertise in art and culture are important for the industry's prosperity. As a result, Noor Al-Dabbagh, the founder of *Banafsajeel*, a curatorial platform, was appointed head of visual arts for the General Culture Authority in February 2018. She is responsible for expanding visual arts events across Saudi Arabia, including supporting education and training programmes and developing regulatory frameworks for exhibitions and events.

In addition to the art-centric state policies like in Saudi Arabia, open immigration policies boosted the emerging art field in the UAE. It became the first Gulf country to have a permanent pavilion at the Venice Biennial art exhibition in 2009. Dubai has transformed into a centre for commercial art, Abu Dhabi has invested in international, large-scale collaborations, and Sharjah has connected local creators to an international art scene (Smithsonian, n.d.). UAE Cultural Advisor Zaki Nusseibeh mentioned that the Emirate's transformation had become an enabler for the young people and a magnet for a cosmopolitan community. UAE has become a multifaceted art hub as it hosts the micro-city of The Louvre Abu Dhabi, a community-focused cultural space called Warehouse 421, Sharjah Biennial, Sharjah Museum of Islamic Civilisation, Art fair of Dubai, Dubai International Film Festival and Dubai Art Opera (Smithsonian, n.d.). To send a message of solidarity, the UAE Ministry of Foreign Affairs acquired pieces worth more than US$ 400,000 created by emerging and established Emirati artists (UAE Ministry of Foreign Affairs and International Cooperation, 2020).

Similarly, the Omani Society for Fine Arts, a part of the Ministry of Culture, Sports and Youth, supports artists and strives to provide an international platform (The Omani Society for Fine Arts, n.d.). The Omani artists can benefit from training courses, competitions, seminars and workshops specialised in various arts areas. Currently, women artists outnumber male members of society. Many Omani women have been involved in international exhibitions such as Brazil (2015), Brunei Darussalam (2014), Russia (2013), Zanzibar (2012) (UNESCO, 2016). In the same vein, the Kuwaiti Minister of Information and Youth Affairs,

Sheikh Salman Sabah Al-Salem Al-Humoud Al-Sabah, said that Kuwait is keen on honouring artists through incentives and awards (Saad, 2013). The National Council for Culture, Art and Letters oversees the art institutions in the country and organises various art events regularly.

Bahrain's support of fine arts through such events as Bahrain Fine Arts Exhibition and fine arts societies and galleries like *Al-Bareh* created a strong synergy and solid foundation for arts to move forward. Moreover, with the patronage of Prime Minister Prince Khalifa bin Salman Al-Khalifa, Bahrain intends to establish itself as the art centre of the Gulf (Bahrain Authority for Culture and Antiquities, 2021). The Ministry of Culture and Information has conceived an ambitious cultural agenda to develop new institutional infrastructures by building museums for archaeological sites. It organised the 'Spring of culture' art event, *Um Kulthum*—The fourth Pyramid exhibition in collaboration with Institut du Monde Arabe (Paris) and conceived mega-structures in 2008-09 when the art scene in other countries was still unfolding. It encouraged independent groups like Elham to express creative talents by organising monthly cultural gatherings in Manama (Fattouh, 2009). In line with the Bahrain Economic *Vision 2030*, the public authority of Tamkeen emphasised the importance of the creative economy (Tamkeen, 2019).

Interestingly, Qatar is the world's biggest art buyer and aims to become the cultural capital of the Middle East and a hub for regional cultural tourism (Qatar Living.com, n.d.). Doha intends to use the heavy influx of people to Qatari shores for the 2022 FIFA World Cup. Qatar is witnessing a burgeoning arts culture, with Doha Film Institute developing and promoting regional and international filmmakers, Qatar Philharmonic Orchestra bringing symphonic music to the region and public and private galleries organising regular exhibits. The art phenomenon in Qatar is enriched by the *Mathaf Arab Museum of Modern Art*, *Sheikh Faisal Bin Qassim Al Thani Museum* and *Al-Riwaq Gallery*, among others.

Women in Art through the Female Gaze

The art movement in Saudi Arabia has a short history; nevertheless, Lama Al-Badna explored the social, political, and economic context through which Saudi women were portrayed in the art. She studied 111 artworks produced by Saudi artists from 1969 to 2019 and opined that Saudi modernisation was reflected in the women's portrayal in art (Obaid, 2021). Despite women in traditional costumes being a central theme of artworks during the study period, the image of the women differed in accordance with ongoing social change, strongly influenced by regional and local events. She says that the artist in the 1960s used to paint portraits of real women; however, later depictions were based on memory and folklore. The obsession with folklore was either an attempt to circumvent women's absence from public places or escape modernity. Secondly, from the 1980s until 2000, the Saudi women's faces were painted blurry as female artists were absent from the media and cultural scene and male artists had minimal interaction with the opposite gender. However, from 2010 onward, Saudi women boldly expressed themselves and became more direct in addressing their struggles and problems with society; they also shifted from the passive expression of their own sorrows to addressing issues related to their reality.

The right to drive for women has been a constant theme in paintings of Saudi female artists. For example, Taghreed Al-Bugshi portrayed a woman driving a motorcycle with a plate with the letters of the word "drive" in Arabic before women won the right to drive. However, after 2018 she painted women in the driving seat with their license plates showing the word MLK, meaning king and AZM, meaning determination reflecting the power and control provided by driving rights (Obaid, 2021). In another painting, she depicted a woman driving to the moon, symbolising the unlimited possibilities. Another artist Skna Hassan painted a woman with a number plate on the door, symbolising her wish to drive and a woman ready to be behind wheels feeling like a queen. Finally, artist Noor Al-Saif painted the Saudi women's frustration of not driving by depicting a woman trying to fill the tank of her toy car at a gas station in 2017 (Aldosari, 2020). Sara Abu Abdallah started as a painter but moved on to photography, film and spontaneous performance. In the video installation *Saudi Automobile*, she painted the wreckage of a crashed pink car and then sat at the driver's seat, claiming ownership of a position the Kingdom restricted to men (Abdallah, 2011).

Issues related to women empowerment, social justice and nature are constantly depicted by female artists. Manal Al-Dowayan has been protesting the existing traditional social norms and political challenges through her art. She worked as a creative director within an oil company and produced art for seven years until becoming a full-time artist in 2010. Her work mostly engages with photographs and installations and has feminist messages at its core. She is internationally acclaimed for her work, including *Suspended Together* and *Light from the Middle East*, which were part of an exhibition at the Victoria & Albert Museum in London. Her installation titled *Suspended Together* presents an assembly of interlocked fibreglass doves covered in permission slip stickers, a poignant representation of Saudi women who needed consent signed by their husbands or male guardians to be able to travel until recently (Singh, 2021).

An interior designer and painter, Samiah Khashoggi, is the founder of the women artist's group *Saudiaat* and *Midrar*, an art hub to enhance women's aesthetic experiences and awareness of contemporary art practices. Her work represents the social issues while emphasising the absence of women from public spaces. For instance, her artwork titled *Mashi* or patches portrays the issue of living with unresolved problems and carrying the burden alone in a quest to present a perfect exterior. She has used multimedia and collage technique to create multiple layers depicting unresolved issues. A subgroup of the series shows a broader man, covering a major portion of the canvas while the woman is thinner with more patches. Cleverly, she has avoided painting the face and expressions as the focus is directed on the body and the hidden scars (Khan, 2014). Culture, women and nature are the sources of inspiration for the acclaimed artist.

Similarly, Hanna Hajjar, an artist and the only female political cartoonist in the Kingdom, works on social and political topics, including gender inequality and economics. Her earliest cartoons dealt with the war in Palestine and called for an end to it. She is one of a few strong female figures working for an Arab publication. While accepting that she has to speak for women as she has the tool of caricaturing, she draws the red line at religion and sex. She has broken the cultural convention and published her sensitive and rejected cartoons on her personal website (Sterns, 2009). One of Hajjar's cartoons of 2009 focuses on the issue of body shaming and undue importance attached to the socially approved standards of beauty that undermine merit while providing opportunity based on appearance (Strukova, 2021).

Sarah Mohanna Al-Abdali, a street graffiti artist in Saudi Arabia, merges graphic design with elements from popular Saudi and Arab culture. She spray-painted graffiti in the historic section of Jeddah, commenting on the overdevelopment in the holy city of Mecca. She grew up with a deep appreciation of the land, architecture and heritage of the coastal region of Hejaz, and it is a recurring theme in her work. She feels that Saudi Arabia is going through many changes, and street art is the perfect medium to experiment (Davis, et al., 2012).

Naseebah Al-Sultan, a member of the Arabic Language Department from Imam University, creates art pieces heavily influenced by nature. She uses acrylic and putty colours to add highlights to her paintings. One of her paintings displayed in the LIFT gallery depicts the public space in Saudi Arabia full of men in pink *ghutra*, a large squire cotton headcover to protect the face during sandstorm clearly depicting the absence of women from the same (Chandra, 2020). The female Emirati artist Sara bin Safwan works as Assistant Curator for Guggenheim Abu Dhabi, and in 2016, she founded an online art platform called *Banat Collective.* The platform focuses on discussing intersectionality and womanhood within the regional context of the Arab world through art and writing. The collective released its first collaborative publication visual art, writing and poetry, in 2018 (Collier, 2019).

The Alem sisters, Shadia and Raja, create classically-inspired portraits to large-scale installations dealing with Islam, woman's rights and the fixity of Saudi society in the era of globalisation. Shadia began her career as a painter before becoming interested in the possibilities of conceptual art, whereas Raja, who is one of the most acclaimed novelists and dramatists in the Kingdom, provides texts to accompany and interact with her sister's creations. In 2011, they were honoured as the first-ever artists representing Saudi Arabia at the Venice Biennale (Lloyd, 2017).

Though the GCC states promote cultural representation through art, they are not open to critical political expressions. Art related to gender and society can be exhibited, but the red line is drawn at the political and security-related art. Soraya Darwesh, a young artist and blogger, says culturally sensitive art can be banned in Saudi Arabia. In November 2013, the Saudi Society for Arts and Culture in Jeddah banned prominent Saudi artists and members of an art initiative called *Edge of Arabia* as their art did not conform to Islamic principles. A year later, Saudi Arabia banned an Islamic comic book, *The 99* by Naif Al-Mutawa, on the grounds of the personification of the prophet (Trenwith, 2014). In addition, Gulf labour artist Walid Raad was denied entry into the UAE for his creations depicting the plight of the migrant population (Abrams, 2015).

In 2020, Kuwait banned an exhibition titled *Like Russian Dolls, We Nest in Our Previous Selves*, by Shurooq Amin (Elgayar, 2020). In addition, Kuwaiti artist, Sami Muhammad's sculpted statue of the first Emir was forbidden from the public display as a representation of human form is forbidden in Islam. Sometimes, state puts restrictions to play along with the conservative elements. As per the artist Badr Fadel Alemdar, fear among the public officials of clashing with conservatives prevents his work from seeing the light of day (Lebel, 2018). There are instances where the authorities are divided on the issue of putting restrictions on art. For example, Kuwaiti legislator Mohammed Hayef al-Mutairi called on the government to stop local artists from making statues, arguing that they had paved the way for the establishment of temples in the Gulf, but he was countered by the fellow MP Ahmed al-Fadel, who dismissed this view as backward (PTI, 2018).

The GCC countries are promoting art to enhance their global image instead of promoting local artists. As the line between art and activism is getting blurry, anything perceived as a threat to national security falls under the anti-terror laws (Mirgani, 2018). As far as the banning of artwork is concerned, the states do not discriminate based on the gender of the artist. Creations by female artists mostly dwell on women empowerment and social issues and remain out of the purview of restrictions. It is restricted only if it questions the authorities or the existing political system. The finer nuances are appreciated by the masses and art enthusiasts equally. Women artists, especially cartoonists, find that publishing in English media gives them a wider canvas than in Arabic as the former sometimes escapes the scrutiny of the authorities Artists tweak their work based on the available window as reaching the audiences is more important than registering dissent or rebellion.

The Motivating Factors

Exposer to Social Media: Women in GCC countries are taking up art as a career option, and a major factor that supports their resolve to carve a niche is their exposure to social media. It provides them with a platform to showcase their work without going out for the physical display of their creation. Several female artists showcase art in virtual galleries and personal websites. In 2020, as the world grappled with the COVID-19 pandemic and a major portion of real-life got confined to home, traffic in the virtual world enhanced manifold. The virtual medium became as solicited as the real one and provided a larger audience for the creation. Over 80 per cent of all Generation Y art buyers bought fine art online in the past year, with almost half of online buyers using Instagram for art-related purposes (Art work Archive, 2021). Through Facebook and Instagram, an artist gets the power to connect with the audience daily and get instant feedback for the finished or work in progress. One right-*click, like* or *follow* can open doors of opportunities.

As per the *Vogue* magazine, today artists use Instagram as their own virtual art gallery, playing both dealer and curator while their fans become critics and collectors (Fleming, 2014). While gallery representation is still prestigious, it is no longer necessary to go through the middleman, allowing the budding artists belonging to humble financial means. Doing away with the gallery also means saving the commission amount that can rather be spent on creating new art or buying new supplies. An artist can use Instagram or your Artwork Archive Public Profile Page as a gallery and collect the full amount on art sales (Artists Guide, 2021). Social media also allows artists to avoid unnecessary hobnobbing with critics or collectors, reduces hassles, and facilitates women artists to display their creations (Art Work Archive, 2021). In addition, with Facebook and Twitter's audience, an artist can now crowd-fund dream projects that otherwise required huge financiers. The only caveat that comes with using social media for art promotion is a lack of control and dilution in privacy that may harm the art brand in the long run (Art Work Archive, 2021).

Social Change: The second factor that encouraged the GCC women to take up art as a full-time career is the seeping social change. Society is getting more open to accepting female artists while parents and families allow women to achieve their dreams. Saudi female photographer Jawahir

Al-Sheikh recalls being told her whole life that her passion would never amount to a job until she convinced her parents to give her a shot at becoming a professional photographer (Tashkandi, 2020). For the Dubai artist Maisoon Al-Saleh, the journey was relatively easy as she belonged to a family of artists; her mother is into fashion, her father is a photographer, and her aunt is a fine artist (Al-Saleh, 2021). Abu Dhabi University and Qatar University conducted research on 200 Emirati businesswomen, the majority of whom conceded that family support is fundamental for success (Sheriff, 2012). Aisha Yousuf, the owner of *Photographya Studio* and Azza Al-Qubaisi, a renowned jewellery designer, vouched for the importance of family support (Sheriff, 2012).

In 2016 more than 90 per cent of respondents out of 1337 agreed that family support is important and believe that women can combine work and family responsibilities. Furthermore, around 60 per cent agree that training, coaching and mentoring would benefit women in entering leadership positions (Knowledge Group, 2021). According to MILLE, a homegrown media brand that features premium and forward-thinking content in the space of fashion, lifestyle, art and culture, although Kuwait, Oman and Bahrain have not experienced radical shifts in their cultural sphere, UAE and Saudi Arabia are leading the way owing to Saudi women gaining the right to drive and appointment of nine female ministers in the cabinet by UAE. In addition, the appointment of the first female ambassador by Saudi Arabia gave hope to young women. More importantly, Sole DXB has turned Dubai into a Middle Eastern fashion capital and the rise of social media influencers with the launch of Instagram, Snapchat and YouTube catalysed the process of women entering public spaces, including art (*Mille World*, 2019).

The Exposer to Foreign Schools: Thirdly, the GCC women are taking up art as a career as they have access to prestigious art schools outside the region. Saudi artist Sarah Al-Abdali studied at Dar Al-Hekma College in Jeddah in the beginning. However, her two-year Master's programme at the Prince's School of Traditional Arts in London allowed her to experiment with various traditional crafts from the Islamic world, dealing in woodwork, ceramics, miniature painting, mosaics and plaster carving (Al-Abdali, 2021). Jeddah artist Fatima al Banawi who won an award for her film *Barakah Meets Barakah,* has a Master's Degree in Theological

Studies from Harvard University. She focused on gender and identity theory in the Middle East and founded a storytelling platform that collects real-life stories from people on the street and turns them into creative productions (Dawson, 2019).

Fakhriya Al-Yahyai conducted a study on the history of Omani women in the fine arts movement and mentioned that the presence of foreign artists in international workshops and exhibiting their work opens new windows for budding artists. She also opines that the returning Masters' and Doctorate holders in Fine Arts played an important role in creating a new generation of artists with a sense of responsibility for developing the art movement. They were the ones who focused on the enhancement of knowledge and quality in making and appreciating artwork as well as developing the art critic movement in Oman (Al-Yahya, 2012). Interestingly, Fakhriya Al-Yahya is also an artist whose art philosophy takes visual and experimental approaches and she tries to showcase the Eastern identity by adopting the philosophy of Islamic culture through the veil.

The financial assistance provided by the GCC countries enables young women to enrol in western schools and attain required skills and training. Najat Makki became the first Emirati female artist to earn a government fellowship to study art abroad in 1977 and went on to receive the Bachelor's and Master's degrees in Relief Sculptures and Metal from the College of Fine Arts in Cairo, followed by a Doctorate in 2001 (*Al-Arabiya*, 2012). Art skills development and rigorous training enable the GCC women to think differently and put their ideas in tangible form with eloquence. The Emirati artist Munira Al-Sayegh completed her studies at London's School of Oriental and African Studies and points at the importance of non-institutional thinking and refining the voice of local and regional artists from the bottom up. She also explores themes of observing change, impermanence and irreversibility in a geopolitical frame and context, and her work has been exhibited in Bolivia, the UAE and the UK (Art Girl's Jungle, 2019). Another Emirati artist Sueraya Shaheen, the Photo Editor of *Tribe Magazine*, has been trained at Sotheby's Institute and studied at the Corcoran College of Art and Design and at Parsons in Paris (Art Girl's Jungle, 2019).

Similarly, Sarah Al-Agroobi is another Emirati artist educated at the Royal College of Art in London who explores notions of culture and identity in Middle Eastern and Western society. Her work has been exhibited regionally and internationally in London, Milan, Istanbul, Venice and Berlin (Collier, 2019). Bahraini artist Ghada Khunji graduated from the Parsons School of Design in New York and later received several awards, including the American Photo Magazine's Image of the Year Award and the Golden Lights Award for Travel. She shifted her lens from the peripheral to focus on the perspective of women hailing from the Arabian Gulf (Khunji, 2021). Finally, Aysha Al-Moayyed from Manama completed her Masters in Fine Arts at Goldsmiths University and has taken part in numerous exhibitions in London, Bahrain and China.

Conclusion

Women in the GCC countries are increasingly pursuing art as a career, majorly owing to the support provided by the state. The countries have been introducing gender reforms that act as stimulants for young girls dreaming of becoming artists. The state policies of the six GCC countries focus on promoting art while opening up as a precursor to attract tourism and investments. Women artists bring a certain nuance to the art world through their specific observation, understanding and experiences. In addition, the exposure to social media, social change seeping into society and access to foreign art schools have acted as motivating factors for the young women seeking to make a career in art. It is the right time for the GCC women willing to enter the art world as professionals as the traditional areas of female dominance like the household have immense possibilities to be depicted on the canvas and celluloid. A female perspective will certainly do justice in bringing it out in the open public spaces catalysing further debates and discussions. The challenge is to push against the cultural and political boundaries set in the region.

References

"Artist's Guide to Social Media Marketing (2021)," Art Work Archive, https://d1zdxptf8tk3f9.cloudfront.net/guides/4/Artwork_Archive_Guide_Social_Media_Marketing.pdf?1568219147, accessed on December 1, 2021.

Qatar Living.com (n.d.) "Arts in Qatar," https://www.qatarliving.com/qatar-guide/arts-qatar, accessed on September 25, 2021.

Abdallah, Sarah Abu (2011), "Saudi Automobile," Sharjah Art Foundation, http://sharjahart.org/sharjah-art-foundation/projects/saudi-automobile1, accessed on September 9, 2021.

Abrams, Amah Rose (2015), "Walid Raad Third Gulf Labour Artist Who's Been Refused Entry to the UAE," Art Net News, May 15, https://news.artnet.com/art-world/walid-raad-gulf-labor-artist-refused-entry-uae-298624, accessed on October 30, 2021.

Al-Abdali, Sarah (2021), *Edge of Arabia*, http://edgeofarabia.com/artists/sarah-al-abdali, accessed on September 19, 2021.

Al-Arabiya (2012), "Arab Artists: Najat Makki Incorporates Gulf Elements in Paintings," September 5, https://www.aishaalabbar.art/usr/documents/press/download_url/6/alarabiya.net-arab-artists-najat-makki-incorporates-gulf-elements-in-paintings.pdf, accessed on October 10, 2021.

Al-Saleh, Maisoon (2021), "Girls Club Asia", https://girlsclub.asia/meet-the-artist/maisoon-al-saleh/, accessed on September 17, 2021.

Al-Yahyai, Fakhriya (2012), "The History of Omani Women in the Fine Arts," *The International Journal of Arts Theory and History,* vol. 7, no. 1, pp. 1-20.

Aldosari, Sheikha (2020), "Women Driving Through the Eyes of 6 Saudi Female Artists, Driving Series by Taghreed Al-Bugshi, I Can Dream, Women Drive a Car, Driving to the Moon, Saudi Women Can Drive and Don't Need a Hero by Skna Hassan, Wait in Red by Noor Al-Saif," *Saudi Women's Stories*, June 27, https://saudiwomenstories.com/2020/06/27/women-driving-through-the-eyes-of-6-saudi-female-artists/, accessed on September 3, 2021.

Art Girl's Jungle (2019), "20 Women at the Top of the UAE Art Scene," *The Art Gorgeous*, March 19, https://theartgorgeous.com/20-women-top-uae-art-scene/, accessed on December 2, 2021.

Art Work Archive (2021), "How Social Media Is Changing Our Art Experience,", https://www.artworkarchive.com/blog/how-social-media-is-changing-our-art-experience, accessed on September 13, 2021.

Bahrain Authority for Culture and Antiquities (2021), "The Fine Arts Movement in Bahrain: The Cultural Achievement of the People of Bahrain," *The Fortieth Annual Bahrain Fine Arts Exhibition*, https://culture.gov.bh/en/events/AnnualFestivalsandEvents/BahrainAnnualFineArtsExhibition/The40thBahrainAnnualFineArtsExhibition/TheFineArtsMovementinBahrain/, accessed on August 29, 2021.

Chandra, Ankita (2020), "Check Out This All-Female Saudi Art Exhibit Opening in Riyadh Soon," *Vogue*, November 18, https://en.vogue.me/art/lift-ksa-ascent-exhibition-female-saudi-artists/, accessed on September 9, 2021.

Collier, Lizzy Vartanian (2019), "20 Women at the Top of the UAE Art Scene: Their Voices Matter in Dubai's Art Circles and Beyond," *The Art Gorgeous*, March 19, https://theartgorgeous.com/20-women-top-uae-art-scene/, accessed on September 11, 2021.

Davis, Catriona, Maktabi, Rima and Abdelhaq, Aroub (2012), "How to Rebel, Saudi Style," CNN, March 23, https://edition.cnn.com/2012/03/23/world/meast/saudi-alternative-culture/index.html, accessed on December 2, 2021.

Dawson, Aimee (2019), "13 Women Who Are Ruling the Rapidly Changing Saudi Art Scene: It's No Secret That Times are Changing in Saudi Arabia," *The Art Gorgeous*, September 5, https://theartgorgeous.com/13-women-ruling-rapidly-changing-saudi-art-scene/, accessed on September 20, 2021.

Elgayar, Aisha (2020), "Kuwait Shuts Down an Art Exhibit: Is the 'Most Open' Gulf Society Closing?," February 25, https://www.al-fanarmedia.org/2020/02/kuwait-shuts-down-an-art-exhibit-is-the-most-open-gulf-society-closing/, accessed on November 1, 2021.

Fattouh, Mayssa (2009), "Bahrain's Art and Culture Scenes: Review of Bahrain's Art and Culture Scenes: Institutions, Galleries, Independent Art Groups," Universes in Universe, October, https://universes.art/en/nafas/articles/2009/bahrain-art-scene, accessed on August 30, 2021.

Fleming (2014), "Why the World's Most Talked About New Art Dealer Is Instagram," *VOGUE*, May 13, https://www.vogue.com/article/buying-and-selling-art-on-instagram, accessed on December 1, 2021.

Greenwald, Michael B (2018), "The New Race for Contemporary Arts Dominance in the Middle East," Belter Centre for Science and International Affairs, Harvard Kennedy School, October, https://www.belfercenter.org/publication/new-race-contemporary-arts-dominance-middle-east, accessed on July 6, 2021.

Khan, Fouzia (2014), "Samiah Khashoggi's 'Patches' Deals With Social Issues," Arab News, May 14, https://www.arabnews.com/news/570401, accessed on September 5, 2021.

Khunji, Ghada (2021), "Edge of Arabia", http://edgeofarabia.com/artists/ghada-khunji, accessed on October 16, 2021.

Knowledge Group (2021), "GCC Women in the Workforce: Status, Challenges, Aspirations Research Findings, Analysis and Recommendations," https://www.knowledgegroup.co/en-us/ResearchInsights/Publication/WhitePapers/DocumentsKG/Women%20in%20the%20workforce%20research_UAE_SM.pdf, accessed on September 19, 2021.

Lebel, Salima (2018), "Kuwaiti Sculptors Struggle Against Views of Idol Worship," *The Daily Star*, November 9, https://www.pressreader.com/lebanon/the-daily-star-lebanon/20181109/281887299326146, accessed on December 1, 2021.

Lloyd, Joseph (2017), "Saudi Arabia's Top 10 Artists and Where to Find Them," *The Culture Trip*, January 12, https://theculturetrip.com/middle-east/saudi-arabia/articles/saudi-arabia-s-top-10-artists-and-where-to-find-them/, accessed on September 12, 2021.

Mille World (2019), "5 Key Social Changes That Transformed the Gulf in 10 Years: Will a New Decade Signal Even More Progression?," *Mille Team*, December 18, https://www.milleworld.com/gcc-social-changes-equality-2019/, accessed on September 19, 2021.

Ministry of Culture, KSA (2019), "From Within," December 8, https://www.moc.gov.sa/en/events/5789, accessed on December 1, 2021.

Mirgani, Suzi (2018), *Art and Cultural Production in the Gulf Cooperation Council*, Routledge.

Obaid, Ruba (2021), "Portrayal of Saudi Women in Art Through the Decades," Arab News, June 9, https://www.arabnews.com/node/1872931/saudi-arabia, accessed on September 2, 2021.

Oman Report (2016), "Diversity of Cultural Expressions", UNESCO, https://en.unesco.org/creativity/governance/periodic-reports/2016/oman, accessed on August 20, 2021.

PTI (2018), "These Modern Sculptors, Their Statues Are Forbidden in Kuwaiti," *Hindustan Times*, November 8, https://www.hindustantimes.com/art-and-culture/in-pics-these-modern-sculptors-their-statues-are-forbidden-in-kuwaiti/story-S4GRGR7v72ZLplHRjzid3J.html, accessed on October 28, 2021.

Saad, Belal (2013), "Kuwait Supports All Citizens With Artistic Talents: Sheikh Salman," Kuwait News Agency, March 30, https://www.kuna.net.kw/ArticleDetails.aspx?id=2301412&Language=en, accessed on August 27, 2021.

Saud, Al-Farhan (2021), "Prince Badr bin Abdullah bin Mohammed bin Farhan Al-Saud, Minister of Culture," Saudi Ministry of Culture, https://www.moc.gov.sa/en/About#hh-msg, accessed on July 6, 2021.

Sheriff, Iman (2012), "Family Support is Key to Emirati Businesswomen's Success: University Study Finds Families to be a Positive Influence," Gulf News, August 11, https://gulfnews.com/uae/education/family-support-is-key-to-emirati-businesswomens-success-1.1058883, accessed on September 17, 2021.

Singh, Amrita (2021), "Rise of the Saudi Female Artists, Suspended Together, by Manal Al-Dowayan," *About Her*, https://www.abouther.com/node/9196/entertainment/art-books/rise-saudi-female-artists, accessed on September 5, 2021.

Smithsonian Magazine (n.d.), "How the UAE Became the Centre for Art in the Middle East," https://www.smithsonianmag.com/sponsored/uae-center-for-art-middle-east-180968375/, accessed on July 12, 2021.

Sterns, Olivia (2009), "Female Cartoonist's Provocative Work Challenges Saudi Society," CNN, http://edition.cnn.com/2009/WORLD/meast/10/27/hajjar.female.cartoonist/, accessed on September 4, 2021.

Strukova, Natalia (2021), "These 6 Female Arab Cartoonists Know how to Challenge Authority: The Stereotypical Image of a Muslim Woman is Crushed by These Decisive Female Cartoonists Who Fight for Their Rights With Pencil in Their Hands," *WM*, http://yonah.org/channel/female-arab-cartoonists-authority/, accessed on September 6, 2021.

Tamkeen (2019), "Tamkeen Targets Bahrain's Art Scene As One of Many Promising Economic Sectors," January 23, https://www.tamkeen.bh/%E2%80%9Ctamkeen%E2%80%9D-targets-bahrain%E2%80%99s-art-scene-as-one-of-many-promising-economic-sectors#:~:text=In%20line%20with%20its%20efforts,promising%20sectors%20in%20the%20kingdom, accessed on October 20, 2021.

Tamkeen (2019), January 23, https://www.tamkeen.bh/%E2%80%9 Ctamkeen%E2%80%9D-targets-bahrain%E2%80%99s-art-scene-as-one-of-many-promising-economic-sectors, accessed on September 2, 2021.

Tashkandi, Hala (2020), "Saudi Women Making Visible Strides in Art," Arab News, March 8, https://www.arabnews.com/node/1638421/saudi-arabia, accessed on July 9, 2021.

Tashkandi, Hala (2020), "Saudi Women Making Visible Strides in Art," Arab News, March 8, https://www.arabnews.com/node/1638421/saudi-arabia, accessed on July 9, 2021.

The Omani Society for Fine Arts Sultanate of Oman, Ministry of Culture, Sports and Youth, (n.d.), https://www.sqhccs.gov.om/affiliates/view/12/70?lang=english, accessed on December 2, 2021.

The World Bank (2020), "Women, Business and the Law 2020," https://openknowledge.worldbank.org/bitstream/handle/10986/32639/9781464815324.pdf, accessed on July 6, 2021.

Trenwith, Courtney (2014), "Saudi Arabia Bans Popular Islamic Cartoon The 99," *Arabian Business*, March 24, https://www.arabianbusiness.com/saudi-arabia-bans-popular-islamic-cartoon-99-543660.html, accessed on November 1, 2021.

UAE Ministry of Foreign Affairs and International Cooperation (2020), "Foreign Ministry supports UAE artists by purchasing their fine artwork," March 30, https://www.mofaic.gov.ae/en/mediahub/news/2020/3/30/30-03-2020-uae-artwork, accessed on August 14, 2021.

Vision 2030, KSA (n.d.), "Vision 2030, Overview, Thriving Economy", https://www.vision2030.gov.sa/v2030/overview/thriving-economy/, accessed on December 2, 2021.

12. Saudi Young Women as Cultural Intermediaries

Priyanka Mittal

Introduction

Saudi Arabia is an authoritarian state situated on the twin pillars of religion and the Al-Saud dynasty. Therefore, the status of women in Saudi Arabia is contingent upon two factors: position of religion and position of government with religion. After 9/11 events in the US and the alleged Saudi involvement in spreading Wahhabism and radicalism world over, the monarchy was forced to change its pro-violence and oppressive image towards constructing a positive reformist image. As a result, it began initiating campaigns that projected a favourable image of women inside the Kingdom. According to Madawi Al-Rasheed, Saudi Arabia used 'charm offensive' campaign to project itself as a modern, pro-women, and forward-looking country through various media campaigns and public relations efforts (Al-Rasheed, 2013, pp. 139 and 151). In this campaign, the position of women was projected through the prism of 'Islam-induced modernity', which did not contradict the pillars of the Saudi state.

But that was not sufficient, as, after Arab Spring 2011, educated youth suffering from high unemployment rates started to protest on the streets. Along with this, women groups fighting for women's rights regarding jobs, equal pay, gender-segregation laws, driving bans, etc., also came in support of the protesting youth groups. Thus in 2011, King Abdullah announced a series of benefits for Saudis worth US$ 10.7 billion, which addressed inflation, housing, education, and unemployment concerns of youth (Murphy, 2011). Along with the reforms packages, the monarch also made subtle changes in judiciary and cabinet positions, appointing the first female deputy in the education ministry, Norah Al-Faiz (Reuters,

2010). Various other structural changes were introduced like opening of workspaces for women and relaxing various religious laws. In addition, certain administrative, judicial, and political reforms and business opportunities were developed for women. In 2016, under Crown Prince Mohammed bin Salman (MbS), *Vision 2030* focused on integrating youth into the economy. For the last two decades, the Saudi establishment has been focusing on harnessing the energy of its youth bulge.

In its *Vision 2030*, Saudi Arabia emphasised on human resources and held great expectations from the youth in attaining its ambitious goal. The Crown Prince MbS explicitly noted that "Our youth are conscious, cultured and creative with high values" (General Authority for Statistics, Saudi Arabia, 2020, p. 3). MbS when he became the Crown Prince in 2017, he belonged to this age group as he was 32 years old. In addition, the Saudi government strived to appoint young members in the cabinet. For example, in 2018, Abdullah bin Bandar bin Abdulaziz Al-Saud, aged 35 years, was appointed as Minister of National Guard. Similarly, in 2017, Abdulaziz bin Saud Al Saud aged 37 years, was inducted into the cabinet as Interior Minister. This approach is indicative of the direction that the Saudi government wants to exemplify by inducting the younger ministers against the old and rigid bureaucratic structured approach.

For its statistical purposes, the United Nations defines 'youth' as those who fall between 15 and 24 years. However, Saudi Arabia considers the population falling in the age group of 15-34 years as a youth, roughly 37 per cent. This age group is the highest percentage amongst all the age groups (General Authority for Statistics, Saudi Arabia, 2020). Moreover, among this age group and percentage, about 49 per cent are women, which points towards significant contribution the women workforce can make to the economy. But only about 31 per cent of women belonging to this age group are employed in the workforce.

In the past four years, several reports state that there has been a significant rise in the number of women workforce. For example, the Saudi female labour force participation rate (LFPR) rose from 17.7 per cent in Q2 2016 to 33.2 per cent in Q4 2020. Moreover, the unemployment rate among female nationals declined to its lowest level in four years at 24.4 per cent in Q4 in 2020 (Al-Khudair, 2021). Thus, in a nutshell, women's presence in the Saudi workforce increased both in share and numbers (Al-Khowaiter, 2021). Often this rise in the women workforce is credited to the *Vision 2030*'s goal of increasing female participation by creating more opportunities in the job market. But the young Saudi women participation rate is less than half of young Saudi males (General Authority for Statistics, Saudi Arabia, 2020).

Though the citizen's unrest during the Arab Spring protests in 2011 in Saudi Arabia settled with reform packages, the phenomenon changed the nature of the protest and negotiations. The Saudi government realised the need to usher in changes in society to appease the youth. It realised that their welfare system was weakening, and gradual inclusion of the youth workforce into the economy was required. The youth culture creates a tangible generational divide since "the new youth culture values self-direction over control, networks over hierarchy, and transparency over secrecy" (Diwan, 2014, p. 2). Thus, the youth, particularly the women workforce, aims to grow in an economy with or without government help. They are seeking newer avenues of self-employment through networks and personal choices. The emerging government investment into creative economy sector acts as an incentive to the women in Saudi Arabia (Al-Khudair, 2019).

Women are emerging as cultural intermediaries having their share of influence, power and capital. Working as filmmakers, artists, painters, musicians, etc., they act as cultural intermediaries to make, remake, subvert, communicate, and circulate cultural identities, representations, and imaginations through strategic communication for social change. The subtle changes pushed through arts, music, and films act as a means of free expression advanced within Saudi culture and tradition. This chapter aims to bring forth the role of women in Saudi Arabia in changing the landscape by acting as 'cultural intermediaries' and their work resulting in social activism. This changing cultural scenario acts as a means of social activism for the female youth trying to push the boundaries and mediate the culture slowly.

Cultural Intermediaries

A creative economy is part of the economic system that develops under the dominant influence of the culture and its resources. The economisation of culture is associated with cultural products like music labels, film making, art and literature production. Such creative goods produced in an economy have high cultural and economic value. Therefore, the creative, cultural, and creative industries hold a special place in any economy, especially after the onset of information and communication technologies (Stachowiak, 2019). The globalised market provides opportunities where the artists could also be entrepreneurs producing specific goods bought by consumers in the market. From the point of view of an artist, the artwork has aesthetic and cultural value; from an entrepreneur's point of view, it needs to be commercially viable. But at the same time, there is an intersecting element of culture and economics system, which plays its role.

The value of the creative economy is often decided by the role cultural intermediaries (CI) play in shaping and regulating it (Jakob and van Heur, 2014). They facilitate the cultural value of goods in an economy, an output of semiotic, aesthetic, artistic and historical values and authenticity (Thorsby, 2011). These CI add value to the goods already existing in the economy. Therefore, they have often been classified as either a set of professions that are supposed to transfer cultural values in a society or as individuals or groups engaged in the transfer of creative goods and cultural values between creators and recipients (Stachowiak, 2019, p. 227). Broadly, they lie at the interplay of culture and economy connecting various national cultures, ethnic groups, tribes, languages using various semiotic codes.

The nomenclature CI has, over the years, delved into complexities, but for this chapter, the understanding of Pierre Bourdieu will be taken. The reference of CI comes from his book *Distinction: A Social Critique of the Judgement of Taste* (1984), where he gave a detailed understanding of the concept. He observed that in the second half of the 20th century, a new profession, CI, developed as a part of 'new petit bourgeois', who create 'average' or 'middle brow culture' which is a simplified version of 'legitimate culture' available to the broader audiences (Bourdieu, 1984, p. 323). Various versions exist about film adaptations of classical drama and literature, popular arrangement of classical music or orchestras, versions of popular tunes, vocal interpretations of classics, etc. (Bourdieu, 1984, p. 323).

Bourdieu further writes about culture dissemination and creation: "New Cultural intermediaries (the most typical of whom are the producers of the cultural programs on TV and the radio or the critics of 'quality' newspapers and magazines and all the writer-journalists and journalists-writers) have invented the whole series of genres half-way between legitimate culture and mass production" (Bourdieu, 1984, pp. 325-326). Bourdieu also calls them 'Need Merchants' who are sellers of the symbolic goods and services (Bourdieu, 1984, p. 365) since they are engaged in specific professions of which they are guarantors and models of values of such products. He writes that "the new petit bourgeois comes into its own in all the occupations involving presentations and representations (sales, marketing, advertising, public relations, fashion, decoration and so forth) and in all the institutions providing symbolic goods and services. These include the various jobs in medical and health assistance and cultural productions and organisations (youth leaders, play leaders, tutors and monitors, radio and TV producers and presenters, magazine journalists), which have expanded considerably in recent years" (Bourdieu, 1984, p. 359).

In their book *The Cultural Intermediaries Reader*, Jennifer Smith Maguire and Julian Matthews (2014) have further complicated the old meanings associated with this term. They write, "CI are tastemakers defining what counts as good taste and cool culture in today's marketplace. Working at the intersection of the culture and economy, they perform critical operations in producing and promoting consumption, constructing legitimacy and adding value through the qualification of goods" (Maguire and Matthews, 2014, p. 1). Thus, CI tends to shape people's beliefs in terms of consumption and possibly convince bodies to invest in culture. As per Nixon and Du Gay (2002), the 'New CI' are "these groups of workers who can exert, from their position within the cultural institutions, a certain amount of cultural authority as shapers of taste and the inculcators of new consumerist's dispositions." For Sean Nixon (1997, p. 181), CI are persons or organisations that move symbols and their meanings, or, more broadly-the cultural value, from one place to another. David Hesmondhalgh (2002, p. 53) suggests replacing the ambiguous term CI with a more specific one, such as 'creative manager', 'creator of Symbols' or 'Creative Practitioner'.

Often the term CI draws some similarities with terms like service class and knowledge class (Negus, 2002, p. 502). However, they also play a predominant role in shaping the image of their nations and cultures and strategies to include what is representative of this image (Mahon, 2000,

p. 471). Using their capital (symbolic and social) which operates within a specific field, CI can determine the power relations in that field. For example, Noha Mellor writes in the context of Arab journalists whom she considers as active CI working in the field. She says "Arab journalists, as active agents, do indeed possess a form of (symbolic and cultural) power, which affects and is affected by the current developments in the region" (Mellor, 2008, pp. 472-473). Further, she says that these journalists form their own 'interpretive community' of practice with shared narratives and discourse about other fields, such as politics and economics.

Generations in any country are defined through experiences and their responses to social events. Sherine Hafez and Susan Slyomovics (2013, p. 82) discuss generational groups as more social than biological groups who share a familiar social and historical process. Therefore, their relation to social events and processes to geopolitical and institutional change gives a particular generation a "certain definitive mode of behaviour, feeling, and thought." The generational divide in Saudi Arabia has been shaped by the new media environment and Arab activism in social and political spaces. This activism has brought forth new forms of civic engagement and political contestation against conservative political culture and traditional social norms of religion in Saudi society. Youth politics has also resulted from advanced communication infrastructure, permitting universal access to social networking sites and the internet. In Saudi Arabia, youngsters find 'spaces' for social engagement and political innovation. According to Kristin Diwan (2014), youth lay the 'groundwork for the transformations to come.' Youth positioning in history enables them to "mediate processes of cultural change" (Cole and Durham, 2007, p. 16). Thus, this discourse enforces the realignment of structures about discipline, institution, and geopolitics related to particular events (Hafez and Slyomovics, 2013, p. 83).

Saudi Women as Cultural Intermediaries and Their Activism

Oil-led development, modernisation, and urbanisation in Saudi Arabia have created isolation for women (Menoret, 2020, pp. 58 and 67). Moreover, the nature of conversations and discussions changed with capital accumulation and power consolidation (Menoret, 2014, p. 8). Thus, practices of urban activism emerged, which were seen as a newer form of engaged citizenship. This has also been highlighted by Pascal Menoret (2014), who uses Jurgen Habermas's concept of the 'plebeian public sphere' to understand the everyday attitudes of Saudi citizens. In his work, *Joyriding in Riyadh*, he explores how thriving sub-cultures in Saudi Arabia is a way of confronting the state towards managing the public sphere, protecting private property enforcing the law (2014, pp. 10-11). Quoting Gramscian concept of Organic Individuals, Sean Foley says "through the language of their culture, they articulate feelings and experiences that the masses cannot easily express" (Foley, 2019, p. 5).

Since any form of political protest against the government is labelled un-Islamic[1] by religious authorities (Reuters, 2011), women groups and activists have resorted to cultural mediums to register their opinions and expressions. As Madawi Al-Rasheed (2013, p. 2) cites Pierre Bordieu (2001, p. 92) who says that "women were drawn into the 'the domains of production and circulation of symbolic goods' like publishing, journalism, the media, teaching, etc. when they were excluded from economic and political activity." Young Saudi women are emerging as filmmakers, artists, sculptors, painters, chefs, musicians, theatre people, sports celebrities, writers, journalists, and TV presenters, which were once fields dominated by men. Thus, women can actively bargain their position against patriarchy and religion, but within the confines of the state.

Women youth activists in Saudi Arabia used their 'capital' to draw an interpretive community with a shared set of rules and ideas. Bourdieu used an inter-dependent and co-constructed trio of—field, capital and habitus—to understand the human activity in a social world (the field of power) (Thomson, 2012, pp. 67 and 70). Thus, each agent within this 'field of power' uses their logic, rules and regularities to interact with other agents having their own 'field of power'. As Patricia Thompson (2012, p. 71) says, "a field is profoundly hierarchised, with dominant agents and institutions having considerable power to determine what happens within it, there is still agency and change." These women filmmakers, painters, fashion designers, etc., have generated their 'field of power', thus drawing their interpretive community, which has subtle power to challenge the state-religious conservative norms. Robert Putnam (2000) offers a distinctive understanding of individuals using their social capital to build community-based relationships.

Urban activism is increasingly seen as a new form of engaged citizenship that works at the intersection of the formal decision-making process and informal urban spaces (Vanhoose and Savini, 2017). Activists and citizens employ informal tactics to test the borders of the legality of the state (Pagano, 2013). However, this practice is considered incompatible with institutionalised planning and a means of disruption to formal policymaking (Lerner, 2012). Since the last decade, Saudi women and activists have realised their shortcoming about free public mobility and limited freedom of speech and expression due to religious and social restrictions. As a result, they have resorted to online means to organise and express their dissent. Patricia Wilson (1997) says that individuals tend to aggregate and develop resistance capacities or propose alternative policymaking ways, as it happened in the case of various online resistance and petition movements. For example, in 2011, the hashtag '#Tal3mrak' movement was used as a sarcastic remark for rich and royal Saudis. Demographically speaking, the two most prominent groups tweeting in Saudi Arabia fall within the age brackets of 25-34 and 18-24.

Moreover, whereas roughly 22 per cent of Saudi Facebook members were female, women made up 37 per cent of the market for Saudi Instagram accounts, and 29 per cent on the Twitter platform in 2019 (Lama, 2019). The debate over the ban on women drivers took on new life in September 2013, when Sheikh Saleh Al-Loheidan, a well-established cleric, warned that driving a car could damage a woman's ovaries and pelvis. In response, the hashtag #WomensDrivingAffectsOvariesAndPelvises was created to deride his curious theory. Several weeks later, during a rare protest against the ban, hashtags such as #Saudi, #Oct26driving, and #Women2Drive were used to rally support (Chappell, 2013).

Similarly, Saudi women bloggers and activists have been using the hashtags #TogetherToEndMaleGuardianship and #StopEnslavingSaudiWomen—to mark their protest against the practice of male guardian laws (Perez, 2016). According to Bayly Philip Christopher Winder (2014), "the Saudi youth, in particular, look to Twitter for conversations that range from apolitical and mundane to partisan and provocative. Calls for reform and jabs at princes exist alongside zealous defences of Saudi tradition." Thus, women and youth activists are producers of strategic communication for social change, suggestive of communication for development and social change. Activists also work as Cultural Intermediaries mediating the cultural and social capitals in society, thus impacting the micro, meso, macro levels of communication for social change (Ciszek, 2017, p. 712).

With *Vision 2030* aiming to transform Saudi cultural and archaeological heritage into a world-class endeavour, women's contribution is seen as indispensable. In Saudi Arabia, women's identity is intertwined as the cultural bearers and front runners of tradition. Therefore women's roles are stereotyped even in media. Women's identity is projected only as mothers, sisters, daughters, and wives in limited frames in the more significant Arab media. Against this, now, Saudi women have been diversifying their roles. With the government's help, women now are seen as celebrity chefs, tourism experts, musicians and in other celebrity roles often, developing their identity independently. For example, Saudi Chef Asma Tabaaji says in her interview that "Saudi women have always been attracted to work in this (chef) area, but within the frame of the productive families' programs. Only a few women have guts to work at restaurants and hotels" (Abouther, 2019). Other Saudi women making a mark for themselves in the food industry are Nour Al-Zaben, Louloua El-Ezzah, and Eman Gazzaz. They independently run their online accounts via Instagram, Twitter, and Facebook-wide followers (Arab News, 2020).

Saudi women's engagement in the tourism sector increases significantly after the launch of *Vision 2030*. According to Minister of Tourism Ahmed Al-Khateeb, 54 per cent of women in the tourism sector are women (*Saudi Gazette*, 2015). In addition, a study found that Mecca city topped in terms of the excellence of women working in the tourism sector and showed a high level of women empowerment (Alasgah and Rizk, 2021). Basmah Al-Mayman is the Regional Director of the UN World Tourism Organisation (UNWTO). She started her career as the founding member of the Saudi Commission for Tourism and National Heritage (The World Bank, 2020).

Saudi women are returning to the architecture, which was banned for women both in studying and practice in the mid-1980s as per Saudi architect Sumaya Dabbagh.[2] Her works have been featured in Sharjah's Mleiha Archaeological Centre (middleeastarchitect, 2018). Other celebrated architects are Azza Al-Deghather (Curtis, 2019) and Nadia Bakhurji[3] (Mirza, 2018). Self-expression through architecture acts as a form of manifestation and tastemaker, making architects cultural intermediaries (O'Callaghan, 2017). Architects emerged as a connection between the product and target market while at the same time producing a cultural and political discourse. Structures of architecture are constructed in the same rules and practices, where people and communities tend to self-govern and regulate themselves, making them think and act in a certain way (Grinceri, 2016).

With the globalised Arab media, Saudi Arabia also witnessed an explosion of local art production, primarily by grassroots arts movements like the Abha arts community. However, the arts community continues to be primarily patronised by Saudi business houses and ruling elite families (Foley, 2019; Al-Senussi, 2016, p. 32). Qualities inherent to the Saudi traditional Islam, society, and monarchy are visible in the artwork. Members of the ruling family establish elite organisations to shape and oversee the growing field. For example, Princess Jawaher bint Majid bin Abdulaziz Al-Saud chaired the Saudi Art Council. Often, the ruling elite's involvement works as cultural intermediates, mediating or acting as 'opinion makers' for the art development. Women artists have used their social and cultural capital to influence the artwork and movements. Manal Al-Dowayan, a contemporary Saudi Artist, is famous for her installation pieces, which primarily examine personal and political issues related to women's rights in ultra-conservative Saudi Arabian laws. She mentions that, in Saudi Arabia, painting and arts as a profession were not considered revered professions, and there was not much infrastructure available (Siegal, 2019). Her powerful art installation, 'Suspended Together' produced in 2011, gives an insight into the impression of movement and freedom of women inside Saudi Arabia.

Safeya Binzager, born in Jeddah in the 1940s had education in Cairo and London (Al-Rushaid, 2020). Considering the time and place she was born, not many women in Saudi Arabia had access to education. Since education to women was more widely available only after the 1960s due to King Faisal's reforms, her educational achievement pointed to the direction that she belonged to an influential family. Safeya Binzager, in 1968, became the first woman to hold an art exhibition in girl's school

Dar Al-Tarbiah. Her works range from oil to etching as mediums focusing on women's lives, wedding ceremony traditions, landscape, and everyday life scenes. Lately, she has been recognised by the UN Environment Programme for her contributions to protecting the national heritage. In 2017 she was bestowed the Order of King Abdul Aziz in appreciation of her contribution to Saudi Culture.

Another profession from which women were debarred entry was singing. Women singing in public is not considered respectable since many Islamic suras interpreters objected to women singing in public. They claim that women singing in public among men can cause *fitna* and chaos. Hence, any form of music and singing was banned on Saudi soil for years, especially after 1979, when reverse-Islamisation took place in Saudi Arabia. But this could not deter women from pursuing their choice and Saudi women were practicing, learning, and teaching music as a profession outside Saudi Arabia. For example, Sawsan Al-Bahiti became the voice of Saudi Opera Singing. She is also a qualified coach at the New York Coaching Center and has been singing opera since 2008 (Yazbeck, 2021). She has also been actively involved in the hospitality and catering industry in Jeddah since 2017 (Singh, 2021). After *Vision 2030* was launched and the General Entertainment Authority was created to support talents and artists, Al-Bahiti launched herself professionally in Saudi Arabia (Nadeem, 2019).

Although cinema was banned since 1979, Saudi elites and women from influential families have been contributing to film production. For example, the first Saudi women filmmaker Haifaa Al-Mansour is well-known for making films on women's issues well within the prism of Saudi society and tradition. Her film *Wajdja* and *Perfect Candidate* have been widely acclaimed on international platforms. The first film is about the aspirations of a young girl to ride a bicycle which is banned for women in Saudi Arabia, while her mother struggles to keep her marriage. The second film is about a young doctor working in a municipal hospital, her struggle to file her nomination for municipal elections, and society's response towards her endeavour. In 2018, she was elected as Saudi Arabia's General Culture Authority member due to her work (Al-Zahrani, 2018). Another significant mention is Ahd Kamel, an actress and filmmaker from Saudi Arabia who worked in films like *Hurma* and *Al-Gondorji*. Her film deals with women's position in Saudi society and she also worked as an actress in Haifaa's film *Wadjda* as a school teacher.

Women TV media personalities like Muna Abu-Sulayman, Badariya Al-Bishr and Lojain Omran have influenced women folk in Saudi Arabia. Muna Abu Sulayman is a TV show host on the women talk show *Kalam Nawaem*, a popular show on MBC which is running for a decade. While Badariya Al-Bishr[4] is a Saudi writer and novelist (Dreyer, 2011), her talk show 'Badria' on MBC has been popular for tackling controversial social issues in Saudi society (Jiffry, n.d.). Lojain Omran is a Saudi television presenter and social media influencer. Her TV programmes include *Good Morning Arabs*, *Ya Hala*, *World of Eve*, etc. She is reported to have more than seven million followers on Instagram (Azaiz, 2017). In 2017, Forbes ranked her 55 out of 100 Arabic celebrities as one of the most influential media personalities in the Middle East (Yazbeck, 2021). These women have been actively moulding people's opinions and taste both inside and outside Saudi Arabia.

Oil income resulted in Saudi Arabia establishing itself as a major media player in the Arab world. Major newspaper publications like *Al-Hayat*, *Arab News*, *Saudi Gazette*, *Asharq Al-Awsat* and popular television networks like *Rotana* and *MBC* are owned and managed by the Saudi ruling family. Thus, media opinion-making creeps into every aspect of decision-making and conveys a favourable Saudi image abroad. These media material practices involve forming everyday values, especially in countries with high social media penetration.

The division of power between Al-Saud and the Wahhabi establishment in the governance of the Saudi state has been detrimental to the growth of women in society. Society and women were seen as internal subjects for the religious bureaucracy to administer. Thus women's exclusion from the public became a visible sign of normalisation. Saudi women's identity was seen in binary—pious, harmonious, moral versus immoral—created to construct gender roles for Saudi society (Al-Rasheed, 2013, p. 44). State behaviour was intertwined with controlling women's behaviour, which separated moral and immoral women; hence, 'this fear shaped state policy' (Al-Rasheed, 2013, p. 49). Madawi Al-Rasheed (2013, p. 23) writes that the oil boom created a 'double exclusion' for women: from the general economy and the domestic sphere. Surplus wealth made the government distribute rents to men and women as a social welfare scheme, and later, men employed domestic workers. Resultantly, women lost their power of expression in the domestic sphere. This 'double exclusion' deprived women of control over their own lives and issues of gender equality. They became 'oil commodities exchanged by men who can afford them.' Thus, women got actively involved in less contradictory and complacent enough not to get caught in state-led religious conservatism.

These CI act as activists who have their own set of specific cultural and social capital, which help them gain legitimacy and influence. Women express their ideas and identities through the limited and restricted spaces in media and art forms. For example, when cinema was not introduced in Saudi Arabia, Haifaa Al-Mansour's film *Wadjda* already became an internationally acclaimed movie. The movie was available through Netflix and other open-source platforms through not screened inside the country. Her film showcases the discriminatory practices of state and patriarchy against women, but without stimulating any criticism of the Saudi state.

Similarly, Manal Al-Dowayan's work *Suspended Together*, directly question the issue of Saudi travel permission needed by women from their guardians. Through her art installation, she tries to bring forth this problem constructively without challenging the Saudi policies and government. Muna Abu Sulayman, a TV show presenter, used TV shows to express her ideas on Saudi women. These women became the face of modern and cosmopolitan Saudi Arabia. These celebrated women emerge as influencers impacting the political and social discourse inside and outside Saudi Arabia. Women take pride in their knowledge of their field, languages and culture and the interpretative aspect of their nationality and culture. They are persistent in asserting their national identity as both Arab and Saudi.

Conclusion

Women's rights activism is multi-faceted, especially because Saudi Arabia is a regionally segregated and diverse nation in terms of geography, tribal factions, and populations hailing from different cultures and traditions. Homogenising the whole Saudi population under the garb of the 'Being Saudi', a singular identity would be confusing. Saudi women have been practicing various forms of women activism, sometimes within the rubric of Islam, Hijazi, Najdi, or largely Saudi-tradition. Their ideas and identity diversify into various practices of advocacy for women's causes. They have organised themselves into a powerful activist bloc mediating change in the conservative Saudi society.

Acting as Cultural Intermediaries, they function as activists who mediate change in society and culture through their work and profession. Saudi women are involved in producing the content and cultural symbols and are the carriers and multipliers of these symbols. Their work gives them the freedom to interpret Saudi laws, religion, culture, and tradition according to their understanding and produce content that is favourable to suit the changing taste of Saudi Youth.

By organising themselves as a powerful bloc, they try to skip government censorship and prohibitions, thus not engaging politically. Instead, the women's cultural intermediaries are trying to create a new symbolic and cultural discourse through their creative work. This creative discourse forms a particular part of Saudi economic and historical narrative, thus becoming political in its own appeal; often directing what Asef Bayat calls 'Social non-movements' refers to the collective actions of non-collective actors.

Notes

1. Protesting through street demonstrations is considered illegal and un-Islamic on the grounds that it may promote *fitna* or social division. Thus any form of challenge to ruling authorities including religious institutions in Saudi Arabia was considered criminal offence. Several human right activities have been condemning and put behind bars for voicing their opinion for example, Raif Badawi, Loujain Al-Hathloul, etc. Back in 1990, women resorted to driving cars in Riyadh to mark their protest against driving ban. These women were implicated for the same. So after 2004 onwards, activists and protesters resorted to traditional form of expressing their opinion through petition writing. The culture of petition writing to king has been active in Saudi Arabia, but now it has changed its character to *hashtag* movements.
2. Her works delivered the King Abdullah Petroleum Studies and Research Center and King Abdullah Metro Station.
3. She is the founder of the Riwaq of the Kingdom and hold a professional partnership with Prince Al-Waleed bin Talal.
4. She is wife of Nasser Al-Qasabi, a famous Arab TV show comedian for shows like *Tash Ma Tash* and *Selfie*.

Reference

About Her (2019), "Saudi Chef Asma Tabaaji Tells Us the Secrets of Her Dishes and Competing with Men in the Industry," https://www.abouther.com/node/12646/people/features/saudi-chef-asma-tabaaji-tells-us-secrets-her-dishes-and-competing-men, accessed on December 25, 2021.

Al Rasheed, Madawi (2013), *A Most Masculine State: Light at the End of the Tunnel*, Cambridge University Press.

Al-Rushaid, Mashael (2020), "The Mother of Art: Meet Safeya Binzagr, The Pioneer of Saudi's Fine Art Movement," *Vogue*, December 10, https://en.vogue.me/art/safeya-binzagr-saudi-fine-art-movement/, accessed on December 26, 2021.

Alasgah, Amnah A. A. and Rizk, Eman S.I. (2021), "Empowering Saudi Women in the Tourism and Management Sectors According to the Kingdom's 2030 Vision," *Journal of Sustainable Finance & Investment*, February.

Al-Khowaiter, Meshal (2021), "Exploring the Rising Workforce Participation Among Saudi Women," Middle East Institute, July 9, https://www.mei.edu/publications/exploring-rising-workforce-participation-among-saudi-women, accessed on November 30, 2021.

Al-Khudair, Deema (2021), "Saudi Unemployment Rate Drops in Q4 2020," Arab News, April 19, https://www.arabnews.com/node/1845036/business-economy, accessed on November 29, 2021.

Al-Khudair, Deema (2019), "Arts and Culture, a Driving Force in the Creative Economy in Saudi Arabia," Arab News, February 7, https://www.arabnews.com/node/1447736/saudi-arabia, accessed on December 29, 2021.

Al-Senussi, Alia (2016), "The Local Evolution of Saudi Arabia's Contemporary Arts Scene," *Identity and Culture in the 21st Century Gulf*, OxGAPS.

Al-Zahrani, Latifa (2018), "Haifaa Al-Mansour Lauds the KSA's Revolutionary," *Women 2030*, May 1, http://women2030.com/node/275, accessed on December 22, 2021.

Arab News (2020), "6 Arab Chefs to Follow on Social Media If You're Self-Isolating," March 15, https://www.arabnews.com/node/1641711/6-arab-chefs-follow-social-media-if-you%25E2%2580%2599re-self-isolating, accessed on December 27, 2021.

Azaiz, Semia (2017), "Social Media Influencers: The Power Players in the Middle East," *Khaleej Times*, July 5, https://www.khaleejtimes.com/technology/social-media-influencers-the-power-players-in-the-middle-east, accessed on December 15, 2021.

Bourdieu, Pierre (1984), *Distinction: A Social Critique of the Judgment of Taste*, Cambridge, MA: Harvard University Press.

Bourdieu, Pierre (2001), *Masculine Domination*, Stanford: Polity Press.

Chappell, Bill (2013), "Saudi Women Get Behind Wheel For Drive-In Protest," *National Public Radio*, October 26, https://www.npr.org/sections/thetwo-way/2013/10/26/240955303/saudi-women-get-behind-wheel-for-drive-in-protest, accessed on December 20, 2021.

Ciszek, Erica L. (2017), "Activists Strategic Communication for Social Change: A Transnational Case Study of Lesbians, Gay, Bisexual, and Transgender Activism," *Journal of Communication*, vol. 67, pp. 702-718.

Cole, Jennifer and Deborah Durham (2007), "Introduction: Age, Regeneration, and the Intimate Politics of Globalization," in Jennifer Cole and Deborah Durham (eds.), *Generations and Globalization: Youth, Age and Family in the New World Economy*, Indiana University Press.

Curtis, Kathleen (2019), "Leading the Way for Female Architects in Saudi Arabia," Syracuse University, February 18, https://www.syracuse.edu/stories/female-architects-saudi-arabia/, accessed on December 28, 2021.

Diwan, Kristin (2014), "Breaking Taboos: Youth Activism in the Gulf States," Atlantic Council.

Dreyer, Christoph (2011), "Interview With the Saudi Writer Badriya AL-Bishr: Anything You Write About Is Made A Scandal, Even Love," May 20, https://en.qantara.de/content/interview-with-the-saudi-writer-badriya-al-bishr-anything-you-write-about-is-made-a-scandal, accessed on December 15, 2021.

Foley, Sean (2019), *Changing Saudi Arabia: Art, Culture and Society in the Kingdom*, Lynne Rienner Publishers.

General Authority for Statistics (2020), *Saudi Youth in Numbers: A Report for International Youth Day 2020*, Statistical Analysis and Decision Support Centre, Saudi Arabia.

Grinceri, Daniel (2016), *Architecture as Cultural and Political Discourse: Case Studies of Conceptual Norms and Aesthetic Practices*, Routledge.

Hafez, Sherine and Slyomovics, Susan (2013), *Anthropology of the Middle East and North Africa: Into the New Millennium,* Indiana University Press.

Hesmondhalgh, David (2002), *The Cultural Industries,* Sage Publications.

Jakob, Doreen and Van Heur, Bas (2014), "Editorial: Taking Matters Into Third Hands: Intermediaries and the Organisation of the Creative Economy," *Regional Studies*, vol. 48, no. 1-5.

Jiffry, Fadia (n.d.), "Badria Al-Bishr: Addressing Hot Button Social Issues Through Talk Show," *About Her*, https://www.abouther.com/node/3351/people/leading-ladies/badria-al-bishr-addressing-hot-button-social-issues-through-talk, accessed on November 30, 2021.

Lama (2019), "Social Media Statistics in Saudi Arabia," Talkwalker, September 3, https://www.talkwalker.com/blog/social-media-statistics-saudi-arabia, accessed on December 23, 2021.

Lerner, Jonathan (2012), "Street Makeovers Put New Spin on the Block: How Community Activists Are Taking City Planning Into Their Own Hands and Creating Pedestrian-Friendly Blocks via Pop-Up Urbanism," *Pacific Standard*, January 16, https://psmag.com/environment/street-makeovers-put-new-spin-on-the-block-38926, accessed on December 27, 2021.

Maguire, Jennifer S. and Matthews, Julian (2014), "Bourdieu on Cultural Intermediaries," in Jennifer S. Maguire and Julian Matthews (eds.), *The Cultural Intermediaries Reader*, Sage Publications.

Mahon, Maureen (2002), "The Visible Evidence of Cultural Producers," *Annual Review of Anthropology*, vol. 29, pp. 467-92.

Mellor, Noha (2008), "Arab Journalists as Cultural Intermediaries," *The International Journal of Press/ Politics*, vol. 13, no. 4, pp. 465-483.

Menoret, Pascal (2014), *Joyriding in Riyadh: Oil, Urbanism and Road Revolt*, Cambridge University Press.

Menoret, Pascal (2020), *Graveyards of Clerics: Everyday Activism in Saudi Arabia,* Stanford: Stanford University Press.

Middle East Architect (2018), "Is Architecture a Returning Profession Among Women in Saudi Arabia?," April 9, https://www.middleeastarchitect.com/news/is-architecture-a-returning-profession-among-women-in-saudi-arabia, accessed on October 30, 2021.

Mirza, Mohammed (2018), "The Story Behind Saudi Arabia's Most Famous Female Architect," *Step Feed*, March 4, https://stepfeed.com/the-story-behind-saudi-arabia-s-most-famous-female-architect-5820#:~:text=Meet%20Nadia%20Bakhurji.&text=Driven%20by%20an%20urge%20to,of%20the%20Kingdom%20, accessed on October 16, 2021.

Murphy, Caryle (2011), "Saudi Arabia's King Abdullah Promises $36 Billion in Benefits," *The Christian Science Monitor*, February 23, https://www.csmonitor.com/World/Middle-East/2011/0223/Saudi-Arabia-s-King-Abdullah-promises-36-billion-in-benefits, accessed on October 18, 2021.

Nadeem, Sadiya A (2019), "Meet Saudi Arabia's First Opera Singer, Sawsan Al-Bahiti," Gulf News, October 12, https://gulfnews.com/world/gulf/saudi/meet-saudi-arabias-first-opera-singer-sawsan-al-bahiti-1.67087019, accessed on October 18, 2021.

Negus, Keith (2002), "The Work of the Cultural Intermediaries and the Enduring Distance Between Production and Consumption," *Cultural Studies*, vol.16, no. 4, pp. 501-515.

Nixon, Sean (1997), "Circulating Culture," In Paul Du Gay (Ed.), *Production of Culture/ Cultures of Production*, Sage Publications.

Nixon, Sean and Gay, Paul G. (2010), "Who Needs Cultural Intermediaries?," *Cultural Studies*, vol. 1, no. 4, pp. 495-500.

O'Callaghan, Judith (2017), "Architecture as Commodity, Architects as Cultural Intermediaries: A Case Study," *Architecture and Culture*, vol. 5, no. 2, pp. 221-240.

Pagano, Celeste (2014), "DIY Urbanism: Property and Process in Grassroots City Building," *Marquette Law Review*, vol.9, no.7, https://scholarship.law.marquette.edu/mulr/vol97/iss2/5, accessed on November 23, 2021.

Deutsche Welle (2016), "Saudi Women Denounce Male Guardianship on Twitter," September 20, https://www.dw.com/en/saudi-women-denounce-male-guardianship-on-twitter/a-19563156, accessed on November 23, 2021.

Putnam, Robert D. (2000), *Bowling Alone: The Collapse and Revival of American Community*, Simon and Schuster Paperbacks.

Reuters Staff (2011), "*Saudi Clerics Condemn Protests and Deviant Ideas*," Reuters, March 6, https://www.reuters.com/article/us-saudi-protests-clerics-idUSTRE7251O220110306, accessed on November 26, 2021.

Reuters (2010), "Factbox: Saudi King Abdullah's Reform," November 22, https://www.reuters.com/article/us-saudi-reforms-factbox-idUSTRE6AL2K120101122, accessed on December 30, 2021.

Saudi Gazette Staff (2015), "54% of Workers in Tourism Are Women: Saudi Minister," *Zawya*, October 29, https://www.zawya.com/mena/en/business/story/54_of_workers_in_tourism_are_women_Saudi_minister-SNG_255437175/, accessed on December 30, 2021.

Seigal, Nina (2019), "Artist Uses Text to Speak About Women's Live," *The New York Times*, December 3, https://www.nytimes.com/2019/12/03/arts/Manal-AlDowayan-Saudi-photographer.html, accessed on December 30, 2021.

Singh, Amrita (2021), "Sawsan Al-Bahiti: The Voice of Saudi Arabian Opera," *About Her,* https://www.abouther.com/node/20471/entertainment/music-film-television/sawsan-al-bahiti-voice-saudi-arabian-opera, accessed on December 22, 2021.

Stachowiak, Krzysztof (2019), "Cultural Intermediaries and Their Role in Creative Economy," *Cultural Studies Appendix*, special edition, no. 2.

The World Bank (2020), "Saudi Women Rising Up in Business in Line With Vision 2030," March 11, https://www.worldbank.org/en/news/feature/2020/03/11/saudi-women-rising-up-in-business-in-line-with-vision-2030, accessed on December 30, 2021.

Thomson, Patricia (2012), "Field," In Michael James Grenfell (Ed.), *Pierre Bourdieu: Key Concepts,* 2nd edition. Routledge.

Throsby, David (2011), *Economics and Culture*, Cambridge University Press.

Vanhoose, Katherine and Savini, Federico (2017), "The Social Capital of Urban Activism: Practices in London and Amsterdam," *City*, vol. 21, no. 173, pp. 1-19.

Wilson, Patricia A. (1997), "Building Social Capital: A learning Agenda for the Twenty-first Century," *Urban Studies*, vol. 34, no. 5& 6, pp. 754-760.

Winder, Bayly P. C. (2014), "The Hashtag Generation: The Twitter Phenomenon In Saudi Society," *Journal of Georgetown University Qatar Middle Eastern Studies Student Association*, vol. 6, pp. 1-8.

Yazbeck, Jeannine (2021), "18 Iconic Saudi Women Helping Shape the Future of the Kingdom," *Vogue*, September 23, https://en.vogue.me/culture/iconic-saudi-women/, accessed on December 30, 2021.

13. Environmental Action in the GCC: Government & the Youth

Prabhat Jawla

Introduction

Climate change presents one of the paramount concerns faced by humanity in the 21st century. The 2015 Paris Agreement on climate change and the 2021 report by the International Panel on Climate Change (IPCC) have unequivocally established that climate is continually warming on account of anthropogenic actions (Intergovernmental Panel on Climate Change (IPCC), 2021; United Nations, 2015). The proposed solutions include restricting the rise in global temperature to below 2° Celsius in the coming years while ideally striving to keep the temperature below 1.5° Celsius (Nyambuu and Semmler, 2020). Climate change is a transboundary phenomenon affecting every continent and region, including the Middle East. The region of MENA (the Middle East and North Africa) has been regarded as one of the most vulnerable to the impacts of climate change (Arab Sustainable Development Report, 2020; Intergovernmental Panel on Climate Change, 2013, p. 1535). The studies projected that in certain parts of the region, temperature could rise by 5° Celsius by the end of the century (Arab Sustainable Development Report, 2020).

In the broadest sense, the region is confronted with the threats of rising sea level, desertification, biodiversity loss, coastal retraction, prolonged periods of drought, changing water salinity, air pollution, marine, and coastal pollution, food security, and a grave water crisis (Abumoghli & Goncalves, 2020; United Nations Development Programme [UNDP] & Global Environment Facility [GEF], 2018; Stang, 2016). Furthermore, as of 2018, the region has had one of the highest per capita greenhouse gas

(GHG) emissions (Climate Watch, 2018). Even though the region faces myriad violent conflicts and hostilities, environmental threats remain significant, which has incidentally received limited attention. Moreover, various auxiliary effects of environmental degradation (desertification of land, depletion of scarce water resources) carry the potential to exacerbate existing conflicts further. Even now, water scarcity concerns have been associated with increased risks of political stability (Amery, 2017).

The Gulf Cooperation Council (GCC)—composed of Saudi Arabia, the United Arab Emirates, Qatar, Bahrain, Kuwait, and Oman—represents the rich and stable states of the wider MENA region and carries some semblance of political and economic uniformity. However, in the region, economically disadvantaged states are disproportionately affected by environmental threats (Intergovernmental Panel on Climate Change (IPCC), 2014) compared to the 'rentier economies' (Springborg, 2013; Mahdavy, 1970). Nonetheless, as the impacts of climate change become more pronounced in the GCC region (threat of submergence of densely populated coastal regions and frequent weather aberrations), these countries have increasingly started to engage in actions, processes, and methods of tackling them (Raouf, 2008).

Among other things, the countries are formulating and adopting long-term national development plans and agendas. A common theme across these different national plans is their insistence on decreasing their dependence on hydrocarbons through economic diversification (Kabbani and Mimoune, 2021). Amidst the fears of the exhaustibility of hydrocarbons reserves, such transitions make sense; however, another major reason the governments are planning and investing heavily in these national visions is to cater to the upcoming younger population, which may no longer rely solely on rentier-benefits like their predecessors.

For the GCC states, the contribution of the young generation would be critical in the upcoming years. Roughly one-third of the GCC population comprises people under 24 years of age (Oxford Business Group, 2016; Economist Intelligence Unit, 2009). In the case of environmental action and accomplishment of the Sustainable Development Goals (SDGs), the youth would have a critical role to play (Arab Youth Center, 2020; Billimoria, 2016). As such, climate change weighs heavily in the minds of the younger generation. According to a 2017 report, 92 per cent of millennials[1] in the GCC are concerned about the environment, while around 20 per cent of these millennials view the fight against climate change as one of the top three priorities (Gulf News Report, 2017).

In such a context, this chapter takes stock of environmental actions in the GCC countries. At the outset, the principal environmental concerns faced by these countries are identified. Then, a review of efforts and initiatives is undertaken from two standpoints: government-led and those led by youth. While doing so, attention is also directed towards notable projects and initiatives that have been vital in addressing the environmental concerns in the Gulf.

Environmental Concerns in the GCC

The environment is an expansive term that encompasses nearly all concerns related to anthropogenic activities; for example, climate change is one of the components of environmental concerns. Environment, however, further includes issues such as desertification, pollution (air and coastal), food security, and water crisis. In this sense, the term environment is a more comprehensive expression for the different environment-related problems.

Although the concerns within the GCC countries are more or less similar, the small littoral states are at higher risks owing to a rise in sea levels, change in water salinity, and access to safe water (Intergovernmental Panel on Climate Change, 2013). Pollution has also emerged as a common cause for concern within the GCC (Bardsley, 2019). The GCC accounts for 2.5 per cent of total global greenhouse gas emissions (Climate Watch, 2018). In 2018, the GCC countries featured as the top six GHG emitters (per capita) in the MENA region, with Qatar with 35.89 tonnes leading, followed by Bahrain (31.19 tonnes), the UAE (27.33 tonnes), Kuwait (27.30 tonnes), Saudi Arabia (18.94 tonnes) and Oman (17.04 tonnes per capita). In the total GHG emissions, the Kingdom of Saudi Arabia (KSA) ranked the highest with 638.12 metric tonnes of CO_2 equivalent (MTCO2e), trailed by the UAE (263.24 MTCO2e), Kuwait (112.97 MTCO2e), Qatar (99.83 MTCO2e), Oman (82.32 MTCO2e) and Bahrain (48.95 MTCO2e) (Figures 13.1 and 13.2).

Figure 13.1: Total GHG Emissions in GCC, 2018

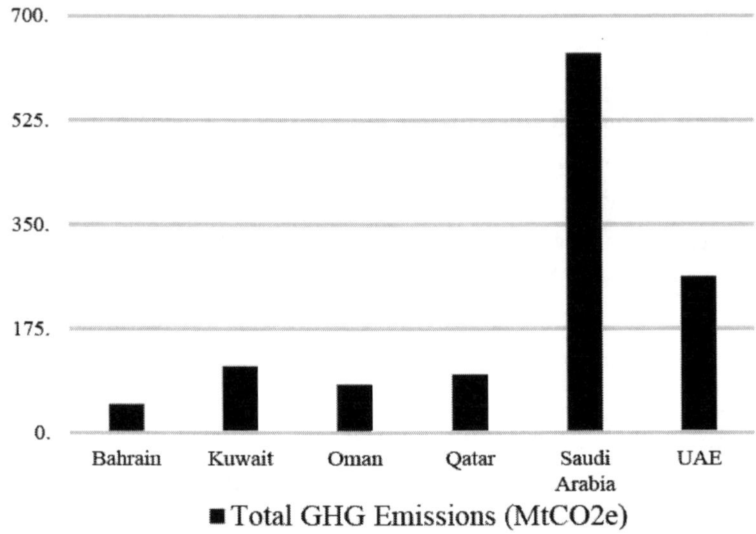

Source: Climate Watch, 2018. *Historical country-level and sectoral GHG emission data (1990-2018).*

Figure 13.2: Per Capita GHG Emissions in GCC, 2018

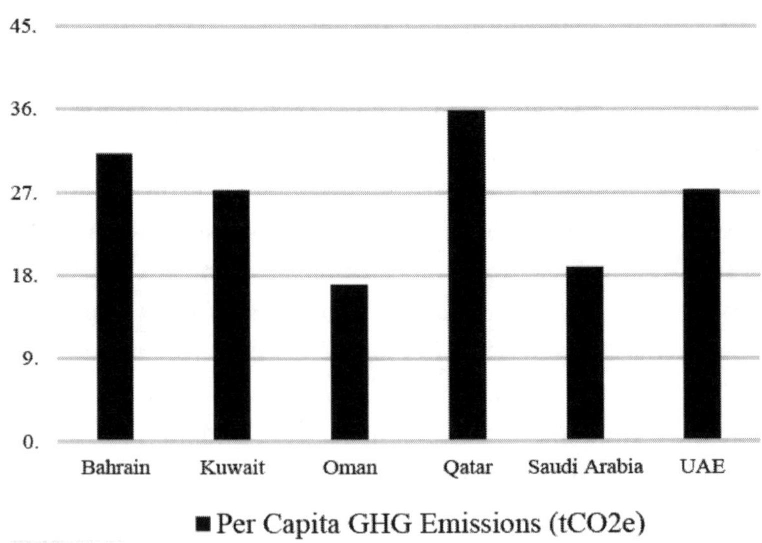

Source: Climate Watch, 2018. *Historical country-level and sectoral GHG emission data (1990-2018).*

Over the last decades, the carbon emissions of all the GCC countries have constantly been increasing, with Saudi Arabia and the UAE being the top emitters. As a result, the cumulative emissions of the GCC have increased from 875.36 MTCO2e to 1245.43 MTCO2e (roughly 25 per cent surge). However, starting in 2015 and carrying into 2016, 2017, and 2018, the growth of emissions in the GCC countries remained low compared to pre-2015 growth rates (see Figure 13.3).

Figure 13.3: GCC Countries GHG Emissions (2008-18)

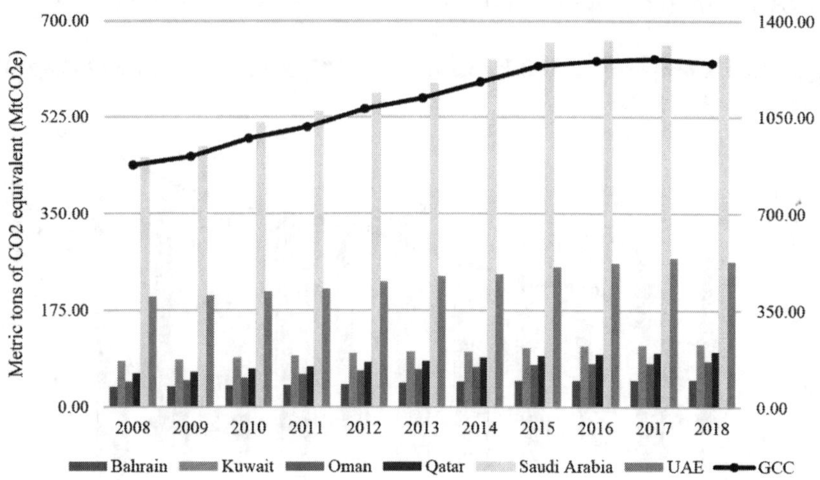

Source: Climate Watch, 2018. *Historical country-level and sectoral GHG emission data (1990-2018).*

Since the MENA region encompasses several large countries and has a larger population share, the gap between the MENA countries and the GCC countries in total emissions becomes wider. Such stark difference occurs due to the substantial emissions that certain MENA countries make. As such, contributions (in cumulative terms) by countries like Iran (828.34 MTCO2e), Egypt (329.40 MTCO2e), Algeria (219.11 MTCO2e) and Iraq (216.19 MTCO2e) upraises MENA's total emissions (Climate Watch, 2018). Comparing the GHG emissions of the GCC, MENA, and the world, it can be observed that emissions of the GCC and the MENA region increased steadily over the last decade, while the global emissions illustrate various sudden increases, including a rapid jump of about 3.86 per cent (highest in a decade) in emissions from 43.02 GtCO2e in 2009 to 44.75 GtCO2e in 2010.

Starting in 2015, the global emission trends picked up the pace with 2016, 2017, and 2018 indicating a steep rise as the emissions climbed from 46.76 GtCO2e (in 2015) to 48.93 GtCO2e (in 2018). However, while the global emission rate continued upward, the year-on-year (YoY) growth of emissions in the GCC has scaled down sharply starting in 2015. Also, within the MENA, the GCC had higher emission rates till 2016, and since then, its emission rates have been lower than that of the MENA region (see Figure 13.4).

Figure 13.4: Comparing GHG Emissions in GCC, MENA & World (2008-18)

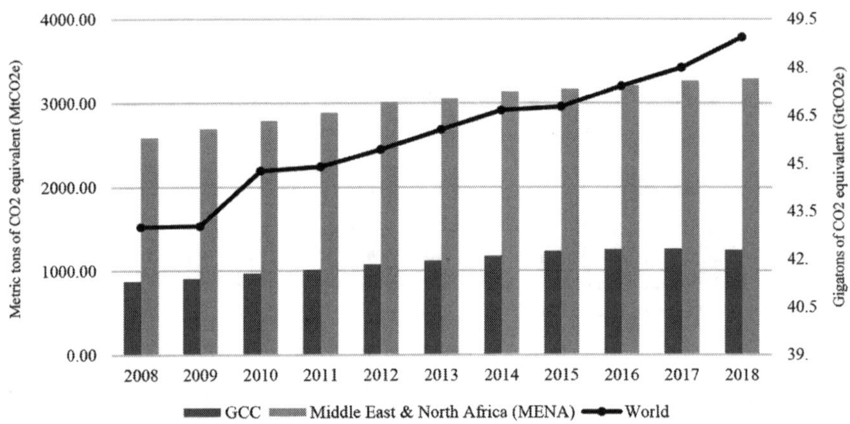

Source: Climate Watch, 2018. *Historical country-level and sectoral GHG emission data (1990-2018).*

Apart from the GHG emissions, there are many other environmental concerns that directly and indirectly impact the Gulf countries. For the most part, the classification of these concerns into proper groups is quite untenable. Nonetheless, the environmental concerns in Gulf countries could be described into three broad levels (see Table 13.1). *Level One* includes macro issues, particularly the climate change phenomenon. The rising sea level (that threatens littoral states), change in water salinity (that impacts fishing and subsequent trade), the exhaustion of non-renewable energy resources is also among the primary concerns, which can be included in this category. The response of the GCC countries (on their respective level) has been to mitigate the adverse impact of such climate change-related concerns by introducing a steady transition from non-renewable to clean energy and pursuing the diversification of their economies.

Table 13.1: Levels of Environmental Concerns in the GCC

	Description	Environmental Concerns	Solutions (proposed & adopted)
Level One	Issues pertaining to large-scale environmental concerns, such as climate change; depletion of fossil fuel reserves.	Rise in sea levels, change in salinity, increased carbon emissions from oil extraction;	Transition to Clean Energy, Decreasing reliance on oil through diversification of economies.
Level Two	Concerns specific to the region, which have long been in existence but have grown more precarious.	Deforestation, desertification, heat waves, drought, sand storms, etc.	Afforestation, Drip irrigation, building robust infrastructures.
Level Three	Concerns that are specific within certain pockets of the GCC countries.	Pollution (Air, Coastal and Marine), Food security, water crisis, etc.	Innovative and technology solutions to the problems of pollution, area-specific projects to provide access to safe water.

Source: Prepared by Author.

Level Two embodies the environmental concerns that are endemic to the region. Although these concerns have existed for some time, the frequency and intensity have intensified in recent years. Prominent examples include deforestation, desertification, aridity, rising periods of drought, and increased frequency of sand storms. The countries have adopted certain measures to alleviate these environmental challenges in the form of afforestation drives, better agricultural practices, investments into drip irrigation, and building robust infrastructures to withstand storms.

Finally, *Level Three* contains localised issues limited to certain settings. For example, air pollution is a problem not in the whole UAE but only in certain cities. The coastal and marine pollution are similar cases. It also covers the predicament of access to fresh water supplies in the countries. Even though food security and water crisis are prominent in the region, some areas are disproportionately affected by these concerns, like in certain parts of Oman and Saudi Arabia. The introduction of an efficient public transport system in Dubai is a palpable solution to the problem of air pollution in the city.

In essence, governments have taken different approaches to deal with these problems and concerns. Even though some of the concerns are specific to certain areas, others are more macro in nature and thus necessitate transboundary cooperation. As such, governments rely on innovation and technological solutions to deal with these problems.

Government-led Actions

The contemporary global environment regime began by government-led initiatives in the 1970s and took present shape after landmark events including the Brundtland Commission (1987), Rio Summit (1992), Kyoto Protocol (1997), Paris Climate Summit (2015), among others (United Nations Environment Programme, 1997). However, from the beginning, the rentier economies of the Gulf demonstrated passivity in engaging with the global environmental regime (Raouf, 2008). For instance, long before the Paris Agreement, the Kyoto Protocol was the principal agreement on climate change, to which all the Gulf countries illustrated hesitancy in joining and did not accede to the Protocol until 2006 (Raouf, 2008). Similar things happened with other issue-specific environment initiatives like the United Nations Convention to Combat Desertification (UNCCD) (1994) (Bauer, 2008). Ideally, desertification should have received popular support within the region, but hardly any enthusiasm was manifested. As it happened, the UNCCD failed to create a tangible action plan to combat desertification (Bauer, 2008) unlike the Vienna Convention for the Protection of the Ozone Layer (1986) and the Montreal Protocol on Substances that Deplete the Ozone Layer (1988) that adopted a unified approach followed by their strict implementation.

However, by the second decade of the 21st century, some changes in the perception of the Gulf countries towards climate change began to emerge. In a certain way, the hesitations prevalent in the 1990s began to diminish as the global environment regime strengthened while the data on climate change became more intelligible and unanimous. The effects of climate change also began manifesting starkly in the region, particularly in the form of increased heat waves and marine degradation. In this direction, the COP18 (Conference of Parties) in Doha (2012), organised under the framework of the United Nations Framework Convention on Climate Change (UNFCCC), was a significant step. The hosting of the world's most significant climate conference speaks volumes of the Gulf nations' changing attitudes and growing concerns. Although controversial, the Doha Conference was significant for it provided the stepping stone for a deal in 2015 (Hedegaard, 2012).

For the Gulf, the COP18 could be regarded as the wake-up call on the climate issue. In light of the Doha Conference, the KSA, Kuwait, and Oman made announcements to produce at least 10 per cent of their energy requirement through renewable energy. Building on COP18, the Gulf countries were actively involved in the COP21 held in Paris in 2015. The same year, the Gulf countries also agreed to the United Nations General Assembly's Agenda 2030 (Sustainable Development Goals [SDGs]) (Abdelraouf, 2015). In short, the perceptions and responses towards the global environmental regime witnessed perceptible changes in the last two decades, driven largely by threats of climate change and fears of resource exhaustion.

Incidentally, just like other sectors in the Gulf countries, governments have largely steered the environmental initiatives, although the pace varies. The earlier government initiatives were incremental and focused on symbolic gestures, such as creating separate ministries and departments dedicated to environmental concerns. However, at present, the governments' interest and participation have increased. Even though one may find exclusive climate-change-related enterprises (like Saudi Green Initiative), most environmental actions in the Gulf have been undertaken as part of the countries' national development plans. Since the environmental issues are wide and varied, addressing them also necessitates a multi-pronged approach. The SDGs are perhaps the best instrument for governments to introduce and execute climate-related initiatives. The UAE's *Vision 2021* could be regarded as the first systemic effort by a Gulf country to address environmental issues. Qatar's *National*

Vision 2030, Kuwait's *New Kuwait 2035*, KSA's *Vision 2030*, Oman's *Vision 2040*, and Bahrain's *Economic Vision 2030* make similar efforts at sustainable development while preserving the environment (Asmyatullin, Tyrkba and Ruzina, 2020).

Part of such ambitious national agendas is to diversify the economy, transit from hydrocarbon to renewables for energy consumption, and address environmental concerns. Accordingly, the Gulf countries have started seriously considering the production and consumption of renewable energy and hold enormous potential for the generation of renewable energy, principally through solar and wind. In this regard, Oman is opportunely situated since it enjoys the highest onshore wind speed range (3-6.3 m s^{-1}), trailed by Kuwait (4.5-5.5 m s^{-1}) and Saudi Arabia (3-6 m s^{-1}) (Alharbi and Csala, 2021). In the case of solar energy, too, Oman receives the highest annual solar radiation (up to 2500 kWh/m^2), followed by the UAE (2285 kWh/m^2), Saudi Arabia (2200 kWh/m^2), and Kuwait (2200 kWh/m^2) (Alharbi and Csala, 2021).

Recently, the Barakah nuclear power plant in the UAE went online. Barakah marks the first nuclear plant in the Arab world, which would produce 5.6 gigawatts of electricity while preventing the release of nearly 21 million tons of carbon emissions every year (Staff Writer, 2020). In 2021, the state-owned 'Qatar Petroleum' has launched a Sustainability Strategy that establishes targets in line with Paris Agreement which proposes to cut-down emission intensity of Qatar's LNG facilities by 25 per cent (Staff Editor, 2021). Additionally, Qatar signed an agreement with France's Total and Japan's Marubeni to construct a US$ 467 million Al Kharsaah solar plant (near Doha), which after completion, capable of producing 800-megawatt electricity (one-tenth of Qatar's energy demand) (Al Jazeera, 2020). In 2021, Saudi Crown Prince Mohammad bin Salman (MbS) inaugurated the Sakaka solar plant in Al Jawf province, during which he also announced the establishment of seven new solar plants. A separate wind energy project in Dumat Al-Jandal is nearing completion in Al Jawf. Combined, these projects would produce 3,600-megawatts of power (Arab News, 2021). Similar initiatives have been undertaken in other countries, with entrepreneurs increasingly engaging in green energy projects (Atlantic Council, 2017).

Saudi Arabia

Launched by Crown Prince Mohammad bin Salman, the Saudi Green Initiative aims to "improve quality of life and protect future generations by increasing reliance on clean energy, offsetting the impact of fossil fuels and protecting the environment" (Saudi Green Initiative, 2021). In association with the Middle East Green Initiative, the Saudi Green Initiative project complements the Saudi national strategy known as *Vision 2030* and is expected to be Riyadh's most concerted long-term effort in environmental action. They would add to the Kingdom's earlier environmental initiatives to increase the vegetation cover and its efforts to transition from non-renewables to clean energy. Essentially, the Kingdom faces concerns related to all three categories. In addition, there are concerns about a rise in sea level in the Red Sea, dust storms and desertification. While expressing the concerns raised by dust storms, MbS admitted that the region incurs a loss of US$ 13 billion annually. *Level Three* includes pollution, is a significant concern for the Kingdom since air pollution has reduced the life expectancy by 1.5 years (Saudi Green Initiative, 2021a).

The Kingdom has pledged to achieve net-zero emissions by the year 2060 (Saudi Green Initiative, 2021b), while also identifying other targets under these initiatives, such as planting ten billion trees across Saudi Arabia, raising protected areas to more than 30 per cent of total area, and inclusion of 50 per cent renewables in country's energy mix by 2030 (Saudi Green Initiative, 2021b). Moreover, these initiatives would ensure increased investments in renewable energy while also trying to revamp and adopt better technologies for the country's existing infrastructure in hydrocarbon production. Under its ambitious *Vision 2030*, the creation of a 170 km Line City in Neom has been modelled on such plans (Yaakoubi and Rashad, 2021).

In the Gulf, Saudi Arabia is the most populous Arab country. It accounts for the highest GHG emissions and also seeks to play a critical role in regional and global affairs. By taking on leadership in the environmental concerns, the Kingdom can address all three concerns simultaneously. As MbS emphasised, the Kingdom "fully recognises its share of responsibility" while wilfully intending to play a more determining role in the climate change crisis. To quote the announcement document, through the Middle

East Green Initiative, "Saudi Arabia will spearhead regional efforts to achieve global targets to combat climate change" (Saudi Green Initiative, 2021a). In this way, the Saudi efforts regarding environmental actions are informed not only by solving the environmental concerns but also by its ambitions to play a leading role in Clean Energy and Climate Change politics. The Middle East Green Initiative would exhibit a critical role in achieving the climate goals. Since most of the environmental actions in the GCC and the wider Middle East are undertaken by individual countries rather than a collective, the Kingdom's Middle East Green Initiative would mark the first transboundary mega-project to tackle the environmental concerns in the region.

United Arab Emirates

The Emirates made one of the foremost actions related to climate change and the environment in the Gulf. The country possesses a vast coastline of roughly 1,300 km and, therefore, falls under high vulnerability due to rising sea levels (*Level One*). For this, the country aims to make huge investments in renewable energy under its Clean Energy Strategy 2035. It further aims to produce the cheapest electricity with the construction of the world's largest solar power plant, conserve biodiversity by focusing on biodiversity tourism and planting one million mangroves, increasing efforts to counter water scarcity. In 2017, the UAE adopted the National Climate Change Plan 2017-2050, which provides a framework for managing greenhouse gas (GHG) emissions, climate change responses, and innovative economic diversification (Government of the United Arab Emirates, 2020).

By far, the UAE is the only GCC country to submit two Nationally Determined Contribution (NDC) reports to the United Nations. Introduced through article 2 of the Paris Agreement, the NDCs are instruments of self-reporting by individual countries about their mitigation efforts and climate actions to achieve the long-term objectives agreed in Paris 2015 (United Nations, 2015). The report outlined the Emirati strategy to reduce the carbon emissions by a quarter (23.5 per cent) of its business as usual (BAU) emissions by 2030 (Al Nuaimi, 2020). The UAE has been active in climate diplomacy as it tries to win a bid to host the COP28 (Murphy, 2021).

Massive infrastructure projects that the country has undertaken in the last two decades had direct consequences for the coastal and marine ecosystems. Incidentally, some environmental concerns (*Level Three*) like air pollution are born out of extensive construction projects. Similarly, marine pollution has increased on account of dredging and the construction of artificial islands. Such concerns have generated early response from the government, as demonstrated by various projects taken up in Abu Dhabi, Sharjah, and Dubai under the UNFCCC's clean development mechanism (CDM) (Raouf, 2008). In 2007, Abu Dhabi's government launched the world's first zero-carbon city project called Masdar City (Walsh, 2011). Since then, the UAE has launched various smart city projects, including the 'Sustainable City' and US$ 8.17 billion worth of 'Desert Rose City' (Buller, 2021; Deulgaonkar, 2016). The UAE's national plan (*Vision 2021*) was momentous, and the earliest of its plans was launched in 2010. A sustainable environment is one of the six national priorities of the seven-year National Agenda, which was adopted as part of *Vision 2021* (Government of the United Arab Emirates, 2021). Besides this, the UAE government has announced a multitude of projects and strategies (much like its National Climate Change Plan) targeting specific environmental concerns like water scarcity, aridity, and marine life in the next 30 years.

Oman

Oman suffers heavily from the climate change phenomenon (*Level One*) as the change in water salinity has disrupted the fishing patterns of the country. A significant Omani population is blessed with a huge coastline engaged in fishery (from fishing to processed products). However, certain remote parts have also been subjected to the water crisis. In light of such challenges, in December 2015, the Oman government announced a long-term project in association with the World Bank titled, *Fisheries and Aquaculture Vision 2040: Sustainable Management of the Fisheries Sector in Oman*. The project aims to create a "profitable world-class fisheries sector that is ecologically sustainable and a net contributor to the economy of Oman" (Sultanate of Oman and World Bank, 2015, p. 1). By inducting support from the private sector, the project would also utilise the expertise of the World Bank. An ambitious project, *Vision 2040,* is meant to bring whole-scale reform in the fishery by making the Omani value chains more efficient and adding value to the sector. Environmental sustainability is an important aspect of the project. As noted in the vision document, "Sustainability is hard-wired into all of the five big steps comprising Vision 2040, and community sustainability is inextricably bound with stakeholder engagement and stakeholder management" (Sultanate of Oman and World Bank, 2015, p. 11).

Criticisms of Government-led Action

It has been argued that the Middle East region started paying attention to environment-related concerns only over the last decade or so (Schaar, 2020). The climate sceptics still question both the sincerity and substance of such mega-initiatives (Sims, 2020; Arab Sustainable Development Report, 2020; Shafi, 2019a). As such, these concerns are not unfounded. For instance, the trends of smart cities that the Gulf countries are investing heavily in also risk becoming ghost towns, if they fail to appeal to the public. Another critical challenge is the lack of integrated policymaking (Schaar, 2020). The GCC was established to "effect coordination, integration and inter-connection between Member States in all fields in order to achieve unity between them" (Gulf Cooperation Council [GCC], 1981). And yet, no integrated measures or regional policy on climate change has been discussed. As far as the SDGs are concerned that are the vehicle of environmental action, the efforts of the Arab region have been stymied by the presence of "structural and entrenched barriers" (Arab Sustainable Development Report, 2020, p. 11). In this regard, some diffidence can also be observed. For instance, the GCC countries lag in their obligations to their SDGs (Arab Sustainable Development Report, 2020). By 2021, Saudi Arabia, Bahrain, Kuwait, and Qatar have not submitted their emission reduction targets in their National Determined Contributions (NDCs) reports to the UNFCCC Secretariat.

Youth-led Action

For decades, environmental issues have inspired youth activism from every section of society in nearly every country. The younger generations are disproportionately impacted and, therefore, increasingly invested in such issues. Perhaps, for such a reason, the *Arab Sustainable Development*

Report (2020) observed that climate change would impose "historical injustice" on the young and future generations (Arab Sustainable Development Report, 2020). As such, of all the major global issues, no other issue has more youth involvement, as does the issue of the environment. Reportedly, 92 per cent of millennials in the GCC believe that the environment is under threat, more than it was 20 years ago (Gulf News, 2017). Like the other countries, the youth in the GCC would be directly impacted by the consequences of actions and inactions related to climate change. "Young people, both in the Kingdom and the world, are demanding a cleaner, greener and more inclusive future, and we owe it to them to deliver on this," emphasised the Saudi Crown Prince (Saudi Green Initiative, 2021a).

Even though the young generation would be the largest employable workforce in the GCC and African[2] countries, the youth insist that their interests are under-represented. As noted in a popular speech by a young girl at COP18, "I speak for half the world. We are the silent majority. You've given us a seat in this hall, but our interests are not on the table" (Vidal, 2012). As more of the younger population enter the workforce, including women, they would constitute the major demography of the workforce in upcoming decades. However, for youth activists, participation through the workforce seems inadequate. For they consider the younger generation a stakeholder in climate change concerns, and therefore, demand a seat at the table. In other words, the youth activists insist that younger generations should not be restricted to the workforce as functionaries of government-led initiatives but should also play a leadership role (Maella, 2012). Here, the meaning of 'leadership role' goes beyond the traditional understanding of leadership based on state-centric structures. Instead, the youths seek to represent and lead through non-state actors such as non-governmental organisations (NGOs), advocacy groups, and social and political activism.

Amidst the increasing population trends, the GCC is bound to remain a "youthful region" (Economic Intelligence Unit, 2009). Overall, in the GCC, the youth comprise nearly one-third of the population. Even though the percentage of the youth population (and also their definition) varies throughout the GCC, in the upcoming decades, the large segments of the population in these countries would be young.

As such, the youth-led environmental action has enormous potential in the Gulf. The adoption of mega-developmental plans by the government would enable a more conducive atmosphere for the youth to develop skills and communicate their views and ideas to a larger population with minimal resources. In addition, the educational and entrepreneurial initiatives that are incubating under these developmental plans allow the newly established groups focused on climate change to collaborate with the governments. So far, the climate change-related initiative has been a mainstay of the government, but there are a handful of civil society and advocacy groups that are taking the lead on environmental action in the GCC countries. The Arab Climate Youth Movement Qatar is a case in point. Kuwait's Eco-Star is another example. Founded by Fatemah Alzelzela in 2019, the 'Eco-Star' is a non-profit that recycles waste from homes, restaurants, and schools at a nominal price of US$ 3 (United Nations Environment Programme, 2020). For each transaction, the group also provides seeds or a plant to foster the habit of planting trees/bushes. Established in 2017, *Zero Hour* is a youth-led movement operating in the UAE that enables conversations around climate change and environmental justice by providing training and resources to young activists. *Connect With Nature* is yet another UAE-based youth-led initiative that seeks to "provide the experiences, knowledge and skills to create future changemakers and environmental leaders" (Connect With Nature, 2021).

Arab Climate Youth Movement Qatar (ACYMQ)

ACYMQ is a youth-led advocacy group based in Qatar that aims to find a "niche space" for environmental discourse in the country. Further, the movement seeks to "solve the climate crisis and to assess and support the establishment of legally binding agreements to deal with climate change issue within international negotiations" (Arab Youth Climate Movement Qatar, 2015). Founded in the lead-up to COP18 meeting in Doha 2012, the movement has focused on grassroots education and awareness on environmental issues while also building awareness through evidence-based policy research on environmental issues. In May 2019, the Arab Youth Climate Movement Qatar became the first independent, youth-led, grassroots association in the country. The vision statement of the group highlights its mission is to

> ... build a movement which fosters understanding of our natural ecosystems, empowers and inspires the community to take effective action in resolving the current ecological crisis, and advocates for evidence-based policies to adapt, mitigate, conserve and protect our ecosystem. (Arab Youth Climate Movement Qatar, 2015)

As such, the group outlines five broad objectives: developing holistic educational programmes, building international partnerships, building a shared vision of Qatar's ecological future, engaging youth, and advocacy to bring policy change through sustained grassroots campaigns (Arab Youth Climate Movement Qatar, 2015). The movement incorporates the support of volunteers from different sectors and educational backgrounds to provide government support in formulating eco-friendly policies. In Qatar, the ACYM is supported by several local organisations, UNESCO Doha, Qatar Foundation, educational institutions, and the Directorate of Climate Change at the Ministry of Municipality and Environment. Moreover, it works with other international climate change organisations like indyACT, 350.org, and Climate Action Network (CAN). Recently, the group has initiated the *Earth Talk Series* to bring environmentalists and development professionals worldwide to discuss environmental issues in a localised context (Arab Youth Climate Movement Qatar, 2015).

The ACYM presents a dazzling example of climate activism and advocacy in the region that expresses the growing concerns of climate change and the necessity for action. The movement regards its vision that the youth should be able to enjoy a climate like their parents and grandparents. Noteworthy is the establishment of the movement that came about during COP18 in Doha. During the COP18, Qatar also witnessed its first climate march attended by around 800 people, especially the youth (Vidal, 2012a). As a result, the movement received widespread international support and recognition during the summit. Since then, it has insisted that Qatar and other Middle Eastern countries should make concerted efforts to recognise the concerns emanating from environment degradation and accordingly should make climate change a priority. In addition, the movement has been able to muster support and collaboration from other Middle Eastern countries like Saudi Arabia, Jordan, Sudan, Mauritania, Libya, and Oman.

Arab Youth Council for Climate Change (AYCCC)

The Arab Youth Council for Climate Change (AYCCC) is a recent initiative that seeks to achieve a "qualitative leap in the interaction of Arab youth with environmental issues" by supporting climate action and encouraging interactions among Arab youths. It is a multistakeholder initiative carried out by Arab Youth Center in association with the UAE's Ministry of Climate Change and Environment (MOCCAE), the Office of the UAE's Special Envoy for Climate Change, private players like Posterity Institute, and several other partners under the aegis of the Arab League (AYCCC, 2021). The council's major goals include supporting fellow Arab nations to achieve their respective climate action goals, increasing awareness about environmental issues, proposing effective green solutions, making recommendations for policy-makers, and representing the Arab youths at various local and international forums by enabling a platform for their opinions and ideas.

In addition, the council aims to promote investment, small and medium enterprises, and start-ups in environment and clean energy (AYCCC, 2021). By providing the young Arabs with skills and knowledge on environment-related concerns, the council aspires to act as a bridge between youth and the decision-makers in the Arab world (Staff Report, 2021). The council has constituted a specialised committee to enlist youths from the Arab world to participate and contribute to its established agenda. It has further announced to biennially host 15-Arab youths from the government and private sector, who are working on challenges related to climate change to voice their concerns by playing a leadership role in the field. Already, the council has tied up with small and micro initiatives in the Arab world.

Even though the council is a semi-governmental enterprise, it carries enormous potential for youth participation. A report by Arab Youth Center acknowledged the underfunding of youth programmes and a fragmented government approach towards youth action. As such, the

AYCCC presents a unique opportunity for the younger people aspiring to bring change in the environment to step in not just as a participant but in a leadership role. To quote from a report from the council, "They [Youth] should not only become part of the solution, they should lead it" (Arab Youth Center (AYC), 2021, p. 2).

Limitations of Youth-led Action

First, the long-running security issues and geopolitical struggles overshadow the role of civil society in the MENA region leaving little room for issues-specific advocacy. Even those civil society groups that function in these countries look to the government for patronage. For their part, the governments have reservations in supporting civil societies as they suspect that the civil societies may become a platform for dissent and censure against the government (Abdelaziz, 2017; Malit and Youha, 2014). On the other hand, the youth themselves in the Arab consider security as their topmost priority, followed closely by education and health (Arab Youth Center, 2020). From the available data,[3] the lesser proportion of youth in KSA (19 per cent) view the environment as a priority, followed by the UAE (8 per cent), Bahrain (6 per cent), and Kuwait (5 per cent) (Arab Youth Center, 2020). As such, the issues of safety and security concerns the youth are far greater than environmental concerns.

Second, the existing literacy and awareness among the population about environmental issues are low, making it even more difficult to advocate these issues (Shafi, 2019). "Arab youth face an additional barrier from educational systems that leave them without the necessary knowledge and tools to mobilise around climate actions" (Arab Sustainable Development Report, 2020, p. 172). In a 2017 report, just half of the millennials in the GCC countries agree that their education has prepared them satisfactorily to combat future challenges, including global warming (*Gulf News*, 2017). Here, the advocacy groups and NGOs could benefit by collaborating with the government. Qatar's patronship of ACYMQ is a good case, wherein the group carried out small-scale operations, worked with volunteers until support from the government and the international groups came. The UAE's AYCCC is another brilliant platform for enabling the youth to educate the public about the environment and support policy change. The role of technology and better educational facilities to the young populace could also be driving rapid changes in social attitudes and norms (Abyad, 2018).

The third is the lack of faith in non-governmental organisations. As pointed out by Neeshad Safi, "the lack of faith in the ability of non-governmental organisations to drive change in most Arab countries. This perception is also exemplified by the fact that there is no framework for non-profit organisations to establish themselves, which significantly hinders them in working to their full potential" (Shafi, 2019a). Amidst this lack of faith, youth's role in non-profits is not fully understood and is limited by existing apprehensions, and consequently, have scuttled youths' success in the past to drive and influence agendas.

Conclusion

The Gulf is expected to face direct as well as indirect consequences of change in the environment. Given their economically strong positions, the Gulf countries are better equipped to adapt to climate change while also having the potential to tackle specific environmental challenges. The governments in all the GCC countries have introduced ambitious national agendas that entail large-scale investments in innovation and R&D to combat challenges emerging from climate change. In doing so, these rentier economies have also pursued a diversification drive to transition from hydrocarbon to renewable energy. Even though Saudi Arabia and the UAE account for the largest GHG emissions, they have been at the forefront of economic diversification and environmental action in the region. In short, the initiatives on environmental action have been largely government-led.

There is a discernible youth enthusiasm to lead and participate in climate and environment-related initiatives. But, the issues pertaining to the environment have been a low priority for the youth, which have been compounded by low awareness and education on climate change. Therefore, the role of the youth in the GCC has been generally passive. Apart from ACYMQ, a few isolated examples stand out in youth-led action on the environment. Nevertheless, this is set to change as the role of youth in climate change action has been increasingly recognised and promoted. Moreover, the expansion of government initiatives carries an enormous opportunity for the young generations to become part of environmental action in the Gulf.

Notes

1. Millennials are defined as individuals aged 18-29.
2. African countries are supposed to be the world's largest young demographic.
3. The data is elicited from *Arab Youth Priorities Survey Report* (2020), conducted and published by the UAE-based Arab Youth Center. The survey included the responses from nearly 7,000 Arab youths in 21 Arab countries. For more, see Arab Youth Center. (2020). *Arab Youth Priorities Survey*. Abu Dhabi: Arab Youth Center Publication. Retrieved September 30, 2021, https://arabyouthcenter.org/en/article/our-research/arab-youth-priority-survey

References

Abdelaziz, Mohamed (2017), "The Hard Reality of Civil Society in the Arab World," Fikra Forum, Washington Institute for Near East Policy, December 11, https://www.washingtoninstitute.org/policy-analysis/hard-reality-civil-society-arab-world, accessed on October 22, 2021.

Abdelraouf, Mohammed (2015), "The GCC and the Paris Climate Change Talks," Trends Research and Advisory, December 1, https://trendsresearch.org/insight/the-gcc-and-the-paris-climate-change-talks/, accessed on September 28, 2021.

Abumoghli, Iyad and Goncalves, Adele (2020), "Environmental Challenges in the MENA Region," United Nations Environment Programme (UNEP), https://wedocs.unep.org/bitstream/handle/20.500.11822/31645/EC_MENA.pdf?sequence=1&isAllowed=y, accessed on September 27, 2021.

Abyad, Abdulrazak (2018), "Demographic Changes in the GCC Countries: Reflection and Future Projections," *Middle East Journal of Age and Ageing*, vol. 15, no. 1, pp. 20-24.

Al Jazeera (2020), "Qatar to Build New Solar Power Plant," January 20, https://www.aljazeera.com/economy/2020/1/20/qatar-to-build-new-solar-power-plant, accessed on September 28, 2021.

Al Nuaimi, Abdullah B. (2020), "How the UAE Is Taking the Climate Change Fight Into 2021," *The National*, https://www.thenationalnews.com/opinion/comment/how-the-uae-is-taking-the-climate-change-fight-into-2021-1.1141985, accessed on September 29, 2021.

Alharbi, Fahad R. and Csala, Denes (2021), "Gulf Cooperation Council Countries' Climate Change Mitigation Challenges and Exploration of Solar and Wind Energy Resource Potential," *Applied Sciences*, vol. 11, no. 6, https://doi.org/10.3390/app11062648, accessed on September 30, 2021.

Amery, Hussein A. (2017), "Water-Demand Management in The Arab Gulf States: Implications For Political Stability," in Jean A. Cahan (ed.), *Water Security in the Middle East: Essays in Scientific and Social Cooperation*, pp. 67-91, London: Anthem Press.

Arab News (2020), "UAE Fires Up First Nuclear Plant in the Arab World," August 1, https://www.arabnews.com/node/1713086/middle-east, accessed on September 29, 2021.

Arab News (2021), "Saudi Arabia's Crown Prince Announces 7 Solar Projects as Sakaka Plant Opens," April 8, https://www.arabnews.com/node/1839676/saudi-arabia, accessed on September 27, 2021.

Arab Youth Center (2021), *Arab Youth Council for Climate Change: Mobilising Youth for a Sustainable Future,* Abu Dhabi, https://climate.arabyouthcenter.org/en, accessed on September 29, 2021.

Arab Youth Center (2020), *Arab Youth Priorities Survey*, Arab Youth Center Publication, Abu Dhabi, https://arabyouthcenter.org/en/article/our-research/arab-youth-priority-survey, accessed on September 30, 2021.

Arab Youth Center (2020), *The State of Arab Youth on SDGs,* Arab Youth Center Publication, Abu Dhabi.

Arab Youth Climate Movement Qatar (2015), *Vision & Mission*, AYCMQ, https://www.aycmqatar.org/aycm-vision-and-mission.html, accessed on September 26, 2021.

Arab Youth Climate Movement Qatar (2020), *About: Earth Talk Series,* AYCMQ, https://www.aycmqatar.org/earth-talk-series.html, accessed on September 26, 2021.

Asmyatullin, Ravil, Tyrkba, Khanifa and Ruzina, Elizaveta (2020), "Smart Cities in GCC: Comparative Study of Economic Dimension," *IOP Conference Series: Earth and Environmental Science*, vol. 459, https://doi.org/10.1088/1755-1315/459/6/062045, accessed on September 30, 2021.

Arab Youth Center (2021), "Arab Youth Council for Climate Change: About the Council," Abu Dhabi, https://climate.arabyouthcenter.org/en, accessed on October 25, 2021.

Bardsley, Daniel (2019), "World Environment Day: Middle Eastern Cities Choked by Air Pollution," *The National,* July 1, https://www.thenationalnews.com/uae/world-environment-day-middle-eastern-cities-choked-by-air-pollution-1.870540, accessed on September 30, 2021.

Bauer, Steffen (2008), "Bureaucratic Authority and the Implementation of International Treaties: Evidence From Two Convention Secretariats," in Jutta Joachim, Bob Reinalda and Bertjan Verbeek (eds.), *International Organizations and Implementation: Enforcers, Managers, Authorities?*, pp. 62-74, Abingdon: Routledge.

Billimoria, Jeroo (2016), "Why Young People Are Key to Achieving the SDGs," World Economic Forum (WEF), September 26, https://www.weforum.org/agenda/2016/09/why-young-people-are-key-to-achieving-the-sdgs, accessed on September 29, 2021.

Buller, Alicia (2021), "The Gulf Is Counting on Its Smart Cities for a Sustainable and Profitable Future," *Computer Weekly*, September 2, https://www.computerweekly.com/news/252506103/The-Gulf-is-counting-on-its-smart-cities-for-a-sustainable-and-profitable-future, accessed on September 29, 2021.

Central Intelligence Agency (CIA) (2021), "Country Profile: CIA The World Factbook", https://www.cia.gov/the-world-factbook/countries/, accessed on September 29, 2021.

Climate Watch (2018), "Historical Country- Level and Sectoral GHG Emission Data (1990-2018)", https://www.climatewatchdata.org/ghg-emissions?calculation=PER_CAPITA&chartType=line&end_year=2018&regions=MNA&source=CAIT&start_year=1990, accessed on September 27, 2021.

Connect With Nature (2021), "About Us: Connect With Nature," Abu Dhabi, https://connectwithnature.ae/about-us#:~:text=Established%20in%202006%20in%20Abu,Al%20Nahyan%20in%20the%201970s, accessed on September 30, 2021.

Deulgaonkar, Parag (2016), "Dubai's $8bn Desert Rose Project at Detailed Design Stage," *Arabian Business*, October 13, https://www.arabianbusiness.com/dubai-s-8bn-desert-rose-project-at-detailed-design-stage-648932.html, accessed on September 28, 2021.

Economist Intelligence Unit (2009), "The GCC in 2020: The Gulf And Its People", Qatar Financial Centre Authority, *The Economist*, September, http://graphics.eiu.com/upload/eb/gulf2020part2.pdf, accessed on September 25, 2021.

Government of the United Arab Emirates (2020), "Second Nationally Determined Contribution of the United Arab Emirates", United Nations Framework Convention for Climate Change, https://www4.unfccc.int/sites/ndcstaging/PublishedDocuments/United%20Arab%20Emirates%20Second/UAE%20Second%20NDC%20-%20UNFCCC%20Submission%20-%20English%20-%20FINAL.pdf, accessed on September 29, 2021.

Government of the United Arab Emirates (2021), "National Agenda," June 6, https://u.ae/en/about-the-uae/strategies-initiatives-and-awards/federal-governments-strategies-and-plans/national-agenda, accessed on September 29, 2021.

Gulf Cooperation Council (1981), "About GCC: Charter", May 25, https://www.gcc-sg.org/en-us/AboutGCC/Pages/Primarylaw.aspx, accessed on September 26, 2021.

Gulf News (2017), "Report: 92% of Millennials in GCC Believe Climate Change Is a Real Threat", January 20, https://gulfnews.com/uae/environment/92-of-millennials-in-gcc-believe-climate-change-is-a-real-threat-1.1964980, accessed on September 29, 2021.

Gulf News (2021), "Arab Youth Centre Launches Arab Youth Council for Climate Change," August 12, https://gulfnews.com/uae/arab-youth-centre-launches-arab-youth-council-for-climate-change-1.81533071, accessed on September 29, 2021.

Hedegaard, Connie (2012), "Why the Doha Climate Conference Was a Success," *The Guardian*, December 14, https://www.theguardian.com/environment/2012/dec/14/doha-climate-conference-success, accessed on September 26, 2021.

Intergovernmental Panel on Climate Change (2013), *AR4 Climate Change 2013: The Physical Science Basis, Contribution of Working Group I to the Fifth Assessment Report of the Intergovernmental Panel on Climate Change,* Cambridge and New York: Cambridge University Press.

Intergovernmental Panel on Climate Change (2014), "AR5 Climate Change 2014: Synthesis Report, Contribution of Working Groups I, II and III to the Fifth Assessment Report of the Intergovernmental Panel on Climate Change", Geneva, Switzerland, https://www.ipcc.ch/report/ar5/syr/, accessed on September 29, 2021.

Intergovernmental Panel on Climate Change (2021), "AR6 Climate Change 2021: The Physical Science Basis, Contribution of Working Group I to the Sixth Assessment Report of the Intergovernmental Panel on Climate Change", New York: United Nations, https://www.ipcc.ch/report/ar6/wg1/downloads/report/IPCC_AR6_WGI_Full_Report.pdf, accessed on September 30, 2021.

Kabbani, Nader and Mimoune, Nejla B. (2021), "Economic Diversification in the Gulf: Time to Redouble Efforts", Washington DC: Brookings, https://www.brookings.edu/research/economic-diversification-in-the-gulf-time-to-redouble-efforts/, accessed on September 29, 2021.

Maella, Reem A. (2012), "The Whole World Thinks Arab Youth Don't Care," *Deutsche Welle*, November 22, https://www.dw.com/en/the-whole-world-thinks-arab-youth-dont-care/a-16398911, accessed on September 26, 2021.

Mahdavy, Hussein (1970), "Patterns and Problems of Economic Development in Rentier States: The Case of Iran," in Michael A. Cook (ed.), *Studies in the Economic History of the Middle East,* pp. 428-467, London: Routledge.

Malit, Froilan T. and Al Youha, Ali (2014), "Global Civil Society in Qatar and the Gulf Cooperation Council: Emerging Dilemmas and Opportunities," Migration Policy Institute, April 9, https://www.migrationpolicy.org/article/global-civil-society-qatar-and-gulf-cooperation-council-emerging-dilemmas-and-opportunities, accessed on October 22, 2021.

Murphy, Dan (2021), "UAE Bid for COP28 Summit Focuses on Economic Opportunities in Climate Action," CNBC, May 25, https://www.cnbc.

com/2021/05/25/uae-bid-for-cop28-focuses-on-economic-opportunities-in-climate-action.html, accessed on September 28, 2021.

Nair, Shalini (2021), "Qatar Petroleum Launches Sustainability Strategy," *Offshore Technology*, January 14, https://www.offshore-technology.com/news/qatar-petroleum-sustainability-strategy/, accessed on September 27, 2021.

Nyambuu, Unurjargal and Semmler, Willi (2020), "Climate Change and the Transition to a Low Carbon Economy– Carbon Targets and the Carbon Budget, *Economic Modelling*, vol. 84, pp. 367-376, https://doi.org/10.1016/j.econmod.2019.04.026, accessed on October 30, 2021.

Oxford Business Group (2016), *The Report: Dubai 2016.*

Petersen, Maxwell (2017), "Energy Innovation and Entrepreneurship in the Middle East," Atlantic Council, April 19, https://www.atlanticcouncil.org/commentary/event-recap/energy-innovation-and-entrepreneurship-in-the-middle-east-2/, accessed on September 26, 2021.

Raouf, Mohamed A. (2008) "Climate Change Threats, Opportunities, and the GCC Countries," *Middle East Institute Policy Briefs*, vol. 12, pp. 1-17.

Schaar, Johan (2020), "What the World Can Do About the Middle East's Coming Environmental Crisis", The Century Foundation, December 14, https://tcf.org/content/report/world-can-middle-easts-coming-environmental-crisis/?session=1&session=1&session=1, accessed on September 25, 2021.

Saudi Green Initiative (2021), "Press Release: His Royal Highness the Crown Prince Announces the Kingdom of Saudi Arabia's Aims to Achieve Net Zero Emissions by 2060", October 23, https://www.saudigreeninitiative.org/pr/SGI_Forum_Press_Release-EN.pdf, accessed on October 25, 2021.

Saudi Green Initiative (2021a), "Announcement Document: Saudi Green Initiative", March 27, https://www.saudigreeninitiative.org/wp-content/uploads/2021/05/27March_EN_HRH_Crown_Prince_Announces_the_Saudi_Green_Initiative_and_the_Middle_East_Green_Initiative.pdf, accessed on September 27, 2021.

Saudi Green Initiative (2021b), "Our Purpose: Saudi Green Initiative", https://www.saudigreeninitiative.org/#purpose, accessed on September 24, 2021.

Shafi, Neeshad (2019), "The Arab World's Best Weapon Against Climate Change? Its Young People," World Economic Forum, January 18, https://www.weforum.org/agenda/2019/01/the-arab-worlds-best-weapon-against-climate-change-its-youth/, accessed on September 24, 2021.

Shafi, Neeshad (2019), "International Perspectives: Arab Youth Climate Movement Qatar," *International Journal of Wilderness*, vol. 25, no. 3.

Sims, David (2020), "Can Arab Cities Be Eco-Sustainable?", *The Cairo Review of Global Affairs*, vol. 37, https://www.thecairoreview.com/essays/can-arab-cities-be-eco-sustainable/, accessed on September 18, 2021.

Springborg, Robert (2013), "GCC Countries as "Rentier States" Revisited," *Middle East Journal*, vol. 67, no. 2, pp. 301-309.

Stang, Gerald (2016), "Climate Challenges in the Middle East: Rethinking Environmental Cooperation," *Middle East Institute Regional Cooperation Series*, Washington DC: Middle East Institute.

Sultanate of Oman and World Bank (2015), "Fisheries and Aquaculture Vision 2040: Sustainable Management of the Fisheries Sector in Oman", Muscat: Ministry of Agriculture and Fisheries Wealth (Sultanate of Oman) and World Bank, https://andp.unescwa.org/sites/default/files/2020-10/Fisheries%20and%20Aquaculture%20Vision%202040.pdf, accessed on September 28, 2021.

United Nations (2015), "Official Text: Paris Agreement", December 12, https://unfccc.int/sites/default/files/english_paris_agreement.pdf, accessed on September 26, 2021.

United Nations Development Programme (UNDP) and Global Environment Facility (GEF) (2018), *Climate Change Adaptation in the Arab States: Best Practices and Lessons Learned*, Bangkok: United Nations Development Programme (UNDP).

United Nations Economic and Social Commission for Western Asia (ESCWA), (2020), *Arab Sustainable Development Report, 2020,* Beirut: United Nations, https://asdr.unescwa.org/sdgs/pdf/en/ASDR2020-Final-Online.pdf, accessed on September 24, 2021.

United Nations Environment Programme (1997), *Handbook of International Environment Law,* Nairobi: United Nations.

United Nations Environment Programme (2020), "Bringing Recycling to Kuwait," December 15, https://www.unep.org/news-and-stories/story/bringing-recycling-kuwait, accessed on September 29, 2021.

Vidal, John (2012), "Youth Activists Bring Energy and Urgency," *The Guardian*, December 4, https://www.theguardian.com/environment/blog/2012/dec/04/doha-climate-conference-diary, accessed on September 28, 2021.

Vidal, John (2012), "Doha Climate Conference Diary: Qatar's First Environmental March," *The Guardian*, December 3, https://www.theguardian.com/environment/blog/2012/dec/03/doha-climate-conference-diary, accessed on September 27, 2021.

Walsh, Bryan (2011), "Masdar City: The World's Greenest City?," *The Time*, January 25, http://content.time.com/time/health/article/0,8599,2043934,00.html, accessed on September 28, 2021.

Yaakoubi, Aziz El and Rashad, Marwa (2021), "Saudi Crown Prince Launches Zero-Carbon City in NEOM Business Zone," Reuters, January 10, https://www.reuters.com/article/us-saudi-neom-project-idUSKBN29F0L8, accessed on September 30, 2021.

14. Youth Dial Technology to Connect Economy and Foreign Policy

N. Janardhan

Introduction

Amid a global gloom in early 2021, Dubai International Airport—one of the world's busiest for international travel—was adding to its surreal boom by letting people pass some of its immigration counters without passports. The idea of contactless technology during the pandemic acquired a new meaning, with an iris-scanner verifying the identity of passengers and eliminating the need for any human interaction when entering or exiting the country's borders (Debre, 2021)

While the use of tech solutions is fast becoming the norm in multiple sectors across the world, deploying fourth industrial revolutions tools in the Gulf Cooperation Council (GCC) countries is striking because the region has traditionally been well-known for oil-dependent economies, with limited interest in diversifying beyond its chief natural resource. But consistent efforts over the last decade and a half to increase the efficiency of their core businesses, develop a non-oil economy, prepare for the global changes induced by energy transition, deal with changing youth-focused demographics, and emphasise e-commerce have increased investment in tech development.

Technology now propels job generation and economic growth in the Gulf markets. Moreover, the region's youth bulge, both among nationals and expatriates, who form a significant share of the population more than the nationals in some countries, offers great potential to promote tech-businesses to ensure workforce rationalisation. Driven by the pandemic, the space for a digital economy, which had already found takers both among the governments and youth in the region during the last decade, is certain to expand exponentially during the decades ahead.

This chapter delves into some of the defining developments in the Gulf's tech-driven agenda, where data is viewed as the new oil. It showcases how governments are preparing long-term plans for technological development as an economic stimulus to satisfy the demands of tech-savvy youth, enhance job opportunities and upgrade workforce efficiency. It justifies, with examples, why many analysts view the region as the next artificial intelligence (AI) hub, with technology playing a humongous role in different sectors of the economy. It also maps the tech-youth interconnectedness with the foreign and security policies of the region to give a holistic picture of the expanse of the impact of technology in the Gulf.

Leap-frog Approach

First-time visitors to the Gulf are bound to be awed by the glitz and glamour of the region's infrastructure and efficient digital governance systems. Some attribute the state-of-the-art facilities and receptiveness to advanced technology not so much to the mere presence of huge oil revenues but to the lack of "legacy infrastructure and systems." It is argued that the latter "allowed the Gulf states to leap-frog and embrace new technologies faster than many countries in the West" (Carrington, 2021).

Dell Technologies' 2020 *Digital Transformation Index* confirms this trend. Saudi Arabia and the UAE are ahead of the rest of the world in implementing cutting-edge technologies. In 2020, 90 per cent of businesses in the two countries fast-tracked digital transformation programmes, ahead of the index's global benchmark of 80 per cent (Dell Technologies, 2020).

The rate of internet penetration in most GCC countries exceeds 73 per cent, compared to the global average of 51 Per cent. This is likely to contribute to the region's estimated e-commerce market compound growth rate of 17 per cent during the 2016-2021 period (Furlow, 2019) In addition, the 2018 Arab Youth Survey found that over 60 per cent of youth in the 18-24 years bracket believe that the digital revolution has been the most important catalyst in the region's development over the past decade (Qasim, 2019). Young people are studying, socialising, shopping and banking online, thus contributing to an advanced digital ecosystem and leading to the pursuit of tech-based careers and business opportunities as a gateway to the future.

As a result, the annual growth in the e-commerce sectors of the Gulf countries and Egypt between 2014 and 2017 was about 30 per cent. An optimistic sales forecast of the region's e-commerce market in 2022 exceeds US$ 41 billion (Fabre and Malauzat, 2019). Though the dual shocks from the coronavirus and low oil prices are likely to restrict consumer demand and market growth in the short and medium terms, the broad trajectory of these growth projections is likely to stay.

In a curious case of countries with the highest dependency on oil in terms of revenues being at the forefront of adopting AI, the UAE announced that it wants to be the "world's most prepared country for artificial intelligence" (Ganji, 2020). To realise this, the government established the world's first AI university in Abu Dhabi and appointed in 2017 a 27-year-old as minister of artificial intelligence, the first time any country in the world established a dedicated AI ministry. Innovation, entrepreneurship and advanced industries are clear priorities for the UAE as part of its ambition to create a diversified knowledge-based economy in line with the UAE Centennial Plan 2071.

Likewise, Saudi Arabia—one of the world's largest oil producers—set up the Saudi Data and Artificial Intelligence Authority to roll out AI in different sectors of the economy. The kingdom is particularly keen to showcase its smart city, NEOM—which is part of its *Vision 2030* programme to diversify the economy—as a technology hub. Not one to be left behind, the Qatar Artificial Intelligence Center was established in 2020.

In reflecting on AI becoming a strategic component of the government's plans, a PWC report predicted that AI's potential impact on the Middle East and Africa would be about US$ 320 billion by 2030. According to the report, AI would contribute about US$ 135 billion to the Saudi economy, translating to about 12 per cent of its GDP (Table 14.1). With the aid of its Artificial Intelligence Strategy 2031, the UAE is tipped to benefit by US$ 96 billion (14 per cent of GDP) by 2030. In addition, Bahrain, Oman, Kuwait, and Qatar are expected to gain around US$ 46 billion from AI (8 per cent of GDP) (Ganj, 2020). The annual growth rates of the contribution of the AI to the economies of the GCC countries between 2018-30 are given in Table 14.2 and in GCC4, it is estimated to be 28.8 per cent.

Reflecting an early start, total AI investments in the Middle East and Africa region between 2008 and 2018 was about US$ 9 billion. Some of the region's cities now intend to use AI to become fully smart, deploying 3D printing for construction and an autonomous transportation strategy. In addition, AI is tipped to influence the following sectors: customer service, public sector, IT management, manufacturing, logistics, supply-chain management, and finance.

Table 14.1: Estimated Gains from Artificial Intelligence by 2030; Select countries

Country	AI Contribution (US$ billion)	AI Contribution (% GDP)
Egypt	42.7	7.7
Saudi Arabia	135.2	12.4
UAE	96	13.6
GCC4 (Bahrain, Kuwait, Oman, and Qatar)	45.9	8.2

Source: PricewaterhouseCoopers (2018)

Table 14.2: Average Annual Growth in the Contribution of AI; Select Countries (2018-2030)

Country	Growth (%)
UAE	33.5
Saudi Arabia	31.3
GCC4 (Bahrain, Kuwait, Oman, and Qatar)	28.8
Egypt	25.5

Source: PricewaterhouseCoopers (2018)

Digital Economy

The metamorphosis of Souq.com (market) into Amazon.ae and amazon.sa, among others, demonstrates the changing ground realities in the Gulf—youth bulge, tech orientation, non-oil and digital economy, job creation, overseas investment, etc. In 2005, when Souq.com was founded, the Middle East had tremendous potential for e-commerce—population over 350 million, half of them less than 25 years old. But it also had its share of drawbacks—a highly fragmented region in terms of laws and customs, logistics, payment infrastructure, low personal computer, and broadband penetration rates. After a slow start, Souq.com evolved with the help of a young and tech-savvy consumer base to become the largest e-commerce provider in the Middle East and one of its fastest-growing businesses. Its success was rewarded with Amazon acquiring it in 2017 for nearly US$ 600 million. To support its operations in the Middle East, Amazon Web Services chose Bahrain in 2019 to host its first data centre in the region, which facilitated job creation.

The Middle East e-commerce market sales were pegged at nearly US$ 70 billion in 2020, up from just over US$ 4 billion in 2016. In a pandemic world, these numbers ascended, with 92 per cent of UAE and Saudi consumers changing their shopping habits to go online. In the UAE, Amazon is now the top e-commerce platform with 46 per cent of shoppers using the service, while Noon is a distant second at 17 per cent (*Fintech News Middle East*, 2021) With young people preferring mobile phones over laptops as their preferred vehicle for shopping, business via apps has overtaken website deals. Since apps were introduced in Souq/Amazon in 2012, more than 70 per cent of the visits and transactions are via smartphone (Mouchawar, 2017). The e-Performance Index for the GCC countries is given in Table 14.3, which shows very high rates of digital transformation. Reflecting the interest in adopting the latest mobile network technology, it is estimated that the GCC countries will have about 62 million 5G subscriptions by 2026, the second-highest in the world after North America (Satelliteprome, 2021). Lured by the tech-business potential in a region, overseas venture capitalists poured in from the West, Asia and even Africa.

In a milieu where most local capital was invested in oil, infrastructure and real estate sectors, attracting in-country investment in the tech arena was not easy. However, once the tech business potential became evident, the region's oil money also began flowing in. Moreover, with 50 per cent of the region's population under 25 years, the tech industry has evolved to become a major provider of meaningful and enduring jobs.

'Speero' illustrates this evolution. When a young Saudi national had trouble getting his car repaired in 2017 because of the reluctance of the garage to buy the spare parts itself and no sellers being ready to deliver the parts directly to the mechanic, the first offshoot of Speero emerged. Along with two other friends, the entrepreneur resorted to technology to start an online automobile parts business. Headquartered in Riyadh, Speero—which first used WhatsApp—now delivers to nearly 100 towns and cities in the kingdom and has logistics offices in Jeddah and Dammam. The company directly links sellers and buyers of new and used automotive spare parts through its website and mobile app, thus ensuring price transparency. The platform now has about 1,000 partners and service providers, with more than 750,000 registered customers across the country, most of them youth. It is backed by local and international investors and plans to expand its business to the UAE soon.

About US$ 1.25 billion was raised by start-ups in the Middle East and North Africa region in the first six months of 2021, a 63 per cent increase during the same period in 2020. The top three countries attracting funding—the UAE, Egypt and Saudi Arabia—accounted for 71 per cent of the total investment. The UAE received 26 per cent of the total funding, while Egypt and Saudi Arabia got 24 per cent and 21 per cent, respectively. The food and beverage sector was the most popular among venture capitalists in terms of dollars invested, while the fintech sector generated the most deals. In reflecting overseas interest in the region's tech start-ups, 31 per cent of the funding came from investors outside the region (Arab News, 2021).

The honours for the biggest tech-based start-up deal during the first half of 2021 went to Dubai-based cloud kitchen Kitopi, which raised US$ 415 million from a group of investors, including Japan's SoftBank Group Corp.'s Vision Fund 2, boosting its value to more than US$ 1 billion, thus becoming a unicorn. The 'Amazon of food'—co-founded by four youth in their late 20s—operates a network of over 60 cloud kitchens in the UAE, Saudi Arabia, Kuwait, and Bahrain (Leon, 2021). The Gulf also has its version of Uber in Careem, which was started by ex-employees of McKinsey in the region and supported by local private equity firm Abraaj. In a mix of ideas, innovation and financing, where creative expatriates are also part of the story, the Gulf also has Aramex, a courier delivery company that has borrowed from the FedEx growth story.

Reflecting the robust tech industry growth, Saudi Arabia announced in 2021 that it would launch a US$ 15 billion public-private partnership fund to advance the digital infrastructure in the kingdom. The plan came amid assessment that telecom and technology operators invest between US$ 3 billion and US$ 4 billion annually in Saudi digital infrastructure, which was viewed as insufficient. The investments in the fourth industrial technology are expected to reach US$ 200 billion in the kingdom by 2030 (Albukhari and Salloum, 2021).

The tech revolution extends beyond e-commerce. The Abu Dhabi National Oil Corporation's digital command centre, for example, generated over US$ 1 billion in business value through cost savings and improved efficiency. In 2019, state-owned defence companies in the UAE formed a US$ 5 billion conglomerate, EDGE, to develop a high-tech defence industry that, according to the group's mission, will "bring innovative technologies and services to the market with greater speed and efficiency" (Warner, 2019).

Table 14.3: GCC E-Performance Index (2021)

Country	Digital Transformation (%)
UAE	67.83
Saudi Arabia	59.01
Qatar	58.50
Bahrain	57.65
Kuwait	55.10
Oman	55.00

Source*:* Adapted from Dubai Chronical (2021)

The ambitious UAE Artificial Intelligence Strategy 2031 seeks to position the country as a leading AI player by building a generation of talented young people capable of employing modern technology (NPAI, 2018). This supports the strategic directions of the UAE government to employ AI to overcome future challenges and develop an integrated development process in line with the transformation that is underway in various sectors. Likewise, Dubai Start-up Hub, an initiative of Dubai Chamber of Commerce and Industry, and Dubai Technology Entrepreneur

Campus are encouraging start-up projects through mentorship support (Dubai Chamber, n.d.).

Abu Dhabi's Hub71 endeavours to stay in tune with the global tech environment by enabling start-ups to grow. It is linked to the government's efforts to diversify the economy as a key driver of the Ghadan 21 programme, which is a catalyst for the emirate's bid to achieve digital transformation. Backed by Mubadala, Abu Dhabi Investment Agency, SoftBank and Microsoft, among others, as strategic partners, Hub71 has a competitive advantage to support start-ups that seek to scale from the national to the global scene. In addition, it is of the several entities selected to endorse global tech entrepreneurs for 'Golden Visas' in the UAE (HUB71, n.d.).

The five- and 10-year visas enable local and global entrepreneurs to set up businesses in the UAE, facilitating long-term market access for global tech talent. It enables residents and foreign nationals to make the UAE their long-term home to build and scale technologies and innovative solutions. In addition to the entrepreneurs, their spouses and children, up to three of the entrepreneur's executive directors could also be covered under the visa, enabling them to live, work and study in the country without an Emirati sponsor. The National Programme for Coders has earmarked 100,000 such visas to the best computer programming talent. Google, Microsoft, Amazon AWS, Cisco, IBM, HPE, LinkedIn, Nvidia, and Facebook are the partners in this public-private endeavour to establish 1,000 tech companies by increasing start-up investments from US$ 410 million to US$ 1.1 billion (Nowais, 2021; The National News, 2021).

Social Media Influencers

In a new trend of the tech-youth interface in the region, young social media influencers—like Alanoud Badr from Saudi Arabia, the UAE's Khalid Al Ameri, Rawan bin Hussain from Kuwait, and Bahrain's Ali Fareed, among others—have risen in number and popularity, earning lucrative incomes in the process (Fakih, 2018). Moreover, the explosion of the 'new' media at the turn of the century enhanced information flow and even served as a 'safety valve' to release pent-up political frustration among the *Khaleejis* (Gulf nationals) over the state of social, economic and political affairs. This was most evident during the Arab uprising in 2011.

However, the current group of tech-savvy media influencers "educate the public, showcase their travels, set fashion trends, and comment on local issues" platforms such as Instagram, Snapchat, YouTube, Twitter, and the like. "This bottom-up celebrity production and self-branding render individual narratives accessible for commercial gain and cultural capital with the potential to reach an audience that rivals that of the television networks" (Fakih, 2018). Many influencers have achieved celebrity status and financial independence by becoming brand ambassadors for various products in a 'new influencer economy'. But their greater accomplishment is breaking social barriers and taboos with their video interaction across a cross-section of society. While many social media users were reluctant even to post profile photos or reveal their real identity, Kuwait's Alabdulmohsen, for example, "shared her daily life and streamed some of her videos from her bedroom, a practice unheard of for women in the Gulf region" (Fakih, 2018).

Recognising their potential in influencing the youth, the region's governments have hosted several forums such as the Arab Social Media Influencers Summit in the UAE, Hashtag Kuwait Conference and *Shoof* (Look Forum) and *Mugharedoon* (Tweeps Forum) in Saudi Arabia. These events bring together "social media influencers with media entrepreneurs, business professionals, and religious scholars to discuss social media content creation, advertising, and social issues such as combating extremism on social media" (Fakih, 2018).

On the flip side, some, like Kuwaiti beauty blogger Sondos Al Qattan felt the consequences of crossing the thin line between black and white in the dual roles of influencer and 'misplaced' activism. She was widely criticised for a "racist rant" against a new law that stipulated an off day for domestic workers. Her views on video cost her several commercial endorsement contracts and created a diplomatic row between Kuwait and the Philippines over the rights of Filipino domestic workers (Gulf News, 2018).

There are several cybercrime laws in the region to bring about a sense of order in a largely 'unregulated' social media influencer market. One such Saudi law imposes fines and prison sentences on the "production, preparation, transmission, or storage of material impinging on public order, religious values, public morals, and privacy, through the information network or computers" (Gulf News, 2018). In addition, in 2018, the UAE made it mandatory for social media influencers to register and obtain a trade license for a fee of about US$ 4,000 (Euro News, 2019). Despite some drawbacks, the impact of the combination of youth, technology, government and citizens is irreversible in the socio-economic realm.

Knowledge-Economy and Shifting Foreign Policy Imperatives

Beyond the intersection of youth, technology and economic diversification, there are a few other dynamics at play—developing a knowledge economy and changing foreign and security policies in the region. With Asia at the forefront of the fourth industrial revolution, the Gulf countries proactively target technological collaboration with China, Japan, South Korea, and India. In an unlikely partnership, Kuwait signed an agreement with Iraq to develop a regional telecommunications corridor of international maritime cables linking "the East and West regions, through the Gulf and from Kuwait, Iraq and Turkey" (CITRA, 2018).

A large part of the Gulf countries' tech and AI strategies are tied to the plans of the global leader in 5G infrastructure—China. The Asian giant, which has taken a huge leap in commercial ties with the region over the last two decades, is also investing heavily in a broad range of advanced technologies and introducing them beyond its borders to expand its economic influence. Other than AI, China has also focused on smart and safe cities and unmanned aerial vehicles (UAVs), which resonate well in the region (Mogielnicki, 2019). The issue of supply meeting the increased tech demand after the advent of COVID-19 has made Gulf economies rely heavily on China. Beijing has provided "industrial internet" at cheaper prices than Western competitors. This, for example, has helped Saudi Telecom Company, which reported an increase of more than 1,000 per cent in bandwidth due to the surge in online education (Zinser, 2020).

To ensure that economic diversification meets its intended goals, especially private sector growth, the GCC countries—which lack a skilled indigenous workforce—are investing in developing a knowledge economy. Several Gulf universities offer educational programmes and training in high-tech fields, such as the UAE University (UAEU) and the Mohamed bin Zayed University of Artificial Intelligence. In 2020, the Abu Dhabi Department of Education and Knowledge announced it would open the first GCC campus of the 42 networks, a global coding and computer programming school (Warner, 2020). Through its strategic partnership with the UAEU in 2019, Huawei agreed to establish an ICT Academy to develop local skills in AI and machine learning. A similar training academy is on the anvil at the Prince Bin Sultan University in Riyadh. Oman's Ministry of Technology and Communications and Huawei will run joint internship programmes, campus recruitment events, and technical training and certification (John, 2020).

Asian multinationals target local employment generation to gain a competitive edge in securing contracts. For example, Huawei signed an agreement with Saudi Arabia's Technical and Vocational Training Corporation in 2014 to provide cloud training to Saudi graduates and hire Saudi trainees each year. It also launched the Saudi Talent Enablement Programme at a job fair with the Saudi Ministry of Communications and Information Technology in 2019; organises a national talent development programme with Tamkeen, the public authority charged with promoting Bahrain's private sector; and runs its Seeds for the Future programme, which develops ICT skills amongst Gulf students, with senior Huawei executives as mentors (Mogielnicki, 2020).

As the leader in 5G technology, Huawei is also a key part of China's Digital Silk Road, an extension of the Belt and Road Initiative. The telecom firms of the UAE, Saudi Arabia, Bahrain, Kuwait, and Oman have signed massive 5G contracts with Huawei since 2019 (Zinser, 2020). The technology targets businesses revolving around cloud computing, ultrafast broadband, and internet of things, including self-driving cars, transportation, etc. The company is involved in several sectors, including Dubai's AI-based 'Police without a Policeman' project (Huawei, 2016).

Similarly, Abu Dhabi Investment Office signed a deal with Chinese AI firm Sense Time in 2019 to base its regional research and development headquarters in the UAE. Beijing is also working with Riyadh on AI-based crowd control tools to manage security at Saudi holy sites, especially during Hajj pilgrimages (Robinson, 2020). Taking this one step further, Huawei has strategically promoted its Safe City surveillance technology to Saudi Arabia to counter extremism (Robinson, 2020). In the defence arena, the UAE purchased the Chinese Wing Loong I drones in 2016 and Wing Loong II in 2018 after the United States refused to sell its latest weaponised drones, citing the impact of the war in Yemen. In 2017, Beijing announced that Riyadh was interested in purchasing about 300 Wing Loong II UAVs. The two governments also struck a deal to manufacture CH-4 drones in Saudi Arabia (Robinson, 2020).

While there are other equally competent players in Asia, it is felt that Chinese academic institutions, private firms, and government entities are well-positioned to support Gulf's emerging tech spheres. For example, universities and research organisations in China play a dominating role in producing inventions and patents for distributed AI, deep learning, and neurorobotics. And Huawei possesses a clear AI strategy, which involves investments in AI research and developing a global AI ecosystem and talent pipeline (Mogielnickl, 2019).

China and Huawei's hi-tech role in the region has become a source of geopolitical tension involving the governments of the region and the United States, which is the chief security guarantor in the Gulf. Washington flagged in 2020 Huawei's role in the UAE's 5G infrastructure projects, claiming that it would make it "difficult" for American and Gulf military forces to communicate securely. "These (Gulf) states have to weigh the value of their partnership with the United States," said US former assistant secretary of state for Near Eastern affairs David Schenker (Cornwell, 2020). Unperturbed, the GCC governments have exercised strategic autonomy, diversified their foreign policy and disallowed politics or ideology to interfere in their economic progress, which is also evident in the UAE signing the Abraham Accord with Israel.

Amid Western scrutiny differences over human rights issues revolving around UAE-Saudi military intervention in Yemen (England and Kerr, 2021), there is a change in the region's arms purchases domain. For example, China's ammunition transfer to Saudi Arabia and the UAE between 2016 and 2020 dramatically increased by 386 per cent and 169 per cent, respectively, compared to the 2011-2015 period. While the numbers indicate a low starting point, not quantity of sales, any increase in China's arms market in the Gulf is a loss for the American and Western arms industries (Bowmann, 2021).

Tech advancements have also made South Korea part of the military apparatus mix, especially with small and medium arms. Its global weapons sales have increased by 143 per cent since 2015, with Turkey and Saudi Arabia being its biggest Middle East customers (Jeong, 2020). The Saudi Arabian Military Industries and South Korea's Hanwha Defence conglomerate signed a joint venture agreement in 2019 to manufacture and sell a range of weapons. It includes a clause to evaluate expanding its product lines to include "rockets, artillery, combat vehicles, naval systems, command and control systems, as well as intelligence, surveillance and reconnaissance-focused products" (Jr, 2019).

This trend of non-traditional players becoming part of the arms suppliers group may intensify, with Israel perhaps becoming a major player in the wake of the Abraham Accord signed with the UAE. A semblance of this change was on display at the 2021 International Défense Exhibition in Abu Dhabi. As a reaction to the Biden administration ordering a freeze on arms contracts signed between the Trump and UAE governments, Abu Dhabi gave the Chinese, Russian and Israeli pavilions greater attention than the American wares (Kahwaji, 2021).

Japan also has a share in the region's tech march. SoftBank Group launched a US$ 100 billion Vision Fund together with Saudi Arabia's Public Investment Fund in 2017. Though the fund reported a huge loss in 2020, which puts the plans for the US$108 billion Vision Fund 2 in a spot, it serves as a benchmark for the region's tech-driven investments in the future (Shead, 2022). In addition, in a demonstration of space diplomacy, the UAE's first home-built KhalifaSat was launched in 2018 from the Tanegashima Space Center in Japan. Further, Emirates Mars Mission's spacecraft was also launched from the same site in 2020 using a Japanese rocket manufactured by Mitsubishi Heavy Industries (*Nikkei Asia*, 2020).

South Korea is another leader in the fourth industrial revolution. It contributed to developing the UAE's first satellites, DubaiSat-1 and DubaiSat-2, in 2009 and 2013, respectively, and lent support in building KhalifaSat (Baldwin, 2018). Marking the completion of the construction of the first of four Barakah nuclear reactors in 2018, the UAE and South Korea elevated their strategic relationship to a "special strategic partnership" (JiAe, 2018). It is important to note that South Korea overcame the US and French bids for the US$ 20-billion Barakah project in 2009 based on lower prices for comparable technology (Bakr and Young, 2009). The Korea-Saudi Vision 2030 Committee targets smart infrastructure and digitisation, among others (Hassan, 2017). And since 2015, Seoul's collaboration with Kuwait has spanned technology-intensive industries, such as smart grids and research and development in energy-efficient buildings (Energy Central, 2019).

Another new Gulf-Asia collaborative tech template that showcases a growing interest in expanding the bilateral to the plurilateral domain is the UAE-Israel-India agreement signed in 2021. This trilateral deal facilitates an Israel-based company, Ecoppia, to produce an innovative water-free robotic solar cleaning technology in India for a project in the UAE (Chaudhary, 2021). With the three governments confident of replicating such collaboration in other sectors, the innovation and international business potential of the UAE-Israel-India trilateral is pegged at US$ 110 billion by 2030 (*Republic World*, 2021). In another deal related to Gulf-India tech collaboration, Saudi and Abu Dhabi sovereign wealth funds invested US$ 3.5 billion in Reliance Industries' Jio (digital) Platforms in 2020 (*Outlook*, 2020).

Challenges and Conclusion

In a fast-changing world where systems are witnessing major disruption and development due to new scientific and technological advancements, governments all over, including the Gulf region, are harnessing this dynamic. With the majority of the population being youth, they are an economic resource that can contribute to social and systemic stability if tapped well. Educated or otherwise, the youth are full of energy and in search of employment. They have fresh ideas and talent that can be shaped through innovative solutions in a world that is 'flat' and getting 'flatter'.

Modern technology has been increasingly targeting youth. Unlike the baby boomers of the 1960s and 1970s, who manoeuvred through tech challenges through creative learning and reskilling, millennials and GenX are starting their careers using platforms created specifically for them by tech companies. The World Bank estimates that the Middle East and North Africa region would need to create 300 million jobs for its youth by 2050. It is estimated that the digital job market can create 1.3 million additional jobs in the GCC region by 2025, including 700,000 opportunities in Saudi Arabia. It is also argued that nearly four million economically inactive women and young men in GCC countries could profit from digital self-employment.

On the other side, there are widespread concerns that digitisation could result in a net loss of jobs. A 2018 report by the World Government Summit and McKinsey found that existing technology could automate 45 per cent of current jobs, saving around US$ 367 billion in salaries in several GCC countries and Egypt. Neutralising these negatives, the same report estimates that in the medium to long term, "the associated labour productivity increases can also be an engine for growth" (Langendorf, 2020).

Another challenge is that given the explosion of internet access among youth, extremist and terrorist groups are lurking on the Web to spread hate, misplaced ideologies and radicalise gullible and vulnerable minds. To counter such attempts, the UAE and the United States combined to use technological tools and launched the Sawab Center, an online engagement and messaging operation that will support the Global Coalition to Counter the Islamic State in Iraq and Syria (ISIS). Since its launch in 2015, the Centre has encouraged governments, communities, and individual voices to proactively counter online extremism and promote positive alternate narratives to ISIS's ideology (Wam, 2020). It uses Twitter, Facebook, Instagram, and YouTube platforms to convey positive counter-messages in several languages.

Overall, advancements in technology in the region will contribute to a knowledge economy, job opportunities, inward and outward investments, employment opportunities, new foreign policy partnerships, and overall economic growth. These far outweigh the cost of associated institutional challenges and pitfalls related to telecom equipment providers, nature of data management, potential loss of jobs in the medium to long term due to automation and geopolitical tension.

Finally, analysts outside the Gulf region often view the governments' push for technological changes to aid growth and job creation in a non-oil economy as a potential tool to enhance political legitimacy, especially among the burgeoning youth population (Alaoui, 2019) However, there is no empirical evidence to back this. While this cannot be ruled out entirely, the changes are likely rooted more in socio-economic-diplomatic factors—modernisation of the region, value addition to the economy, improving the standard of living, fulfilling the aspirations of a tech-savvy generation enhancing synergies with international partners.

References

Alaoui, H. (2019), "Youth, Technology, and Political Change in Saudi Arabia," Hoover Institution, 22 April, https://www.hoover.org/research/youth-technology-and-political-change-saudi-arabia, accessed on December 29, 2021.

Albukhari, I., and Salloum, J. (2021), "Saudi Arabia Plans $15bn Technology Fund With Private Investors," Arab News, 29 July, https://www.arabnews.com/node/1902036/business-economy, accessed on December 29, 2021.

Arab News (2021), "Saudi Startups Raise More Than $250m by Mid- Year: Report," 18 July, https://www.arabnews.com/node/1896236/business-economy, accessed December 24, 2021.

Asia Nikkei (2020), "UAE's Mars Orbiter Successfully Launched by Mitsubishi Rocket," 20 July, https://asia.nikkei.com/Business/Aerospace-Defense/UAE-s-Mars-orbiter-successfully-launched-by-Mitsubishi-rocket, accessed on December 27, 2021.

Bakr, A., and Young, C. M. (2009), "South Korea Wins Landmark Gulf Nuclear Power Deal," Reuters, 27 December, https://www.reuters.com/article/us-emirates-korea-nuclear-idUSLDE5BQ05O20091227, accessed on December 28, 2021.

Baldwin, D. (2018), "First UAE-Made Satellite Delivered to South Korea," Gulf News, 15 February, https://gulfnews.com/uae/first-uae-made-satellite-delivered-to-south-korea-1.2174095, accessed on December 28, 2021.

Bowmann, B. (2021), "China's Surprising Drone Sales in the Middle East," Defense News, 23 April, https://www.defensenews.com/opinion/2021/04/23/chinas-surprising-drone-sales-in-the-middle-east/, accessed on December 25, 2021.

Carrington, M. (2021), "Letter From the Gulf: Can the GCC Leap-Frog the West in AI Adoption?," *The AI Journal*, 30 March, https://aijourn.com/letter-from-the-gulf-can-the-gcc-leap-frog-the-west-in-ai-adoption/, accessed on December 23, 2021.

Chaudhary, D. R. (2021), "India, Israel and UAE Sign Maiden Trilateral Deal to Push W Asian Partnership", *The Economic Times*, 6 May, https://economictimes.indiatimes.com/news/india/india-israel-and-uae-sign-maiden-trilateral-deal-to-push-w-asian-partnership/articleshow/82432369.cms?from=mdr, accessed on November 29, 2021.

Communication & Info. Technology Regulatory Authority [CITRA], Government of Kuwait [GOK] (2018), "CITRA Signed With the Iraqi Ministry of Communications the Agreement of the Regional Corridor Project," 15 February, https://citra.gov.kw/sites/en/Pages/NewsDetails.aspx?NewsID=33, accessed on November 30, 2021.

Cornwell, A. (2020), "Gulf States Should Consider U.S. Ties When Dealing With China Official," Reuters, 7 May, https://www.reuters.com/article/us-health-coronavirus-usa-gulf-idUSKBN22J2WA, accessed on November 30, 2021.

Debre, I. (2021), "At Dubai Airport, Travelers' Eyes Become Their Passports," AP News, 7 March, https://apnews.com/article/dubai-airport-iris-scanner-verify-identity-4c8f2fb1f62df394e29e8365b3bd105e, accessed on December 28, 2021.

Dell Technologies (2020), "Measuring Digital Transformation Progress Around the World," https://www.delltechnologies.com/en-in/perspectives/digital-transformation-index.htm, accessed on December 29, 2021.

Dubai Chamber (n.d.), "Dubai Startup Hub," https://www.dubaichamber.com/what-we-do/dubai-startup-hub, accessed on December 29, 2021.

Dubai Chronical (2021), "GCC e-performance Index 2021 Examines Progress of Arab Gulf Countries Digital' transformation," 11 May, https://www.dubaichronicle.com/2021/05/11/gcc-e-performance-index-2021-examines-progress-of-arab-gulf-countries-digital-transformation/

Energy Central (2019), "Korean Group Wins $95m Kuwait Power Grid Deal," 18 June, https://energycentral.com/news/korean-group-wins-95m-kuwait-power-grid-deal, accessed on December 25, 2021.

England, A. and Kerr, S. (2021), "More of China, Less of America: How Superpower Fight Is Squeezing the Gulf," *Financial Times*, 20 September, https://www.ft.com/content/4f82b560-4744-4c53-bf4b-7a37d3afeb13, accessed on December 28, 2021.

Euro News (2019), "License to Influence: UAE Law Regulates Social Media Players," 21 July, https://www.euronews.com/2019/07/19/license-to-influence-uae-law-regulates-social-media-players, accessed on December 24, 2021.

Fabre, C., and Malauzat, A. L. (2019), "E-Commerce in MENA: Opportunity Beyond the Hype," Bain & Company, 19 February, https://www.bain.com/insights/ecommerce-in-MENA-opportunity-beyond-the-hype/, accessed on December 26, 2021.

Fakih, M. (2018), "Social Media Influencers in the Gulf Arab States," AGSIW, 7 November, https://agsiw.org/social-media-influencers-in-the-gulf-arab-states/, accessed on December 26, 2021.

Fintech News Middle East (2021), "Amazon's Growing Foothold in the Middle East," 9 February, https://fintechnews.ae/7570/fintech/amazons-growing-foothold-in-the-middle-east/#:~:text=Amazon%20is%20aggressively%20expanding%20its,2020%2C%20and%20the%20launch%20of, accessed on December 28, 2021.

Furlow, R. (2019), "The Gulf's Economic Development Is Going Digital," Atlantic Council, 22 August, https://www.atlanticcouncil.org/blogs/menasource/the-gulfs-economic-development-is-going-digital/, accessed on November 30, 2021.

Ganji, H. (2020), "Transition From Oil to AI: Middle East Can Be the Next Great AI Hub," Readwrite, 4 October, https://readwrite.com/2020/10/04/transition-from-oil-to-ai-middle-east-can-be-the-next-great-ai-hub/, accessed on December 29, 2021.

Gulf News (2018), "Kuwait Influencer Not Sorry for Filipino Worker Remark," 23 July, https://gulfnews.com/world/gulf/kuwait/kuwait-influencer-not-sorry-for-filipino-worker-remark-1.2255987#:~:text=Global%20brands%20working%20with,did%20not%20require%20an%20apology, accessed on December 24, 2021.

Hassan, R. (2017), "Saudi-Korea Vision 2030 Committee Launched with Access to 400 Companies," Arab News, 1 November, https://www.arabnews.com/node/1186981/saudi-arabia, accessed on November 28, 2021.

Huawei (2016), "Huawei and Dubai Police Join Forces to Make Dubai a Safer City Through Innovation," 30 May, https://e.huawei.com/ae/news/ae/2015/2016/201605300841, accessed on December 28, 2021.

HUB71 (n.d.), "Welcome to Abu Dhabi's," https://hub71.com/, accessed on December 29, 2021.

Jeong, H. W. (2020), "South Korea's Evolving Ties With the Middle East," Asia Society, 28 July, https://asiasociety.org/asias-new-pivot/south-korea, accessed on December 28, 2021.

JiAe, S. (2018), "Korea, UAE Agree to Become Special Strategic Partners," *Korea.Net*, 26 March, https://www.korea.net/NewsFocus/policies/view?articleId=156352, accessed on December 29, 2021.

John, O. (2020), "MTC and Huawei Ink Partnership to Develop Oman's ICT Ecosystem," *OER Live*, 7 May, https://www.oerlive.com/, https://www.oerlive.com/it/mtc-and-huawei-ink-partnership-to-develop-omans-ict-ecosystem/#:~:text=MTC%20and%20Huawei%20Ink%20Partnership%20to%20Develop%20Oman's%20ICT%20Ecosystem,-By&text=The%20Ministry%20of%20Technology%20and,digital%20society%20and%20IC, accessed on December 29, 2021.

Jr, B. D. (2019), "SAMI, Korean Conglomerate Agree to Defence-Focused Joint Venture Company," *Arabian Business*, 1 July, https://www.arabianbusiness.com/industries/transport/423138-sami-korean-conglomerate-agree-to-defence-focused-joint-venture-company, accessed on December 27, 2021.

Kahwaji, R. (2021), "IDEX: Low-key US Presence Opens Doors for Israel, China," *Breaking Defense*, 23 February, https://breakingdefense.com/2021/02/idex-low-key-us-presence-opens-doors-for-israel-china/, accessed on December 26, 2021.

Langendorf, M. (2020), "Digital Stability: How Technology Can Empower Future Generations in the Middle East," ECFR, 24 March, https://ecfr.eu/publication/digital_stability_how_technology_can_empower_future_generations_middle_e, accessed on December 28, 2021.

Leon, P. D. (2021), "Kitopi's Mohamad Ballout Is Aiming to Have His Cloud Kitchen Platform Dominate MENA and the World With a US$415 Million Funding Round Led by SoftBank," *Entrepreneur*, 9 August, https://www.entrepreneur.com/article/379649, accessed on December 28, 2021.

Mogielnicki, D. R. (2020), "Enabling the New Frontiers of Gulf-Asia Economic Ties," AGDA, December, https://www.agda.ac.ae/docs/default-source/Publications/eda-insight-nov-2020-eng-robert.pdf?sfvrsn=6, accessed on December 29, 2021.

Mogielnickl, D. R. (2019), "China Could Be the Big Winner of Saudi Arabia's Race to Become a Tech Hub," Foreign Policy, 8 October, https://foreignpolicy.com/2019/10/08/saudi-arabia-racing-high-tech-hub-china-is-ready-to-join-in/, accessed on November 27, 2021.

Mouchawar, R. (2017), "Souq.com's CEO on Building an E-commerce Powerhouse in the Middle East," *Harvard Business Review*, September, https://hbr.org/2017/09/souq-coms-ceo-on-building-an-e-commerce-powerhouse-in-the-middle-east, accessed on December 29, 2021.

National Program For Artificial Intelligence(NPAI), Government of UAE (2018), "UAE National Strategy For Artificial Intelligence 2031," https://ai.gov.ae/wp-content/uploads/2021/07/UAE-National-Strategy-for-Artificial-Intelligence-2031.pdf, accessed on December 26, 2021.

Nikkei Asia (2020), "UAE's Mars Orbiter Successfully Launched by Mitsubishi Rocket," https://asia.nikkei.com/Business/Aerospace-Defense/UAE-s-Mars-orbiter-successfully-launched-by-Mitsubishi-rocket, accessed on December 26, 2021.

Nowais, S. A. (2021), "Minister Outlines Vision to Attract Global Talent to Live, Work and Retire in UAE," *The National*, 6 May, https://www.thenationalnews.com/uae/government/minister-outlines-vision-to-attract-global-talent-to-live-work-and-retire-in-uae-1.1218098, accessed on December 28, 2021.

Outlook (2020), "Jio to Complete 25% Equity Dilution With Saudi Fund's Equity Buy: Report," 15 June, https://www.outlookindia.com/newsscroll/jio-to-complete-25-equity-dilution-with-saudi-funds-equity-buy-report/1867180, accessed on December 28, 2021.

PricewaterhouseCoopers (2018) "Potential Impact of Artificial Intelligence in the Middle East," https://www.pwc.com/m1/en/publications/potential-impact-artificial-intelligence-middle-east.html , accessed on December 28, 2021.

Robinson, W. (2020), "The Rise of Chinese AI in the Gulf: A Renewal of China's Serbia Model," Washington Institute for Near East Policy, 13 October, https://www.washingtoninstitute.org/policy-analysis/rise-chinese-ai-gulf-renewal-chinas-serbia-model, accessed on December 24, 2021.

Satelliteprome (2021), "GCC to Have 62m 5G Mobile Subscriptions by 2026: Ericsson," 9 July, https://satelliteprome.com/news/gcc-to-have-62m-5g-mobile-subscriptions-by-2026-ericsson/, accessed on December 28, 2021.

Shead, S. (2020), "SoftBank's Second Vision Fund Hangs in the Balance After the First One Posted a Record $18 Billion Loss," *CNBC*, 22 May, https://www.cnbc.com/2020/05/22/softbanks-vision-fund-ii-in-jeopardy.html, accessed on November 29, 2021.

The National News (2021), "UAE Sets Out Plan to Provide 100,000 Golden Visas for World's Best Coders," 11 July, https://www.thenationalnews.com/uae/government/2021/07/11/uae-sets-out-plan-to-provide-100000-golden-visas-for-worlds-best-coders/#:~:text=%E2%80%9CWe%20launched%20a%20national%20programme,Sheikh%20Mohammed%20wrote%20on%20Twitter, accessed on December 26, 2021.

Wam. (2020), "UAE-US Sawab Center Launches New Social Media Campaign Exposing Daesh Lies," *Khaleej Times*, 23 November, https://www.khaleejtimes.com/government/uae-us-sawab-center-launches-new-social-media-campaign-exposing-daesh-lies, accessed on November 30, 2021.

Warner, K. (2019), "Crown Prince of Abu Dhabi Unveils One of Middle East's Biggest Defence Groups," *The National*, 6 November, https://www.thenationalnews.com/uae/crown-prince-of-abu-dhabi-unveils-one-of-middle-east-s-biggest-defence-groups-1.933512, accessed on November 30, 2021.

Warner, K. (2020), "Abu Dhabi Opens a Coding School With No Classes Or Teachers," *The National*, 2 September, https://www.thenationalnews.com/uae/education/abu-dhabi-opens-a-coding-school-with-no-classes-or-teachers-1.1071865, accessed on December 29, 2021.

Zinser, S. (2020), "China's Digital Silk Road Grows With 5G in the Middle East," *The Diplomat*, 16 December, https://thediplomat.com/2020/12/chinas-digital-silk-road-grows-with-5g-in-the-middle-east/, accessed on December 28, 2021.

Index